RAILWAY WALKS

LNER

JEFF VINTER

Consultant to BBC's *Railway Walks* series

In memory of Brian Lyndon
historian, railway rambler and companion

First published 1990
This edition published 2009

The History Press
The Mill, Brimscombe Port
Stroud, Gloucestershire, GL5 2QG
www.thehistorypress.co.uk

British Library Cataloguing in Publication Data.
A catalogue record for this book is available from the British Library.

ISBN 978 07524 5105 3

Typesetting and origination by The History Press
Printed in Great Britain

CONTENTS

LOCATION OF WALKS   vi

KEY TO MAPS   vii

ACKNOWLEDGEMENTS   viii

PREFACE   ix

INTRODUCTION   xi

1   The Alban Way   1

2   An Essex Byway   14

3   The Midland and Great Northern Joint Railway, Norfolk   28

4   The Spa Trail   45

5   The Hornsea Rail Trail   61

6   The Hudson Way   79

7   The Vale of York   93

8   The Scarborough and Whitby Railway Path   109

9   The Waskerley Way   126

10 The Derwent Walk   142

APPENDIX A
Useful Addresses   156

APPENDIX B
Official Railway Walks   158

BIBLIOGRAPHY   169

INDEX   171

LOCATION OF WALKS

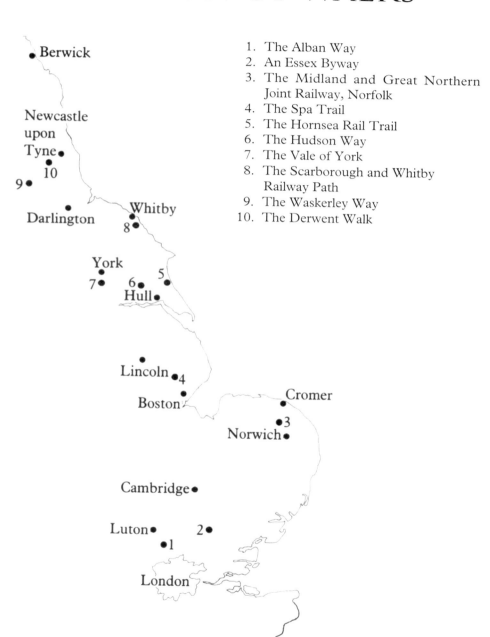

1. The Alban Way
2. An Essex Byway
3. The Midland and Great Northern Joint Railway, Norfolk
4. The Spa Trail
5. The Hornsea Rail Trail
6. The Hudson Way
7. The Vale of York
8. The Scarborough and Whitby Railway Path
9. The Waskerley Way
10. The Derwent Walk

Berwick

Newcastle upon Tyne
9
10

Darlington
Whitby
8

York
7 6 5
Hull

Lincoln 4
Boston
Cromer
3
Norwich

Cambridge

Luton 2
1

London

KEY TO MAPS

Railways

——————————— Railway path
– – – – – – – – Course of trackbed (no public access)
▬▬▬▬▬▬▬ Operational railway

Stations

———■——— With buildings and platforms
———●——— With platforms only
———○——— Station site (few remains if any)

Features

Viaduct or major bridge
Tunnel with through access
Tunnel with no through access
SH Goods or engine shed
SB Signal box
LC Level crossing with keeper's cottage, crossing gates or rails in situ

Other Routes

═══════════ Any metalled road
.... Track or path

Facilities

☕ Public house nearby

Note: The relevant Ordnance Survey maps are identified in the 'Transport and Facilities' section of each chapter.

ACKNOWLEDGEMENTS

As with *Railway Walks: GWR & SR,* a large number of individuals and organizations have again lent a helping hand. Particular thanks are due to the following:

For accommodation and sustenance: Julian Marko of Durham; Nigel and Melissa Winstanley of Scunthorpe; and Andrew Pike of Cublington. The preparation of this book entailed many weeks of apparently ceaseless travel – it was good to have a few 'homes from home' along the way.

For access to books: Alan Vinter, my father; Pete Walker and Geoff Sargeant, fellow railway ramblers; and Robert Turner and the staff of Winchester Library. Once again, the quality of the histories in this volume owes much to the excellence of the library's huge Railway Collection.

For his personal reminiscences: Robert Stephenson of Market Weighton. The time constraints of the project prevented a more systematic form of interviewing, but thanks are also due to the many and multifarious fellow walkers I bothered along the way.

For proof-reading and corrections: my wife, Jenny; and Roger Wright of Durham County Council.

For information on railway walks: Rhys ab Ells, whose *Railway Rights of Way* once again proved a reliable and invaluable work of reference; the staff of Sustrans Ltd, Bristol; Roger Wright of Durham County Council; Ian Ingles of Humberside County Council; Allen Oliver of the Northumberland Railway Walks Society; Paul Hibberd, whose researches for Railway Ramblers uncovered the excellent Alban Way; Mr. N.B. Collin of Hull, who provided much useful background information on the old railways of Humberside; and Richard Lewis, Ralph Rawlinson and Phil Wood, stalwarts of Railway Ramblers, who have helped to keep me up to date with railway path developments throughout the UK for many years.

For sheer perversity: the summer weather – grim for the walks (outdoors, 1988) but fabulous for the writing-up (indoors, 1989). How on earth did it know?

For tea, sympathy, transport and rescue services: my wife, Jenny, fellow visitor to all the places mentioned in this book. Without her practical and unfailing assistance, this project would have been infinitely more difficult, if possible at all. The achievement of this, the second volume in the series, owes a great deal to her support.

JV

PREFACE TO 2009 EDITION

My exploration of disused railways on the eastern side of England owes a great deal to two late friends: Brian Lyndon (to whom this book is dedicated) and Julian Marko. Brian was a great help to me in East Anglia, while Julian ensured that I walked almost every railway path that had been created in the north east up until the time of his early death in 1994. Working on this book again brought back many happy memories of days spent in their company.

Time constraints prevented a complete rewrite, which logically would have required a prolonged tour of the country to identify all that had changed. When I started this series 20 years ago, my wife and I went on the road for over six weeks. A repeat of this was not practical due to work commitments and the fact that the commission from my publisher arrived in the middle of winter. However, to compensate the reader, I have revised completely the content of Appendix B, 'Official Railway Walks', which is now fully up to date. Additionally, the entry for each walk now includes a short 'thumbnail description', which I hope will help those who use this book to plan railway walks of their own.

This enlarged reprint appears in a changed world. Railway managers are no longer expected to shut down parts of the system that provides their livelihood. While some freight lines have closed (usually as a result of mines and factories closing), many of these are now accessible as 'rail trails', especially in the north east – a testament to the constructive approach now taken to abandoned railway infrastructure. This is a vast improvement on the former practice of selling off old railways in small pieces, which destroyed their linear integrity. Let us hope that this change is a permanent one.

On the public transport front, the provision today is broadly similar to what it was when this book first appeared. Bus services have shrunk back in some rural areas, but often the major services are better, especially in terms of frequency. Rail services have improved, although the fares are too high, as anyone with a family and an economic car will know.

The licensed trade is now in a sorry state, which presents a threat to those welcome 'refreshment stops' in town and country, which are often a highlight of a day's walking. Pub closures continue at a quickening pace, especially in rural areas. The news that Tetley's famous brewery in Leeds is set to close in 2010 was a shock, and demonstrates what happens when international corporations take over indigenous companies that once served local markets and local tastes. If you use this book 'in the field', do support the local pub – but choose a genuinely local ale. That way, you'll help both the landlord and the local brewer.

So, is the weather half decent? Fancy stretching your legs? Get out and take a look at your local railway paths!

Jeff Vinter
Chichester
February 2009

INTRODUCTION

The London and North Eastern Railway was formed on 1 January 1923 by the Railways Act of 1921. Its main constituents were the Great Northern, Great Eastern, Great Central, North Eastern, North British and Great North of Scotland Railways, but a number of smaller concerns, such as the Horncastle Railway, went into the melting-pot with them. A few minor lines even managed to retain their independence, two examples being the Derwent Valley Light Railway in Yorkshire and the narrow-gauge Southwold Railway in Suffolk.

The result of this vast amalgamation was something of an unwieldy colossus, for the LNER could be no more uniform and homogeneous than the vast region it served. It was an empire of extremes, even within the same geographical area. In the south, for example, thousands of commuters might travel daily from the urban parts of Essex into London but, a few miles further east, fruit trains would chuff contentedly through remote country halts where the passenger shelters were made out of used carriage bodies. Similarly in the north, the Tyne and the Tees might resound to the roar of industry, but goods trains still plied their way across the high and deserted Durham moors, where snow blockages were not unknown even in May. The final descent into Stanhope involved the use of two inclined planes, constructed in the early 1830s! As one might expect, the LNER's railway paths (if one can call them that) reflect the variety which existed when they were still in use as operational lines. The two extremes are the Stanhope branch, now the lonely Waskerley Way, and part of the former East Coast main line between Selby and York.

The pity is that so little of the network of abandoned railways has been preserved in this way. The walks described in this book can really be regarded as the lucky ones, although the small number of lines which have been preserved as working steam railways are arguably even luckier. However, the fact remains that the majority of disused lines are now hopelessly fragmented and unlikely ever again to offer useful service to the community. If one stretches the definition of a railway to include all sorts of tramways, some 10,000 miles of abandoned trackbed now thread their way across the country's landscape. Of this potentially vast national resource, barely 10 per cent can be walked, let alone cycled or traversed by wheelchair users.

Railway enthusiasts are a funny breed, for once a line has been carved along a particular route, they never forget it, and make regular pilgrimages years after its closure. A number of television programmes have probably made the

Somerset and Dorset one of the most famous railways in this category, though the north has other examples, such as the Waverley and Stainmore routes. It is difficult to explain the attraction of these old lines unless one has actually travelled over them. The late Sir John Betjeman always claimed that you could see far more countryside from the window of a train than from a car, and there is a great deal in this. Outside the major cities, the railways were frequently unaccompanied, except perhaps by a river when that offered the best way of negotiating some natural feature; as a result, they frequently offered a unique view over a pristine cross section of the English landscape. Perhaps, therefore, these incurable enthusiasts are merely seeking to recapture the views and images of some favourite, now impossible, journey.

Of course, the navvies who constructed these lines – often with nothing more than picks, shovels and the sweat of their brows – believed that they were building them for good. Unfortunately, the last fifteen years have seen a considerable decrease in the number of abandoned railway routes left intact, and one feels at times impelled to retrace past journeys if only to prove that they were something more than a dream. Road planners and others have swept away huge viaducts and embankments, infilled cuttings, and razed station sites to the ground; in so doing they have destroyed features which thousands of men and women still remember vividly. They have actively severed points of contact with the past, leaving our memories to become even more ethereal and intangible. The preservation of old routes and buildings is more than just fancy: it gives us a sense of where we, as a nation, have come from. And who is to say that these abandoned routes will not be put to some valuable new use in the future? One only has to look at the growing canal network, now appreciated in its own right as a unique combination of industrial archaeology and leisure amenity, to realize that we are being extremely foolhardy if we consign our past heritage to the dustbin simply because it happens to be 'out of fashion'. That was one of the most serious mistakes made in the 1960s, and it is high time we started to put it right.

Those who are not old enough to be moved by these considerations can explore old railways for another reason, that of 'defeating Dr Beeching'; more on his stewardship of British Railways later. I have to admit that my own explorations stem largely from this source. When in the West Country Dr Beeching and his successors decreed, 'Thou shalt not pass this way again', I was soon moved to dust down my hiking boots in order to find out what kind of places these extinguished railway lines once served. It was this inquisitiveness which led me to discover such diverse and delightful places as Bridport, Padstow, Hornsea, Alston, Southwold, Barnard Castle . . . the list goes on and on. And as for all those beautiful lonely places along the way which have no name except on the largest of maps, I could not begin to list them.

For all these reasons and more, railway enthusiasts keep on returning to their favourite scenes from the past. As a result, there are now several books on our library shelves which illustrate the fate of railway lines which have, literally, been put out to grass. Of course, there are evocative scenes where, perhaps, a railway family still lives in the same building and keeps it as though the trains might return tomorrow; but, sadly, there are many more cases which speak volubly of neglect and tragically lost opportunities. Consider a sample: the abandoned trackbed, waist-high with brambles and nettles; a cutting, slowly filling up with modem domestic detritus – television sets, refrigerators, washing-machines; a majestic station building, such as Louth, neglected and vandalized for years until it is physically disintegrating. It is a terrible reproach to us, as a nation, that we let these things happen. How much better would the quality of all our lives be if we could only find the will and the imagination to utilize our industrial heritage in some constructive new way.

The trackbed itself is probably the easiest feature to put to new use. Two official reports considered this aspect of abandoned railways in 1970 and 1982 respectively. The 1970 publication was the so-called Appleton Report, produced by Dr J.H. Appleton (a reader in Geography at Hull University), but it was largely overshadowed by its 1982 successor, the Grimshaw Report. This was produced by John Grimshaw and Associates, a firm of engineering consultants based in Bristol. It was a vast document, consisting of a main report supported by no less than thirty-three separate annexes, which showed in pragmatic detail how a number of major traffic-free railway paths could be constructed from disused lines which were already largely in public ownership. It says much for the practical and realistic approach of these annexes that various local authorities have already converted some of them into *faits accomplis*.

Two problems prompted this gigantic piece of work: the first was that of derelict industrial land, which we have looked at already; the second was that of road-traffic accidents involving pedestrians, cyclists and other vulnerable road users. John Grimshaw saw, quite rightly, that the two problems could be solved by using one to cure the other. He was (and still is) also concerned about open spaces in and between large urban centres. In a society where people have become conditioned to travelling from one building to another in the insulated cocoon of a car, the space between has become less and less important. As a result, developers have often taken a myopic view of the environment surrounding sites, while architects have designed buildings with 'zero attention ... to anything except what goes on within the walls'. The report highlighted the need to encourage pedestrians and cyclists off the roads and on to abandoned railways, once the routes had been suitably treated and brought up to standard. To this end, Grimshaw set up two organizations: the Railway Path Project and Sustrans Limited. The Railway Path Project deals with surveys and field studies, its clients being local authorities and even government departments, while Sustrans deals with the construction side of the work. Grimshaw outlines their policies thus:

From the start we set out to design a high quality route which would be smooth and dry throughout the year. These might be regarded as 'trunk' paths and are particularly popular in the winter when so many field paths are difficult to use, and with those who need an easier walk. All the gates and access points are arranged so that wheelchairs and prams as well as cyclists can freely use the paths. (*Byway and Bridleway*, No. 4, 1989)

Abandoned railways are ideal for this treatment because they are level and often segregated entirely from road traffic. The same can also be said of canal towpaths, and it is no accident that Sustrans has upgraded the towpath of the Kennet and Avon Canal between Bath and Trowbridge. Bit by bit, and with the support of interested local authorities, Grimshaw's organization is beginning to show that a network of safe, attractive and traffic-free routes could be created from the very things which society has discarded. And what a pleasure it is to see planning conceived in terms which accommodate pedestrians, cyclists, young families, the elderly and the disabled.

A well-constructed railway path invariably proves popular. The character of the route certainly changes, but that is no bad thing, since a railway line which is truly abandoned can be a rather forlorn and depressing place; personally speaking, I would much rather see it develop some new form of life. The best of these conversions are very pleasant 'experiences', charged with a sense of purpose and usefulness. In walking the lines described in this series, I have met wheelchair users, mothers teaching their children how to ride bicycles, local residents exercising their dogs, women on their way to the shops, youngsters on bicycles loaded with rods and poles for fishing, groups of ramblers, even whole sponsored walks! The plain fact of the matter is that the paths are well used and have become a valued part of the local infrastructure. What we desperately need is more of them and a commitment to link them together so that they can be of more than purely local significance.

Sustrans is well aware of the need to integrate what has been done already and has ambitious plans to create a long distance cycleway from London to the Avon Gorge, beyond Bristol. A more or less continuous path now exists from Trowbridge to Pill (near Avonmouth), while, at the eastern end, a start has been made in the Thames Valley; the key to joining the two together is the incorporation of the full length of the towpath of the Kennet and Avon Canal. Two equally interesting possibilities beckon in the north. The first is a 'Trans-Pennine Trail' in which Barnsley Borough Council has a large hand (further details appear in Chapter 7); while the second is a mammoth London to Inverness cycleway. This may be a case of optimism run wild, but no one could accuse John Grimshaw of not having a goal to work toward, and a number of county councils along the way know that he has his eye on 'their' old railway lines!

The construction of a Sustrans path depends largely on the area through which it will pass. John Grimshaw again explains the company's policy:

In rural areas we generally aim to to build a 2 metre wide path finished in limestone or whin dust, whereas in urban areas the heavier use warrants an asphalt path 3 metres wide. On paths of this type the level of use can be quite high. For instance, we estimate that about one million journeys are made each year over various lengths of the Bristol and Bath path [their pilot scheme]. Pedestrians and cyclists are in roughly equal numbers.

It is significant that all motorized vehicles are barred from these routes and the access points are specifically designed to keep them out. The same generally goes for horses, except where the former trackbed is wide enough to accommodate separate provision for both types of user. Horseriders do, unfortunately, create problems: though a number of councils permit them on the routes, there is no getting away from the fact that horses' hooves do serious damage to the surface of the paths, especially if the animals are ridden hard. The end result is extremely selfish: while horses may still be able to negotiate a path with a pitted surface, cyclists certainly cannot, and it is not particularly pleasant for pedestrians either. Durham County Council has already had to close parts of the Derwent Walk in order to repair damage caused by horses (see Chapter 10) and it is my opinion that they should be kept off railway walks altogether – particularly if the users are to include groups such as the disabled and children. At the end of the day, these paths should exist for those who are prepared to get about under their own steam – forgive the pun. Horseriders already have the use of an extensive network of bridleways throughout the country: plenty of those have been made difficult for cyclists by the pot-holing effect described above, so it hardly seems unreasonable to ask that they are given a network of routes free from such defects.

So much for abandoned trackbeds. Abandoned railway architecture can present a more difficult problem, simply because it was so specifically designed for its original purpose. What on earth can one do with a disused signal-box, for example, or a 120 ft high stone viaduct? And what of the larger disused stations like Manchester Central or Nottingham London Road? Mercifully, a large proportion of disused railway properties are on a domestic scale and can be converted quite happily into private homes. The popularity of this type of residence has not escaped the notice of cartoonists working for the national press. In August 1988, for example, the Daily Telegraph carried a cartoon by 'Matt' in which a yuppie couple were rushing along in their sports car, the wife holding a newspaper on which the banner headline read 'TRAIN FARES UP'. Her response to this was: 'Marvellous, there'll be loads more disused stations to convert.' The joke is apt enough, and one only has to walk along the Hornsea Rail Trail or the Scarborough and Whitby Railway Path to see the evidence of various conversions. Gatehouses as well as station buildings are admirably suited to this purpose.

Some of the buildings which might be too large for a single family have been adapted to a wide variety of new functions. The old station at Thorpe Thewles, for example, on the former line from Stockton to Wingate, is now the Station House Field Centre on the Castle Eden Walkway: it is equipped with a main lecture room and exhibition area, and offers facilities for study, seminars and experimental work. Whitby West Cliff now provides a depot and offices for the Yorkshire Water Authority; Durham Gilesgate is a warehouse and trade outlet for Archibalds, the local builders' merchants; while Hornsea Town station on the bracing east coast has been converted into a number of very superior flats. Further uses which will be encountered elsewhere in the country (and perhaps at other former LNER stations which I was not lucky enough to discover) include guest-houses, tea-rooms, pubs, shops, offices, even churches and chapels. Taken as a whole, there seems no logical reason why station buildings on this scale should not be found some worthwhile new use after the trains have gone. The real problem begins with disused stations at the top of the range. Just imagine for one moment that Newcastle Central was suddenly closed completely: should it be demolished or could some new use be found for it?

Perhaps it is fortunate that there are relatively few disused stations of this size. Those that do exist are well known amongst railway historians: Bristol Temple Meads (Brunel's original Great Western Railway terminus), Bath Green Park, Manchester Central, Birmingham Snow Hill and Nottingham London Road spring readily to mind. Birmingham Snow Hill is the odd one out here, for after years of neglect most of the structure was demolished and turned into a rather tatty car-park; British Rail then decided that it needed the station after all, built a new one and relaid the tracks! This raises some interesting questions which readers may like to muse over in their own time.

The original Bristol Temple Meads is now a museum and exhibition centre. In the north-east, Darlington North Road – although a smaller station – has been saved by having a similar new use found for it. In 1985, Tony Byrne was a director of the Bristol Marketing Board and his remarks to a contemporary conference on the railway heritage were particularly revealing:

> I would add that it has been an enormous pleasure . . . to see a very dramatic development of attitude over the last five years in the people we work with in British Rail, so that we are all now treating this great railway complex as an area of exceptional commercial and tourist opportunity rather than a huge headache. (*The Future of the Railway Heritage*, 1985)

What a welcome sentiment! Sainsbury's clearly adopted a similar approach to Bath Green Park, which they now own. During the day, the great train shed is a covered car-park for customers at their nearby supermarket but, during the evening, it is available for concerts. The platforms now accommodate an indoor market and are usually lined with traders' stalls, while the former public rooms and offices accommodate a variety of other retail businesses including a café-cum-pub and a clothes shop. There is even a small museum, which contains an exhibition on the extensive restoration and conversion work which had to be carried out. Manchester Central has likewise been converted into an 'event centre', capable of holding 'trade exhibitions, public exhibitions, pop shows, sports events and so on'. Returning to the 1985 railway heritage conference, the investment banker who presented the Manchester case-study had this to say about preserving our architectural heritage during a period of government austerity:

> We need to seek out contemporary commercial uses which can be accommodated within historic walls, and which will generate revenues, create activity and bring these buildings back into our daily lives.

The restoration of Nottingham London Road was perhaps the boldest venture of all for, as James Taylor, the city council's principal planning officer, freely admitted, no end use had been determined when the project began. The principal intention was to clean up a prominent city-centre eyesore and ultimately revive an under-utilized building together with its adjoining sixty acres of land. The council used Community Programme labour, financed by the Manpower Services Commission, an obvious spin-off being the skills training provided by the project. Mr Taylor reported as follows:

> Over the last year 88 different workers have been engaged on the project and, of those leaving the scheme, some 38 per cent have found regular employment. All the workers have received varying levels of training in building and conservation techniques which should better qualify them to seek permanent employment. Compared with the despondency which is often rife on Community Programme schemes, there seems quite a good spirit on this job and some genuine interest and pride in the end results.

Sustrans has experienced the same 'pride in the job' on its railway path construction projects, which were financed in the same way. In view of the benefits to be derived – skills training, the rehabilitation of derelict buildings and industrial land, the provision of facilities for ordinary people which will actually enhance their health – it seems a great pity that the Community Programme has now been closed. Something is urgently needed to replace it. While the Department of Transport cannot be expected to finance the restoration of derelict buildings, can it not fund railway path construction from its budget for road-building? After all, it places a price on road accidents: every injury and fatality is costed in terms of police time, hospital time and so on. Railways paths actually tempt pedestrians and cyclists away from the roads and, in so doing, actively prevent road accidents and all the associated expenses. Why, therefore, cannot some of the savings be channelled into building more of them?

From the above, it will be seen that abandoned trackbeds and stations can be found worthwhile new uses, given some imagination and commitment. But what of the other paraphernalia of old railways, the bridges, viaducts, goods sheds, signal-boxes and all that peculiar technology of wires, rods and levers on which the system once depended? Here we are on more difficult ground. Bridges and viaducts certainly ought to be retained so that future users of the trackbed can be segregated from road traffic, but a number of practical considerations intervene. A good number of bridges have been demolished, either because a local authority wished to eliminate a long-term maintenance liability or because a former railway structure restricted road visibility. The same applies to disused viaducts, although the arguments are almost always conducted in terms of maintenance costs: the funds available through agencies such as BR's Railway Heritage Fund are simply inadequate to cope with all the demands made on it. On the other hand, many of these viaducts cannot be demolished because they are listed structures so, sooner or later, we are going to face a dilemma: to preserve or to destroy? In the end, it will probably depend on the value the local authority places on its industrial heritage. Railway ramblers in Durham and other enlightened counties have little to fear, but the same cannot be said of those areas where cost-cutting is the prime consideration – justifiable though that may be in other respects.

A number of goods sheds remain because their design makes them perfectly suitable for use as warehouses or even as garages for farm equipment. One shed, at Caton in Lancashire, has even been converted into a Catholic church! I wonder if the congregation includes any appreciative railway enthusiasts. Signal-boxes are something of a problem due to their highly individualistic construction. A few now do service as elevated greenhouses or information centres on official walks, but most have been demolished. One or two, such as that at Cherry Burton, still stand gauntly in abandonment, but it is now twenty-five years since it was closed and it cannot survive indefinitely in its present state. Nearly all of the associated equipment has vanished without trace: a few signals survive here and there, sometimes as barely recognizable armless stumps, but the associated rods, cables and pulleys have all vanished – no doubt recovered by BR for use elsewhere. Mile-posts and gradient posts have fared marginally better, but they are popular prey for private collectors (who do at least give them a decent home): very few survive on the walks described in this book.

Tunnels are another major feature of railways, but practically none of those used by the LNER are now open to walkers, who must travel to the south and west if they wish to indulge in this particular pursuit. The only exception which springs to mind (although it was never used by the LNER) is the original tramway tunnel at Grosmont, the small bore of which reveals that it was constructed with horses rather than steam locomotives in mind. The company which built it was the early Whitby and Pickering Railway, incorporated by an ambiguous act which had separate sections, some permitting and others forbidding the use of steam on the line! It is easy to understand the reluctance of local authorities to allow public access through such tunnels, particularly if there is a history of water seepage, with the consequent danger of bricks becoming dislodged from the roof; they accordingly provide a detour if a sealed tunnel blocks the way, as, for instance, at Ravenscar on the Whitby–Scarborough walk.

The other obvious engineering structures along an abandoned railway are cuttings and embankments which, generally speaking, have survived extremely well: cuttings tend to become secluded nature reserves, while embankments remain lofty, unnatural perches which give extensive views of the surrounding countryside – often where none would otherwise exist. A number of the LNER's embankments, particularly in the north-east, actually started life as timber-built viaducts. Hurbuck embankment on Durham County Council's Lanchester Valley Walk is a case in point: its origins are revealed by its sheer size and the extreme steepness of its sides. In its previous incarnation, it was Knitsley Viaduct. There is a photograph of it (the only one I have ever seen) on page 608 of W.W. Tomlinson's *North Eastern Railway*, a monumental work which remains a well-loved classic.

We have now covered all of the obvious railway remains, except the old railway fencing and the remains of the tracks themselves. Railway fencing was usually made from concrete posts and wire, a simple arrangement which has lasted remarkably well; earlier types have been replaced as part of the normal round of maintenance. As for the tracks, observant walkers can still expect to find the tell-tale remnants of sleepers, rails, fishplates, chairs and keys. Provided they are little used, minor level crossings are a good place to start looking for these relics, as the rails are often preserved in the tarmac: the local authority will see no point in going to all the trouble and expense of digging them out if they are crossed by nothing more than a few cars and the odd farm tractor. Fishplates, chairs and keys are a little more unusual, but many lines were dismantled by contractors who were not particularly thorough: a walk along the north end of the Hornsea Rail Trail reveals some of what they left behind, still peeping through the new ash surface. It is even possible to find some of the nuts and bolts which once held the fishplates to the rails. If he or she were unbelievably assiduous, incredibly strong and (it has to be admitted) a bit daft, a latter-day collector could probably gather enough material from England's railway footpaths to construct a couple of sidings in the back garden.

The introduction to *Railway Walks: GWR & SR* in this series gave a general history of railway closures, and it is not proposed to repeat all of that material here. Suffice it to say that, since long before Dr Beeching, closures have been a characteristic feature of the industry. In the nineteenth century, tramways and railways used to come and go with the quarries and industries that spawned them. For an early twentieth-century example, one only has to look at the lonely

Rosedale branch on the North Yorkshire Moors: this closed as long ago as 1929, when the quarries had been exhausted by the extraction of ten million tons of Rosedale ironstone. The two world wars also had a debilitating effect on the industry. On the one hand, the demands of wartime service strained the railway companies' finances and left them with a huge backlog of maintenance; on the other, they delivered a hefty impetus to the development of an alternative transport technology – the internal combustion engine. It is for these reasons that we find local bus services beginning to compete with branch-line trains from the 1920s. A small trickle of passenger withdrawals (and occasionally complete closures) followed as a direct result. One such casualty was the much-loved Southwold Railway, which closed its narrow-gauge line on 11 April 1929.

By the 1950s, the railways were competing with both petrol and diesel traction on the roads, and car ownership was on the increase. The government responded with a bold Modernisation Plan, which sought to provide much needed improvements in locomotives and rolling stock, while cutting out some of the dead wood. This meant that a number of little-used branch lines lost their passenger services, but, overall, the results were highly beneficial, with the railways enjoying something of an Indian summer. It is difficult to say where these developments would have led had they not been stopped. The lure of roads, with their apparent freedom and convenience, would probably have ruined the railways anyway. In any event, the Macmillan Government became increasingly concerned about the financial losses being incurred by the nation's rail network – a concern which mounted steadily as the world entered the bold decade of the sixties. An advisory group was set up to investigate ways of resolving the problem and it soon became clear that its most prominent member was Dr Richard Beeching, who believed that British Railways should close down all loss-making branch lines and duplicate trunk routes, switching its effort instead to the high-speed transport of passengers and freight. Dr Beeching was accordingly appointed Chairman of British Railways from 1961 and, in 1963, published his infamous report, *The Re-Shaping of British Railways*. This heralded the greatest wave of railway closures that Britain has ever seen and, it is to be hoped, ever will see.

Most railwaymen at the time appreciated Dr Beeching's politeness and clarity of thought, and it must be said that he was responsible for the development of the railway's InterCity business, which is so important today. On the other hand, many of them were very concerned about the butchery being inflicted on their industry and could not see how a technical director from ICI was qualified to mete it out; it was even claimed that his speciality was soap-powders! One can imagine how the railwaymen felt. Beeching knew that he would be regarded as the 'axe man', although he always claimed that he was performing careful surgery rather than wholesale slaughter. Many railway enthusiasts today regard him as a sort of demon, but, in the final analysis, he was only doing his job. The decade of the 1960s was the age of the car: railways, like Victorian architecture, were going out of fashion. Had Dr Beeching not fulfilled his role, it is certain that the government would have found someone else to do it instead. Despite this, however, there are three regrettable factors about Dr Beeching's reign: firstly, he ushered in a prolonged period of gloom and despondency in the industry; secondly, serious questions have been raised about the timetabling, accounting and statistical methods which accompanied the closure of several doomed lines; and thirdly, no attempt was made to find any way in which the trackbeds thus abandoned could be re-employed in the public domain. Perhaps the saddest thing of all is that 'the man from M' made the wholesale closure of lines an acceptable feature of railway management; at times in the post-Beeching years, it has almost seemed as if the general idea is to close railways down rather than keep them running. It took until the mid-1970s for the flood of closures to return to a trickle.

This, then, is how we inherited our network of abandoned railways. The proportion along which we can now walk or ride our bicycles is undoubtedly too small, but there are encouraging signs, particularly in the work of Sustrans Limited and the growing awareness of local authorities that empty trackbeds offer valuable recreational opportunities. Given that nobody in 1963 seems to have considered the idea of railway paths and cycleways, it is almost miraculous that we have so many. So, get out and enjoy them! Local and national government will only be encouraged to develop more of these facilities by the observation that they are being well used; and if some feature of the route seems below standard, send a letter to the relevant authority and suggest how it could be improved.

To finish on a practical note, a few points need to be made about preparing for the walks in this book. While the obvious pitfalls (if any) are mentioned in each chapter, you must have some regard to the weather and terrain. If you are venturing on to high moorland, the coast or a wind-swept plain, do ensure that you are equipped with adequate clothing. Nothing is more calculated to give you a headache than a cold wind whistling around your face and the back of your neck – I can heartily recommend a scarf and woolly hat. The footwear required depends on the route selected: plimsolls or light shoes are perfectly adequate in summer on routes with a fine surface, but they can cause agony if you discover that you have selected a path with a knobbly surface of gravel. The only route which I found in the least bit uncomfortable, for instance, was the gravelly middle section of the Hornsea Rail Trail, but that was my own fault for not wearing shoes with thick enough soles. I only encountered significant waterlogging once, in Essex, on the Braintree–Bishop's Stortford walk, so I can see no real need to struggle around in wellington boots. Personally speaking, I find light-weight fell boots or Clarks' Polyveldts the best bet as they are light and very comfortable. At fifteen to twenty miles each, some of the walks I undertake are rather long and conventional hiking boots feel more like something a diver wears by the time I have reached the end. The sensation of having lead weights swinging at the end of your legs is not one I can recommend!

An Ordnance Survey map is an invaluable companion and readers will soon find that I have identified all significant points on these walks by providing a six-figure grid reference. Not only does this pin-point places in a way which is thoroughly unambiguous, it also eliminates a lot of otherwise tedious detail from the narrative. For that matter, it enables walkers to return by a different route if they wish, creating their own circular rambles. The Landranger Series is particularly recommended, and sheets can be borrowed from most large libraries. The relevant sheet numbers are given in the final section of each chapter.

If you intend to follow my footsteps literally and make a linear walk, it is absolutely essential that you cheek the public transport details thoroughly before setting out. Many a good walk has been turned into a nightmare by arriving at the end only to discover that the last bus went several hours ago. Since the deregulation of bus services in October 1986, the level of provision – particularly in rural areas – can change with alarming speed. While the details provided are current at the time of going to press, they cannot be regarded as fixed in perpetuity. A judicious telephone call to the relevant operator or the public transport information office of the local county council can save a lot of heartache later. Of course, these dire warnings can be ignored if you and a friend can undertake the expedition jointly with two cars, placing one at the far end of the walk before you set out. There are places where this is the only practical solution and, if this is the case, I have not shrunk from saying so. Now, however, nothing more remains but to introduce the walks themselves. Happy rambling!

1
THE ALBAN WAY
St Albans to Hatfield

Introduction

Before the railway age, the towns of St Albans and Hatfield enjoyed trade and prosperity as a result of their situation on major coaching routes – St Albans on the Holyhead Road (A5) and West Coast Road (A6), and Hatfield on the Great North Road (A l). Their size and importance attracted the attention of Victorian railway-builders, so that, during the nineteenth century, they were placed on separate main lines, with two branches from St Albans and three from Hatfield. The St Albans branches ran to Watford and Hatfield, while the Hatfield branches radiated out to St Albans, Dunstable and Hertford. Nowadays, only the line from Watford to St Albans survives, the others having closed to passengers in 1951 and 1965. Rationalization this close to London may be considered surprising, but it is unlikely that all of the Hertfordshire branches could have survived. In rural parts of the county, there was simply not the traffic; Ayot station on the Hatfield-Dunstable line, for instance, closed permanently after a fire in 1948. In urban areas, there were cheaper and more frequent buses, and there were sometimes faster and more convenient railways – two complaints which particularly affected the branch from St Albans to Hatfield.

Despite this, the line managed to eke out an existence of just over a hundred years, during which time it served the local community faithfully if only on a modest scale. It ended up as a string of private sidings and tiny halts, a sure sign that the railway was struggling to attract every last penny of revenue. Some of its freight traffic was unique, the two most notable commodities being orchids from Sanders' Nursery (very fashionable until the mid-1920s) and thousands of copies of Salvation Army periodicals destined for Army citadels and public houses throughout the land. This, one supposes, made it almost a missionary railway, a veritable 'railroad to heaven'. I have certainly come across nothing else like it throughout the length and breadth of the country.

History

The first railway in the St Albans area was the London and Birmingham Railway, which opened its line from London to Tring in 1837 and extended it to Birmingham in 1838. Passengers from St Albans had to take a horse-drawn coach to Watford and change on to the train there. In 1850, the Great Northern Railway opened its main line from King's Cross to Hatfield and Peterborough, and this gave clear notice to the L & B (now part of the newly formed London and North Western Railway) that there was to be competition for the St Albans traffic. In particular, the journey to Hatfield was about one and a half miles shorter than that to Watford, a significant consideration given the high cost of coach travel. The LNWR responded by building a line from Watford right into the south-west corner of the city, and this survives today as the St Albans Abbey branch: it was authorized on 4 August 1853 and opened for traffic on 5 May 1858. The Abbey branch was bad news for the Great Northern, which claimed to have lost all of its two-thirds share of the St Albans traffic after it opened. Much as it might have wished to retaliate, the GNR was unable to do so for several years while it pursued its expansion and development plans in the north of England. This tied up a lot of its energy and spare capital, and when it did turn to St Albans again, it restricted itself to encouraging various local landowners to float an independent company called the Hatfield and St Albans Railway. The significant features of the GNR's agreement with this concern were that it would put up £20,000 of the estimated £88,000 construction costs, and would operate the line, when complete, in return for half of the gross receipts. The Hatfield and St Albans Railway was duly authorized by an Act of Parliament on 30 June 1862 which, *inter alia*, gave the GNR running powers into St Albans' LNWR station. The minute-book of the board of directors has survived and, from this, we know that the company planned to construct the line as a single track with provision at all of the overbridges for subsequent doubling. By September 1863, a contractor had been appointed and most of the land purchased, but a serious development occurred in that year, the significance of which the shareholders, and perhaps the directors, failed to appreciate. This development was the planned construction of the Midland Railway's line from Bedford to London. While the Midland had no malice against the local company, its running powers over the Great Northern main line were practically useless; the GNR gave Midland trains at Hitchin very low priority and it is said that, on one occasion, the queue of waiting Midland trains was five miles long. Under these circumstances, the Midland had no alternative but to construct its own route to London via St Albans, which would offer the city its most direct access to the capital yet. Unfortunately, this was to have a disastrous impact on its two branch lines.

The directors of the Hatfield and St Albans Railway considered the threat, but decided, most unwisely, to persevere; they must have realized that the construction of the Midland line would mean that, in the long term, their own railway could hope for little more than local traffic between the two places named in its title. In August 1865, the company's shareholders were told that their line was nearly complete and, on 16 October that year, trains began running from Hatfield to St Albans London Road; the opening was greeted with few celebrations, due to the railway's parlous financial circumstances. On 1 November 1866, passenger trains finally ran through from Hatfield to St Albans Abbey station, but they had a very short-lived hold on the city's railway traffic, for the Midland line from Bedford to St Pancras opened in July 1868, and the effect was immediate. None the less, the Hatfield and St Albans Railway was at least complete, though only a modest affair, and saddled with debt from the start. It featured very few engineering works, the exceptions being a cutting north-west of Hatfield station, an embankment across the Ver Valley and a brick bridge over the River Ver within St Albans. There was only one intermediate station, at Springfield, but this was not ready for the opening due to difficulties in providing the station-master with a house. St Albans London Road was the largest station on the line and possessed, initially, a passing loop, a small motive-power depot and a turntable, but these facilities gradually disappeared when the railway found them to be superfluous.

Traffic on the Hatfield and St Albans Railway was disappointing even before

St Albans Abbey station, 16 March 1957. The train is formed of a first generation railbus manufactured by Park Royal; note the line of coal wagons in the left of the picture

A.E. Bennett

the Midland line opened, and this created serious financial difficulties for the company. The cost of building the line was put at £113,000, but only £85,000 had been raised by the two share issues; the shortfall was met by loans, which the low level of receipts proved inadequate to service. Bankruptcy loomed as early as May 1866, a mere seven months after the first passenger train had pulled into St Albans London Road. In 1870, a creditor brought action against the company and it was found to be insolvent; a receiver was appointed but he had little more success in managing it than the directors. The fundamental problem remained its great burden of debt, and there appeared to be no chance that this could be repaid in a reasonable amount of time. As a result, the directors eventually decided to approach the Great Northern and accept whatever they were offered. The final agreement was formalized by an Act of Parliament on 1 November 1883, whereby the GNR took over the line in return for paying all its outstanding debts as well as the cost of winding up the company and redeeming its shares at 23 per cent of their face value.

When relieved of its disabling debts, the line must have fared much better. Little material evidence exists, but it can be assumed that it ran fairly successfully until the 1920s, when road competition began to steal its trade. In 1879, Springfield station was renamed Smallford to avoid confusion with another Springfield in Scotland, but it actually served the village of Colney

The basic facilities at Smallford station photographed in April 1955. The substantial brick overbridge was built to accommodate a second line of rails, although this was never added

A.E. Bennett

Heath anyway! As was so often the case, the main architect of confusion was the railway company itself. In July 1895, a new siding was laid at Hill End to receive materials for the construction of a new asylum, later the Hertfordshire County Mental Hospital. In 1899, one Joseph Fenwick Owen established a brickworks here which possessed its own internal tramway and brought a fair amount of freight traffic on to the line, while a new passenger station was opened at Hill End on 1 August that year; its timber buildings lasted until 1954 when they were destroyed by fire. A new halt was also opened at Nast Hyde on 1 February 1910. A level crossing and gatekeeper's cottage had been provided here since the line's opening, but now a modest, timber-built platform and shelter were added for the benefit of Great Nast Hyde House and Nast Hyde Farm, though traffic levels can never have been great. Further west, in St Albans, the Salvation Army Printing Works were established in Campfield Road in 1901. The railway carried ingoing goods in the form of newsprint for the Army's publications, while outgoing goods took the form of print runs of *The War Cry* and *Young Soldier*. A former employee reckons that a single consignment of *The War Cry* weighed between 15 and 20 tons and required two or three wagons. A private halt was provided for the benefit of Salvation Army staff, but by 1938 it was listed in the public timetable and must have been open to members of the public as well.

Bus services began to affect the line's business in the mid-twenties. The National Omnibus Company started a service from St Albans to Hatfield in 1925, while the Albanian Bus Company started a service from St Albans to Colney Heath in 1927. These rapidly reduced the amount of traffic from the three main stations on the line. According to a document in St Albans Library, traffic in 1938 had slumped to the point where an average of fourteen passengers per day were being conveyed by seventeen separate trains. While this source may be unreliable, there was little doubt that the passenger service was not paying its way, and the London and North Eastern Railway, owner of the line from 1923, withdrew it in September 1939 as a wartime economy measure. However, the economy was short-lived, for, in December 1940, a limited passenger service was restored in order to conserve valuable petrol supplies. Rail fares were even pitched lower than those of rival buses in order to encourage business. Ambulance trains began running to Hill End Hospital and, in about 1941, a cold store was opened just west of Smallford. This was part of the wartime strategic plan to keep food supplies away from port areas, which were an obvious bombing target. Finally, on 1 August 1942, a new halt was opened at Lemsford Road, on the north-west edge of Hatfield, for the convenience of workers at the nearby De Havilland aircraft factory.

Unfortunately, the line's wartime value was quickly forgotten after 1945, and decline again set in. The Smallford cold store soon switched to road transport, although a rail-connected banana warehouse was added at about the same time. Passenger levels continued to decline and the passenger service was accordingly withdrawn on 1 October 1951. Freight services lingered on until the 1960s, with Hill End and London Road sidings closing in October 1964. The Fleetville and Salvation Army sidings closed in December that year and, by May 1965, the only remaining traffic was the occasional delivery of bananas to the warehouse in Smallford. This lasted until December 1968, when the line was closed. The rails were removed in 1969 and now even the banana warehouse has been demolished.

The Line Today

After 1969, there were lengthy discussions as to what should be done with the old railway. Most rail-over-road bridges were demolished, but, generally, road-over-rail bridges were retained. Eventually (and after protracted negotiations with British Rail), the district councils of Welwyn-Hatfield and St Albans bought the trackbed for conversion into a footpath and cycleway. The eastern section was converted first; it was designated 'The Smallford Trail' and opened on 8 December 1985. However, the western section from Hill End to St Albans Abbey station was left, pending a decision on its possible use for a new relief road. In the event, this plan was rejected and conversion work commenced in 1986. The route was opened officially on 17 April 1988, and the whole length from St Albans to Hatfield was named 'The Alban Way'.

The conversion of the last two miles within St Albans involved major clearance work, resurfacing, landscaping, demolition of an air-raid shelter and the removal of an enormous amount of domestic refuse – an unwelcome but all too common presence on abandoned railway land. Over 130 workers were employed on the scheme, both volunteers and unemployed people sponsored by the Manpower Services Commission. The district councils' joint press-release also mentioned the 'practical help of several commercial companies who adjoin the route'. At the Salvation Army siding, for example, a local company gave a strip of its car-park so that the cycleway could pass through. Support like this is invaluable and shows just what can be done when there is sufficient goodwill and commitment.

I approached the Alban Way with some hesitation after the rather sterile conversion carried out on the Silkin Way at Telford, but left feeling that an exceptionally good job had been made of it. In parts of St Albans, it was difficult to remember that this was actually an urban walk, particularly by the River Ver and in the delightful tree-lined avenue which passes under the Midland main line just south of St Albans City station: it gave the impression of a green lane into the countryside. Only in Hatfield did tarmac intrude, and even there one could still feel grateful that it was possible to trace the course of the old railway with so little difficulty.

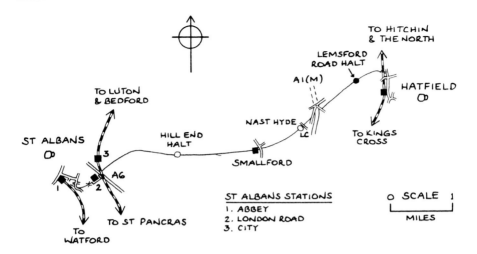

THE ALBAN WAY

The Walk (6½ miles)

The Alban Way starts at grid reference 149062, off a minor road a short walk from St Albans Abbey station, terminus of the six and a half mile branch line from Watford. The station once possessed an overall roof, but that and the original buildings have all been swept away in the name of rationalization and efficiency. Trains from Hatfield used to terminate in a bay to the north-east, offering a cross-platform connection on to waiting Watford trains. Despite the many changes, the station still reveals the LNWR's original intention of continuing towards Luton. The easiest way to find the start of the walk is as follows. Proceeding out of the station, turn right and then right again into Prospect Road. Follow Prospect Road to a T-junction with Cottonmill Lane and there turn right again. Pass a small cul-de-sac on the right and look out for a gap in the hedge (again on the right) just before a bridge over the disused railway. This is the start of the route and soon leads down on to the disused trackbed. After all those right turns, it will come as no surprise to discover that you are barely a hundred yards from your starting point, the Abbey station, which is visible to the north-west.

The line rapidly curves away to the north-east and crosses the River Ver on a fine skew bridge; this is one of the few major structures which was not built from the outset to accommodate double track. Today it is a quiet and leafy spot with a good view of the abbey to the north-west. A hundred yards or so further

A skew bridge carrying the Alban Way over the River Ver in St Albans. The attractive abbey can be seen from the trackbed at this point

on, an earth track is crossed, which the Ordnance Survey map identifies as a public footpath. It is of minimal significance nowadays but, some two hundred years ago, this used to be the main road from London. The line is then blocked by private occupation, but a detour negotiates the obstruction: the path skirts round the south side of London Road station (grid reference 155065) and offers a glimpse of a water-tower through the trees. The station, a fine imposing building, is now in private hands and the owner is busy restoring a number of military vehicles from the Second World War – no small undertaking.

Immediately beyond the station, the path swings back on to the trackbed and a backward glance reveals the two platforms between the trees. The down platform on the left was originally served by a passing loop, but this proved superfluous and had been converted to a siding by 1890. Thereafter, all trains used the up platform on the right. The line now passes under London Road and the Midland main line in quick succession; the railway bridge is particularly large and is reminiscent of the huge vault of a church. It carries quadruple track and close inspection reveals that it is, in fact, two bridges – the first built in 1868, when the line opened, and the second added in 1894, when the track was quadrupled. The view ahead is of a grand avenue of trees, yet this is right in the middle of St Albans, with over a mile of solid urban development to the right and left; in summer, it is scarcely believable.

At grid reference 161069, the railway crosses Camp Road; the spot is impossible to miss because an underbridge has been demolished here. When the railway was at its height, the walker would have met, from west to east, the Salvation Army halt, Sanders siding (on the left), the missing bridge and the Salvation Army siding (on the right). All this is much changed now, but a useful landmark is the car-park through which the walk passes, where the owners have given up about 4 ft of their land in order to maintain the route's continuity. St Albans Orchid Nurseries extended to the left until the business moved away and the greenhouses were demolished in 1953. In its heyday, it sent large quantities of orchids to King's Cross in specially ventilated 'orchid vans' provided by the Great Northern Railway. These were loaded in Sanders siding, the site of which has just been passed.

The site of Hill End Halt is met at grid reference 175070 but precious little of the station remains. This is hardly surprising, for it was of timber construction and burned down in 1954. As the line was not in passenger use at that time, it was not replaced. The site now accommodates a car-park for path users, and in August 1988 still housed a depot used by the Manpower Services Commission

This plaque near the former Salvation Army siding commemorates the opening of the Alban Way on 17 April 1988. The first part of the route (between Hatfield and Hill End) opened in 1985 and was known initially as the Smallford Trail

construction team. Only at the eastern edge of the site was a short fragment of platform still visible, on private land. From here on, the path is the earlier Smallford Trail, opened in December 1985. The views finally begin to open out as the line enters a short stretch of countryside before reaching the out-skirts of Hatfield.

Smallford station still stands at grid reference 199073. The track layout here was extremely simple, with a single through-line and a single siding. Somehow, the railway managed to find enough activity to justify the provision of a small signal-box, but it did not last long. The platform still survives, much overgrown, with its timber building now used as the office for a scrap merchant who occupies the old station yard. Immediately after closure, the station was used as a ladies' hairdressing salon, so its current employment involves a certain loss of dignity. Continuing east, the line offers attractive views across open fields (wheat-filled in summer) before reaching the site of Nast Hyde Halt at grid reference 210078. The gatekeeper's cottage, a neat, two-storey brick building, still survives in private occupation, but the trackbed beyond has been incorporated into a small housing estate. The street names, such as Haltside and The Sidings, reflect the history of the site, and three cheers for there not being the ubiquitous Beeching Close! The Alban Way may be followed through this development until the A1(M) is encountered just south of Hatfield Tunnel. Autophobes had better shut their eyes to this, for six lanes of motorway now plunge beneath Hatfield Aerodrome, and a large chunk of the old railway, not surprisingly, has been obliterated. It is also just as well not to enquire how much it all cost. Happily, the Alban Way offers walkers an entirely segregated route on towards Hatfield town centre and station. From the western embankment of the motorway a track leads away to the left. Follow this as far as a T-junction with a main road, and there turn right. Follow the road across the tunnel mouth and, on the east side, use the subway provided to pass under it and regain the old trackbed. There are several strategically placed waymarking signs to ensure that you do not lose your way; once again, all credit to the councils concerned.

From here onwards, most of the trackbed has been tarmacked and provided with street lighting, as it is now an arterial route in a network of residential footpaths. Here and there, though, the walker still finds himself on a slight embankment which confirms that this is indeed the course of the old railway. At grid reference 223090 the bridge over Lemsford Road has been removed, but the remains of Lemsford Road Halt still survive on the other side. The railway company originally considered building the platform out of sleepers, but this plan was rejected as it was wartime and the sleepers could do more useful service elsewhere. In the event, the halt was made entirely from concrete (including a small porter's room) at a cost of £1,757. The platform edging slabs have all been removed, but their arched supports still remain in a long line. This is one of those scenes occasionally encountered on old railways which smacks of surrealism.

The tarmacked path comes to an abrupt end at grid reference 228093 but the trackbed continues in a deep cutting which curves to the south on a tight, 12 chain radius to approach Hatfield station. Ironically, this is the most rustic and untouched part of the entire walk and it is difficult to imagine that, up above, you are surrounded by urban housing. The path ends just short of the former junction with the Great Northern main line. Steps on the left lead out of the cutting and into a small recreation ground. Cross this diagonally to the left, and, on reaching a narrow road, turn right. Cross the main line by a pedestrian bridge and then turn right again. Hatfield station is now just over a quarter of a mile straight ahead. Much of the station's historical interest was swept away when it was modernized for electrification, but the entrance to Hatfield House and the Royal Palace of Hatfield still stands opposite. Hatfield House is the family seat of the Marquis of Salisbury and home of the Cecil family; the Royal Palace is most famous for having been the childhood home of Queen Elizabeth I.

Further Explorations

Hertfordshire is a rather surprising county for railway walks. Given its proximity to London and the prevailing 'land hunger' referred to elsewhere in this series, one might have expected much to have been sacrificed whereas, in fact, much has been preserved. There has certainly been a healthy awareness of the potential of disused railways as recreational routes, as an officer of St Albans District Council told me in 1988: 'The opening of the Alban Way represented the completion of our programme since 1982 of converting disused railway lines to footpaths/cycleways.' Nevertheless, sacrifices of former railway land have been made, but the walker is left feeling that the overall policy has been one of compromise and reason.

The Alban Way is the county's longest railway path to date, but the Cole Greenway from near Hertford North station to Cole Green (four miles) should be worth a look, as also the Ayot Greenway from Ayot Green to Sheepcote Lane on the edge of Wheathampstead (two and a half miles). The countryside around Ayot Green is particularly attractive and has strong literary connections; George Bernard Shaw lived at nearby Ayot St Lawrence. The Upper Lea Valley Through Walk is also useful, for it strings together several lengths of disused railway between Ayot Green and Harpenden (including the Ayot Greenway) and is a sensible way of making a coherent walk from a number of otherwise disconnected sections. On the west side of Harpenden, two and a half miles of the old 'Nicky' line to Hemel Hempstead are also reputed to be open as a footpath. The length concerned runs from Harpenden junction (grid reference 132153) to the Redbourne bypass (113128). While these routes are all relatively short and in places fragmentary, they are at least geographically close, so perhaps the county council could prepare a single leaflet giving details of them all? It has already demonstrated initiative in this respect by obtaining sponsorship from London Country Buses to produce an attractive and informative leaflet on the Ayot Greenway.

Other than its railway walks, Hertfordshire also contains a substantial length of the Grand Union Canal. This runs diagonally through the west of the county, passing through Watford, Berkhamsted and Tring. Its towpath offers another source of interesting walks with an industrial archaeological flavour, but, for those who want a break from walking, there are also narrow-boat trips on *The Arcturus*. These run from Ironbridge Lock in Cassiobury Park, Watford (grid reference 089974), every Sunday afternoon from Easter to October, and on Tuesday and Thursday afternoons in August.

Transport and Facilities

Map:	Ordnance Survey: Landranger Series Sheet 166 (recommended)
Buses:	Arriva Southern Counties
	Arriva Shires and Essex
	www.arrivabus.co.uk
	Telephone: (Traveline) 0871 200 22 33
Trains:	National Rail Enquiries
	www.nationalrail.co.uk
	Telephone: 08457 48 49 50

This walk could hardly be more convenient for rail travellers, for the two ends are located within a few hundred yards of operational railway stations at St Albans Abbey and Hatfield. For good measure, St Albans City on the Bedford line is also a short walk from the old London Road station on the Alban Way. All three stations enjoy a good service seven days a week.

Bus services are similarly convenient. There are a number of services between St Albans and Hatfield, including:

a. Routes 300 and 301. These run from Monday to Saturday and provide a basic service of every twenty minutes, with a slight 'thinning-out' in the evening.

All of these services run until 11 p.m. so there is no excuse for missing the last bus!

This level of public transport makes the Alban Way one of the best provided railway walks in the whole country. The price of this is that the walk passes through an area which is urban or at best 'semi-rural', but it does mean that facilities are never far away. St Albans and Hatfield have no shortage of pubs, shops and cafés, and there is a bustling Saturday market at St Albans which practically brings the city centre to a standstill. The city's other claim to fame is the Campaign for Real Ale, whose headquarters are tucked away in an innocent-looking residential road; the organization is understandably pleased at the availability of traditional draught beer in virtually all the local pubs. McMullens of Hertford are the local brewers and they produce a fine, light mild called 'AK', which is very refreshing after a stroll along the railway path. At the other extreme, as one might expect, a number of pubs offer a staggering range of traditional ales from all over the country. The tiny village of Tyttenhanger is a good place to start looking, but don't expect to do much walking afterwards!

2
AN ESSEX BYWAY
BRAINTREE TO TILEKIIN GREEN

Introduction

Essex is a real mixture of a county. To some extent, all counties are, but the contrasts in Essex seem rather more exaggerated. Southend-on-Sea, the home of Access credit cards, has a liberal helping of tower blocks which can be seen for miles in the surrounding countryside. The town's Victorian railway stations sit cheek by jowl with modern civic architecture, while the A127 to London is still punctuated with giant 'road-house' pubs, which once catered for coachloads of day-trippers from the capital. Yet away from the bustle of the seaside and brash modern towns like Basildon and Billericay, Essex is a county of backwaters, of marshy river estuaries, weather-boarded cottages and ancient churches. To someone unfamiliar with the area, it might seem unbelievable that it could possess branch lines so rustic that railway historians write lyrically about their idiosyncrasies. Even the station names reflect this rural character: the Thaxted branch, for example, possessed the delightful Sibleys (for Chickney and Broxted) and Cutler's Green Halt. However, if we could turn the clock back a hundred years, we would find somewhat less enthusiasm among the directors and shareholders of the Great Eastern Railway. Some of these rustic branch lines did little for the company's prosperity, and the subject of the present chapter was dismissed as 'that wretched Dunmow line, as terrible a waste of money as any railway perpetrated'.

Many of these lines were 'infills', added after the main Essex railways had already been built. In the days before good roads, every community wanted a railway of its own, however illusory the profits might eventually turn out to be. The principal interest was to improve on the horse-and-cart as a means of transport, and against this even a mixed train which stopped to shunt wagons at every intermediate station scored quite well. Most of the companies were home-spun affairs, hopelessly undersubscribed and short of money, usually baled out and taken over by the philanthropic Great Eastern Railway. It was just as well that the GER was masterly at squeezing every last drop of potential out of such lines! Tiny halts were opened wherever there was the remotest prospect of passengers; anything and everything was carried as freight. In this respect, it is fitting that the final traffic conveyed over the branch line from Braintree to Bishop's Stortford was green bananas!

History

Despite some early proposals in 1835 and 1845, the area of central Essex west of Braintree was bypassed by the Railway Mania. The reasons are not hard to find, for it was a rural district short of revenue potential, and the only community of any size was Dunmow. Despite this, there was still interest in providing a line, mainly amongst farmers who wanted better transport for their crops of grain, sugar-beet and root vegetables. In 1861, when Braintree and Bishop's Stortford were already well established on the railway map, the unfortunate residents of Dunmow had to rely on a horse-drawn coach, which connected at Bishop's Stortford with a slow train from Norwich. This inconvenient arrangement allowed just over four hours in London before long-suffering passengers had to begin their marathon journey back home.

Such poor communications did a lot to keep interest in the railway project alive, but a scheme in 1858 to construct a London, Dunmow, Clare and Bury St Edmunds Railway met with no more success than its predecessors. Once again, a major problem was the rural area through which the line would pass and the lack of any clear revenue potential. The next scheme was far more realistic and modest. The Bishop's Stortford, Dunmow and Braintree Railway deposited plans on 30 November 1860 for an eighteen-mile branch line linking the three towns and making a connection at Dunmow with the proposed Ongar-Dunmow extension of the Epping Railway. The company was incorporated in 1861 with an authorized share capital of £120,000, of which the Eastern Counties Railway agreed to subscribe £40,000. However, the townsfolk of Bishop's Stortford and Braintree demonstrated their lack of enthusiasm for the scheme by failing to take up shares, with the result that only £6,000 had been subscribed by January 1862. The company struggled to keep the scheme alive and, for a time, it looked as if the contractors would accept part payment for their services in company shares. However, they eventually withdrew and it was left to the Great Eastern Railway to break the stalemate in summer 1863 by presenting a bill before Parliament to lease or purchase the line. This was duly passed, and new contractors had been appointed by August 1863. Construction work finally commenced in November that year and was followed by a belated sod-cutting ceremony on 24 February 1864: the enthusiasm which this aroused was in complete contrast to the lack of interest in the original share issue.

Perhaps local people were relieved that their pockets had been spared.

By autumn 1866 the major earthworks had been completed, and the railway inspector, Colonel Yolland, visited the line in November 1866. This turned out to be the first of three inspections before the line was finally approved for public use on 18 February 1869. The long delay between the first and third visits reveals a lack of commitment on the part of the GER, for some directors were convinced that their new line was a waste of time and money. Passenger services commenced on 22 February 1869, although the opening was not well attended: locals had become so used to the sight of their new line standing complete but unapproved that it caught them by surprise when the trains finally began to run.

The branch now settled down to a placid existence of just over a hundred years. Stations were provided at Rayne, Felsted, Dunmow and Takeley; the last two also possessed passing loops but, by some quirk, that at Takeley was authorized for goods trains only. The initial passenger service was two trains per day, but goods traffic (particularly agricultural produce) soon became a more important source of income. The connection to Ongar, potentially a lucrative agricultural line in its own right, was never built. Passenger traffic remained resolutely light, but despite this staffing levels were generous, perhaps even excessive: in 1906, for example, Rayne had a complement of seven full-time staff. A new station was added at Easton Lodge in the early 1890s. Although

The wayside station at Takeley, seen looking west towards Bishop's Stortford. Originally provided with a passing loop, this was removed in the late 1950s

P.J. Kelley

open to the public, it was constructed at the expense of the Countess of Warwick who lived nearby; the Prince of Wales, later Edward VII, was a frequent visitor. On 7 November 1910, a new halt was opened at Hockerill on the outskirts of Bishop's Stortford but, although convenient for the nearby golf-course, it was only a short walk from the main station on the Cambridge line, so traffic could not have been particularly good. By the end of 1914, passenger services had increased to six trains per weekday with three on Sundays, a remarkable provision in view of the light loadings.

Services were at first unaffected following the outbreak of the First World War, but Sunday passenger trains were withdrawn in 1916 and weekday services reduced in 1918. The Sunday trains were never restored, but by 1919 all other services were back to their pre-war levels, and the Great Eastern was still boldly attempting to develop traffic. Two more stations were opened in 1922, at Bannister Green and Stane Street (near Takeley): these were exceptionally small rail-level halts, and special steps had to be carried in the guard's compartment to enable passengers to alight or board. Colonel Yolland's remarks are not recorded! However, the war effort had severely strained the finances of all Britain's railways and, on 1 January 1923, the old Great Eastern became a part of the new London and North Eastern Railway.

An important development occurred in 1926 when a new sugar factory opened at Felsted; this was part of the government's plan to reduce the country's dependence on imported foreign produce. The factory was soon receiving up to 90 per cent of its sugar-beet supply via the branch, and a goods loop had to be constructed at Felsted station to handle the extra traffic. The factory even had its own internal rail system, which was operated by a number of industrial tank-engines. In the early 1930s, there were considerably more goods trains on the Dunmow line than on the connecting Witham-Braintree branch, but by 1936 freight services on both lines had been consolidated into a basic pattern of two trains daily,

The Second World War brought increased activity, as it did to so many other branch lines throughout the country. The line was used for diverted passenger trains from Liverpool Street to Colchester when the Great Eastern main line was damaged by enemy action, and thousands of tons of hard core travelled via Dunmow for the construction of a new airstrip at Saling, west of Braintree. When the airstrip was complete, it was supplied with trainloads of bombs, which rumbled over the branch under cover of night. In 1948 the line passed to the Eastern Region of the newly created British Railways, but by this time bus competition was beginning to hit hard. The buses took twenty-five minutes longer than the train, but they were cheaper and more frequent. At the same time, competition from private cars was increasing, so that by the turn of the decade, it was not uncommon for some trains to run entirely empty for at least part of their journey. Passenger services were accordingly withdrawn on 1 March 1952, the last train being the 8.15 p.m. from Bishop's Stortford to

Dunmow station photographed in 1957. The site did not change much over the years, with the facilities shown here little altered from those of its earliest years. The route of the old railway now forms the A120 at this point, and the familiar landmark of the grain store in the background is still present

Braintree hauled by a class F5 2-4-2 locomotive of GER ancestry. (The F5s were known colloquially as 'Gobblers', due to their insatiable appetite for coal.)

Passenger services may have gone, but the line was still far from finished. In 1941 a new rail-connected cold store had opened at Hockerill, and in 1948 there were still four freight workings daily. Occasional passenger specials also ran, including excursions to the Essex coast and school trains to and from Felsted School at the beginning and end of each term. In 1956, the line again proved its worth as a diversionary route during the electrification of the Shenfield-Chelmsford line, when through trains to Ipswich were routed over it in the late evening. An unwelcome development occurred in September 1962, when steam was withdrawn from the branch and all workings were taken over by modern diesel locomotives. Unfortunately, these were too large to negotiate the points which led into the sidings at Hockerill and so the cold store traffic was lost for what was, in the final analysis, not a very good reason. To balance this, Geest opened a rail-connected banana warehouse at Easton Lodge in the same year, and this received up to 300 tons per week of green bananas for ripening.

In the mid-1960s, there was a flurry of interest in developing the line; there was optimistic talk of reintroducing passenger services and operating rubbish trains from Dunmow to Chelmsford. However, nothing came of this and a final wave of economies was introduced instead. Goods facilities were withdrawn at Rayne and Felsted in 1964, then Takeley suffered the same fate in 1966. In the same year, a group of BR engineers examined the viaduct east of Dunmow and declared it unsafe for further use. Traffic on the line did not justify the cost of repairs and the section from Dunmow to Felsted was accordingly closed completely on 10 April 1966. The line was then worked in two halves, the eastern section being the first to go entirely. After the condemnation of the viaduct only the British Sugar Corporation at Felsted continued to use the branch, and volumes declined inexorably as traffic switched to the roads. The last trickle of dried beet pulp disappeared in 1968: the section from Braintree to Felsted closed officially on 1 April 1969 and was lifted during the course of 1970. The western end of the line fared slightly better. Dunmow station remained open for occasional agricultural traffic, but by 1968 this had become so infrequent that it was uneconomic. All facilities were withdrawn on 1 April 1969, the rails lifted as far as Easton Lodge and the station buildings demolished. The site was even proposed for use as a rubbish tip – the ultimate ignominy. By now the only remaining traffic was banana deliveries to Easton Lodge, but these were also shrinking due to increased road competition. By the end of 1971, even Geest had deserted the branch. The last known working was an enthusiasts' brake-van trip from Bishop's Stortford to Easton and back on 27 July 1972. By autumn of that year, the track had been lifted from Easton Lodge to Stansted Airport, although the last two miles into Bishop's Stortford were 'moth-balled' for two years pending a decision on their possible electrification as a passenger line to the airport. In the event, however, nothing came of these proposals and the remaining stub was lifted during the course of 1974.

The Line Today

Essex County Council acquired the trackbed from British Rail in the late 1970s, largely with a view to highway improvements. In 1980, it was divided into two sections, Braintree to Great Dunmow and Great Dunmow to Bishop's Stortford: the former was managed positively as a linear country park, but the latter was retained simply as a 'holding operation' until its future use could be determined. In 1983, the council was still talking in terms of its absorption in improvements to the A120, an extremely busy road which conveys large volumes of traffic to and from Stansted Airport. At the end of 1987, however, the council dropped a sudden bombshell. One of the proposed routes for the improved A120 was to follow the eastern part of the line, from Braintree to Great Dunmow, and it was said that certain county planners favoured this because the authority already owned the land. A vigorous campaign of opposition then followed and, early in 1988, Essex County officers took their members for a walk along the trackbed and showed them what would be lost if they chose that route. In the event, a relatively expensive option was selected which kept north of the line and cut it only at Rayne and Dunmow. From the railway rambler's point of view, the advantage of this was that the western end of the branch, long under the threat of conversion into a road, was finally and unexpectedly spared. Walkers had been allowed to follow it on a permissive basis, but now its future might be secured as part of a properly constituted railway path.

With this in mind, it was pleasing to see publicity literature in summer 1988 describing 'The Braintree to Bishop's Stortford Disused Railway Line' as a 'fifteen-mile nature walk'. On the negative side, the facility looked as if it had suffered a touch of planning blight, with drainage repairs and clearance urgently required in a number of places. This was not to be wondered at, for there had previously been little justification in spending public money on a path which was likely to be the site for a major new road. However, the threat is now past, and the walk deserves to be properly maintained. Apart from showing the 'other' face of Essex, it is also the nearest long-distance railway path to London.

The Walk (15 miles)

The present-day Braintree railway station is in fact the second in the town and was built specifically to facilitate a connection with the new Dunmow line; the original stood at grid reference 763229. Immediately west of the station, a car-park now occupies part of the former trackbed (a reflection on the importance of commuting from the town), but beyond that lies the start of the

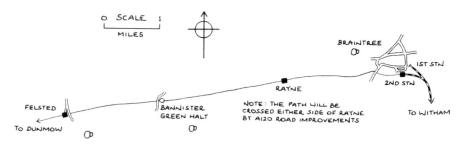

BRAINTREE TO FELSTED

Rayne station on the former branch line from Braintree to Bishop's Stortford. The building was boarded up in 1988, but had been occupied previously. A few lengths of rail remained in place just out of the picture to the left

railway path proper. The first half-mile has a very urban feel and is rather narrow in places, its use having perhaps been curtailed by recent doubts over its future. The most notable feature is a little 'orchard' which has sprung up along the line, perhaps the result of some apple core tossed from a train window many years ago.

Just east of Rayne, the trackbed has become very overgrown in the cutting which leads to the village station, but a detour has been provided along its northern side. The station itself was unoccupied in 1988 but in generally sound condition; it is of similar design to others on the line and includes a small integral canopy. Its appearance belies the fact that it hasn't seen a train for over twenty years: at the west end, the rails are still in place over a minor level crossing; the goods yard is still obvious, though weed-infested and overgrown; and the blackened goods shed still waits for deliveries that will never come. On the south side of the site, half buried in undergrowth, there is even a gradient-post complete with both arms; others on the branch survive only as limbless stumps and are sometimes unrecognizable.

Continuing west, there are good views across surrounding farmland, with plenty of cereal crops in evidence, as well as, in late summer, the occasional field of blackened broad beans. No trace remains of the tiny halt which once served

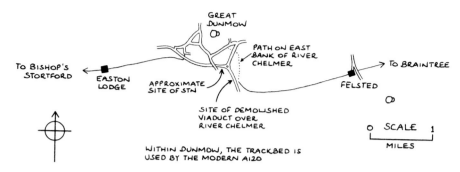

GREAT
DUNMOW

PATH ON EAST
BANK OF RIVER
CHELMER

To BISHOP'S
STORTFORD

EASTON
LODGE

APPROXIMATE
SITE OF STN

To BRAINTREE

FELSTED

SITE OF DEMOLISHED
VIADUCT OVER
RIVER CHELMER

SCALE

0   1

MILES

WITHIN DUNMOW, THE TRACKBED IS
USED BY THE MODERN A120

FELSTED TO EASTON LODGE

Bannister Green, its most likely situation being by the overbridge at grid reference 691217. I managed to resist the temptation to patronise the nearby Three Horseshoes, a visit I made to ill effect on a previous occasion! Between here and Felsted, I encountered two waterlogged sections, which were soggy reminders that the railway ran at right angles to the natural drainage of the land; it would be nice if the council could remedy these trouble spots, perhaps with a raised causeway as has been done west of Dunmow.

Felsted station, privately owned and in excellent condition, is situated to the west of the village at grid reference 665212; in summer the building is adorned with flowers, recalling the days of 'Best-Kept Station' competitions. The sugar factory, for so long a major source of traffic for the branch, is still in business, but it has been joined by a car scrap-yard, which occupies a short length of trackbed just west of the station. Those who think that the railway has been ill served by progress will be gratified when they see the fate meted out to moribund motor cars. Continuing west, the track passes below Little Dunmow, but there are signs that it has been less well used as it approaches Great Dunmow. By the time Langleys is reached (grid reference 639209), the route is running along a high embankment which once led on to the seven-arch Langleys Viaduct. Do not be misled by the Ordnance Survey, for the viaduct was demolished in 1977 even though the 1986 impression of their Landranger map shows it still astride the valley of the River Chelmer. It had to be removed in the interests of safety, for people refused to stop trespassing on it. This means that the walker is left standing at the top of a huge wall of earth which ends abruptly and inexplicably. In the view ahead, there is no evidence that a railway to Dunmow ever existed: modern road improvements have seen to that. Fortunately, the council has provided a flight of steps whereby the walker can descend the embankment to a riverside path at grid reference 637210. Turn right here and follow the river for approximately three-quarters of a mile. Pass under the first bridge (this conveys the A120 and is not a good place to stop) and leave the river by the second, at grid reference 634219. This is a convenient spot to take a break, with a car-park and riverside picnic area provided; the centre of Dunmow lies just over a quarter of a mile to the south-west.

On the subject of Langleys Viaduct, it is worth mentioning the late Brian Lyndon, who was an Essex man and keen railway rambler in these parts. The first time he did this walk, he gave his parents a nasty fright because they didn't quite catch the fact that the rails had been removed; they must have developed a rather strange view of railway rambling as a death-defying pursuit in which participants played chicken with 1,000 horsepower diesel locomotives. On arrival at Langleys, where the viaduct had only recently been demolished, he found various shapeless fragments of masonry lying in the river where it used to pass overhead. With the aid of a large stick, he hastily manoeuvred some of these into position as stepping-stones, perhaps the last time that the viaduct did service for rail-related passengers. He also found the platforms of Dunmow station on the south side of the town's new bypass, much against his expectations and the conventional wisdom of local guide-books.

As noted above, the remainder of the branch from Dunmow to Bishop's Stortford was for a long time in the care of the County Highways Department, which was expecting eventually to turn it into a new road until, happily, this threat was lifted in 1988. Improvements cannot be made overnight, however, and parts of the route should be regarded as 'rough stuff': wellington boots and a strong jacket are sensible precautions. The trackbed may be regained at grid reference 623217; access is from a minor road called High Stile at the west end of Great Dunmow village. The walk starts as a narrow path amidst thick woodland but soon opens out into a wide cutting spanned by an attractive three-arch bridge; surprisingly, this carries nothing more than a farm track. One of the attractions of this section is that the low level of maintenance and intervention has produced a much wilder environment: there are plenty of rabbits and hares in evidence, often startled by the walker's passing and I even disturbed a bird of prey which was feeding on a dead chaffinch. On the negative side, the line also draws close to the A120 which means that there is often a background buzz of traffic although this should be reduced when the new road opens to the north.

The site of Easton Lodge station (marked as 'Greencrofts' on the Ordnance Survey map) is met at grid reference 603213. Apart from being the Countess of Warwick's halt, Easton Lodge also possessed one of the two level crossings on the line. The gates, as might be expected, have long since disappeared, but the gatekeeper's cottage and a little wooden hut still survive, both in good condition. Three-quarters of a mile further west, an overbridge has been infilled following requests to strengthen it for local farm traffic. These requests date back as far as 1965 but nothing was done until 1976 when the line had closed; since then, steps have been provided up one side and down the other to help walkers on their way.

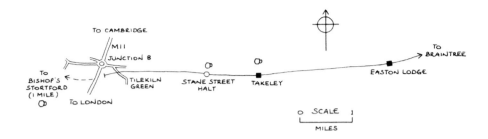

EASTON LODGE TO TILEKIN GREEN

At Canfield End, a large sand and gravel working is situated to the south of the line and walkers should not be alarmed by the sight and sound of huge earth-moving vehicles trundling by on the other side of the hedge. In 1983, these vehicles were using the trackbed without authorization, and it is good to see that the council has taken steps to sort this problem out. After the quarry, the line takes on a semi-urban look as it approaches Takeley: back-gardens run down to the trackbed and, here and there, the odd gate has been added so that

Takeley station at the west end of the line has not fared as well as its neighbours, though it has escaped the demolition inflicted upon Dunmow. The distinctive style of architecture used along the line is clearly evident in this photograph

dog-walkers can get straight on to the line from their gardens. Takeley station still stands at grid reference 563211, though it has clearly seen better days. In 1988, the station-master's residence was boarded up, but the ticket office and booking-hall were still in use, perhaps as offices for the adjoining coal yard. This is still a going concern, with large staves made from old timber sleepers – once a common sight at railway stations throughout the country. Coal was the last freight traffic handled at Takeley, the final delivery arriving in spring 1966. The coal-merchant is unusual in not having abandoned his old railway haunt.

The last three miles of the walk pass along the northern boundary of Hatfield Forest and can be rather overgrown, though not impassable. Given that the forest is managed as a country park, it would be helpful if the rangers' duties could extend to clearing the railway path two or three times during the summer months. On leaving the forest, the path once again takes on a more open aspect, until an underbridge is reached at grid reference 519213. This is Tilekiln Green and effectively the end of the walk for, although the trackbed can be followed a quarter of a mile further west, it is soon severed by the mighty M11 just south of junction 8. It is best to stop now! Steps lead down to a minor lane: the A120 and local buses are just a short walk to the north.

Further Explorations

Generally speaking, Essex is not well endowed with railway walks; the county is close to London and this seems to induce a 'property hunger' whereby redundant industrial land is gobbled up with remarkable haste. Despite this, the line from Maldon to Witham is being converted, though only at the slow pace that funds permit, while the whole of the Brightlingsea branch is available to walkers, excepting the regrettable absence of the bridge over Alresford Creek. This has the unfortunate effect of dividing the line into two discrete and unconnected halves. When all allowances have been made, many walkers will feel that the admonition of old school reports is justified: 'Could do better.' Surely more resources could be found for promoting and developing facilities in rural Essex rather than for propelling visitors through it as fast as possible? Indeed, should not the fact that the county is so close to London be seen as a justification for such a policy? After all, it does still retain a large number of green fields within a relatively short distance of the capital.

Those who wish to track down more of the county's railway past need look no further than the Colne Valley, home of two separate railway preservation groups. The Colne Valley and Halstead Railway originally ran from Chappel and Wakes Colne (on BR's existing Sudbury branch) to Haverhill, the full length of the line being opened in 1863. It lost its passenger service in 1962, but odds and ends of freight traffic continued to use it until April 1965. This was a highly individual railway, which managed to remain independent of the Great Eastern until both companies were absorbed into the LNER in 1923, and it is not surprising that it ranks highly in local affections. The new Colne Valley Railway was formed in 1973 and, 'by extraordinary enthusiasm and hard work', its volunteers have created a new station at Castle Hedingham, which features the original Castle Hedingham station on one platform and an exact reproduction of Halstead station on the other. It should be added that Castle Hedingham station had to be dismantled, moved from its original site and then re-erected brick-by-brick. Trains currently run over one mile of track towards Haverhill and there are plans to add another mile in the near future.

At the Colchester end of the same line, the East Anglian Railway Museum is now established at Chappel and Wakes Colne station, which it shares with British Rail. This museum, which also possesses a short length of operational line, seeks to inform as well as entertain and, to this end, includes exhibits which unravel the intricacies of signalling and explain the inner workings of the steam engine. It is open throughout the year and its modest admission charges represent good value for money. Last but not least, a third section of the Colne Valley line, the short stretch from Yeldham to Hedingham, is open as a public footpath. I presume that this is a district council initiative, since the county council seems unaware of it. Taken as a whole, the fact that so much of the line has survived is quite remarkable and speaks volubly of the enthusiasm which the Colne Valley and Halstead Railway created.

Transport and Facilities

Map: Ordnance Survey: Landranger Series Sheet 167 (recommended)

Buses: First Essex
            www.firstgroup.com/ukbus/southeast/essex
            Telephone: (Traveline) 0871 200 22 33

Trains: National Rail Enquiries
            www.nationalrail.co.uk
            Telephone: 08457 48 49 50

The two ends of this walk are still served by rail, although there was a time when the branch from Witham to Braintree seemed doomed to closure: happily, a vigorous local campaign improved business on the line to the extent that it justified electrification. The services to both Bishop's Stortford and Braintree are good: there are two trains per hour for Bishop's Stortford, and one for Braintree, with slight reductions on Sundays.

As for refreshments, Braintree and Bishop's Stortford possess all the facilities one would expect of a market town, while Dunmow has some pleasant tea-rooms; I trust that they offer the local preserves from Elsenham or Tiptree! Those in search of good ale will have no difficulty in finding Ridley's beers, which are brewed at Hartford End, just south of Felsted. The Three Horseshoes at Bannister Green is a good place to sample the company's products, although on a summer's day walkers might find its village-green setting so agreeable that they get no further. This part of Essex is certainly a far cry from the brash modernity of the county's urban sprawl.

3
THE MIDLAND AND GREAT NORTHERN JOINT RAILWAY, NORFOLK
NORTH WALSHAM TO AYLSHAM AND ATTLEBRIDGE TO HELLESDON

Introduction

The Eastern counties were dominated by the Great Eastern Railway, a benevolent monopoly which, by and large, has received a very favourable press from railway historians. The company was formed on 7 August 1862 by an amalgamation of minor companies which often seemed more bent on politics and intrigue than running their affairs properly. One of its constituents was the Eastern Counties Railway, which adopted some rather strange practices, particularly when it came to banking heavy trains up the incline between Romford and Brentwood. A banking engine would approach the struggling train while it was in motion and effectively ram it from behind. On one occasion, in August 1845, the effect of the collision was so great that it detached and derailed the last coach. and it was only by a 'special interference of providence' that it did not topple over an embankment. One of the luckless victims lost his ticket in the ensuing confusion and was charged for his journey a second time on arrival at Chelmsford.

While operational irregularities such as this were mercifully rare, the pattern of little companies embroiled in parochial schemes (and frequently disputes) was repeated throughout East Anglia. In many cases, there was not much traffic to compete for and very little capital to invest in the railways which promised to tap it. In the north, much of Norfolk was thinly populated and prone to the vicissitudes of agriculture: particular problems followed the repeal of the Corn Laws in 1846, which removed protection against cheap foreign corn, and the development of canning and refrigeration in the 1870s, which led to large-scale imports of meat and dairy produce from America, Australia and New Zealand. Both of these developments seriously affected the local economy and have a direct bearing on why so many East Anglian railways took such a long time to be completed.

Despite this, north Norfolk was unusual in that it attracted a major interloper into traditional Great Eastern territory – the Midland and Great Northern Joint Railway. The M & GN developed an extensive network, the majority of which was swept away on a single day, 28 February 1959: this pre-dated the major closures of the 1960s and was difficult for many local people to accept. However, most of the railway walks in the county (and many road improvement schemes) have utilized the M & GN's trackbed, so it can be argued that the sacrifice has produced a number of modern benefits. From the historical perspective, the individual walks do not make much sense if viewed in isolation: they were part of a vigorous and distinctive railway network, and it is the history of that network which will now be traced.

History

London and Norwich were connected by rail on 30 July 1845. The effect was more or less immediate for, within six months, the last London-Norwich horse-drawn coach service was withdrawn, thus completing the displacement of some seven hundred horses. The rural area north of Norwich was not to be excluded from the benefits of rail communication and, in the same year, a North of Norfolk Railway was proposed. However, this plan met with dire warnings about the 'probable dearth of traffic' and was soon abandoned; it is no accident that, for the next thirty years, Norwich remained a boundary north of which railways did not develop.

Development when it did come was seriously hampered by financial difficulties and painfully slow as a result. The problem is well illustrated by the Norwich and Spalding Railway, formed in 1853. The company's title proclaimed its long-term intention of constructing a line across the region from east to west, but it only succeeded in getting as far as Sutton Bridge – fifteen miles east of Spalding and a full forty-five miles from its intended destination of Norwich. The problem was repeated elsewhere, as companies often failed to complete their lines, or else took many years to do so. From a constructional point of view, the Lynn and Fakenham Railway (authorized in 1876) was probably the most successful: not only did it open a line from King's Lynn to Fakenham on 6 August 1880, it also opened an extension to Norwich on 2 December 1882.

The Midland Railway and the Great Northern Railway were established just west of Norfolk at Peterborough, and it is not surprising that they acquired an

Ex-LMS 2-6-0 No. 43080 waits at Gedney station on the former Midland and Great Northern line between Spalding and South Lynn on 14 February 1959. This was one of the first routes where concrete was used for a variety of lineside structures, including the signal-posts shown here
A.E. Bennett

interest in some of the smaller concerns struggling to develop in the area. The Great Northern, for example, worked the Norwich and Spalding line to Sutton Bridge in return for half of the gross receipts. The harbour traffic at King's Lynn and the prospect of developing trade in north-east Norfolk were the incentives, together, no doubt, with an element of empire-building. The companies' ambitions were favourably viewed in the area, there being widespread support for an enterprise independent of the monopolistic Great Eastern Railway. On a more practical level, landowners wanted better transport for themselves and their produce, while it was an established fact that railways enabled coal to be brought into the county more cheaply than other means of transport: this would help existing industries and perhaps encourage new ones to develop.

The MR and GNR developed their hold on the lines in north-east Norfolk in three stages. The first occurred in 1866 when they formed the Midland and Eastern Railway from the three companies which owned the route from Bourne to King's Lynn via Spalding: this was to remain their main route of access into Norfolk until closure in 1959. It was followed in 1882 by the formation of the Eastern and Midlands Railway, which incorporated the M & E and brought into

British Railways class 4MT No. 43107 at Aylsham North station in the summer of 1958. This small market town had a second station on the Great Eastern line from Wroxham to County School which lost its passenger service as early as September 1952

N.E. Stead Collection

the fold four other local companies, the most important of which was the Lynn and Fakenham Railway with its long route from King's Lynn to Norwich City. The E & M then consolidated its position by 'filling in the gaps' with local lines from Melton Constable to North Walsham and Cromer respectively. Finally, the Midland and Great Northern Joint Railway was formed on 1 July 1893 by an Act which allowed the MR and GNR to take over the Eastern and Midlands completely. The master plan was thus complete and represented a 'sensible and mutually beneficial compromise' for both of the principal companies. The final network consisted of just over 182 miles of track, linking sixty-five stations and halts, although a number of extra halts were added in the 1930s to cater for the growing traffic to holiday camps. The full, entangled complexity of its development can be appreciated by referring to the table at the end of this section to see when the railways on the accompanying map were built and acquired.

Between 1883 and 1924, the M & GN was dominated by William Marriott. Marriott started his working life as an employee of the London contractors

Wilkinson and Jarvis, who constructed the lines from King's Lynn to Norwich and from Great Yarmouth to North Walsham. He completed his apprenticeship in 1881 and became engineer to the Eastern and Midlands Railway in 1883. He added locomotive superintendent to his duties in 1884 and carried both of these offices into the new M & GN in 1893. He became traffic manager of the line in 1919 and finally retired in 1924. Marriott kept the railway going through good times and bad, and developed a mighty reputation for economy and inventive flair. He could turn his mind to anything, from new types of rail-joint to concrete fabrications, and it is no exaggeration to say that his concrete shop at Melton Constable produced everything from signal-posts to prefabricated offices. Some of these products were even exported to Ceylon! Melton Constable, of course, is the other name associated with the railway, for it became its headquarters and a veritable 'Crewe of north Norfolk'. In 1881, its population was a mere 118 souls but, by 1911, this had increased almost tenfold. The railway was compelled to build a large number of houses in the village, for it was so remote and isolated that there was no other way of inducing employees to stay!

The original locomotives on the line were of the 'bumpkin' variety, as befitted a network of rural branch lines, but, from 1882 onwards, a variety of express locomotives were delivered starting with four Beyer Peacock 4-4-0s. These were followed by improvements to the track (including some doubling) and the installation of tablet catchers on locomotives, all of which helped to elevate train speeds from 32 to 44 mph. These matched some of the best offered by the Great Eastern Railway and were a source of considerable pride. In the 1880s, holidays for the masses became commonplace, and the M & GN brought in a large proportion of visitors to the area; indeed, the number of Midlanders who holiday in Norfolk today reflects a habit established by the railway over a century ago. By 1884, the Midland Railway was advertising Norfolk farmhouse holidays, while by the 1890s wherries were being converted for leisure use on the Broads. Of course, all of this traffic was seasonal, but the railway ran a variety of day excursions to make the most of the holiday-makers who were already there: other coastal resorts or places of interest inland, such as Norwich, were the most popular destinations. On the freight side the main traffic was coal, befitting the MR and GNR, which were great coal-carrying railways. As for 'exports', the local fish industry made a healthy contribution with fish workers' specials and many express fish trains in the autumn.

Melton Constable was put through its paces during the First World War, for the works repaired over 500 wagons and 70 locomotives on top of building 70 wagons for the GNR. This involved considerable overtime, some of it accompanied by Zeppelin raids. Unfortunately, the railway's supremacy in transport was challenged within a year of the war ending. As we have seen elsewhere, the war effort greatly accelerated the development of road vehicles, and by 1919 buses from Norwich and Yarmouth were running to most of the places served by the M & GN. Many stations, such as Norwich City and

Whitwell & Reepham, were badly sited, making the railway particularly vulnerable. Additionally, the north Norfolk coast had failed to develop in the way that had been anticipated: the population of Lower Sheringham grew from 300 in 1881 to just over 4,000 in 1901 but then remained static, while Mundesley, which possessed a magnificent station with three through-platforms and a bay, failed to develop until after the railway had closed. Only the growing number of holiday camps and the opening of several new camp halts in the 1930s offered much hope in the inter-war years.

The Second World War brought about a revival in the railway's fortunes, for it served a dozen East Anglian airbases, and the emphasis on home food production brought some agricultural traffic on to the rails. After 1945, however, the decline continued as before. Particularly damaging was the fact that large sections of the north Norfolk coast were not cleared promptly of wartime mines: this inflicted a serious blow on the hitherto reliable summer trade. The first casualty was the line from Cromer to Mundesley, which closed to passengers and freight respectively on 7 and 18 April 1953. Yarmouth Beach to Gorleston followed on 21 September 1953, and then it was the turn of the short line to Cromer High which closed to passengers on 20 September 1954, although freight services were retained until 1960. Closure of the highly uneconomic Melton Constable-Great Yarmouth section was also discussed in this year but deferred for reasons which I have been unable to discover. Despite these and other less obvious economies, however, losses continued to spiral: the steady drift of freight on to the roads continued unchecked, while, on the passenger side, the only remaining traffic of any size was the summer Saturday holiday trade and the transport of schoolchildren during term times – hardly a sound financial basis for continued operations. As a result, the death blow was delivered on 28 February 1959, when the whole section from Bourne to Yarmouth via King's Lynn and Fakenham closed completely, along with passenger services on the connecting line from Melton Constable to Norwich City.

Most of the M & GN network was thus wiped out at a stroke, but even further contraction was yet to come. On 12 September 1960, British Railways opened a new connecting curve at Themelthorpe, which enabled trains to reach Norwich City via the shorter Great Eastern route and, as a result, the section from Melton Constable to Themelthorpe was closed completely. The line from Melton Constable to Sheringham was kept on temporarily for the sake of the scattered communities along its route, but closure came here too in 1964 – to passengers on 6 April and to freight on 28 December. The line from North Walsham to Mundesley also disappeared in this year, closing to passengers on 5 October and to freight (as at Sheringham) on 28 December. By now, car ownership in East Anglia was the highest per capita in the country and, excepting the four miles from Cromer to Sheringham, the M & GN had been reduced to a mere stub from Themelthorpe to Norwich City, which could only be reached by its rival's metals. Then Norwich City was closed to freight on 3 February 1969. Lenwade

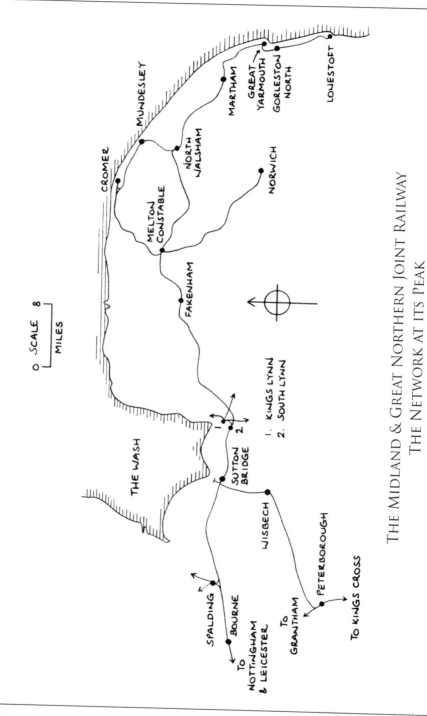

THE MIDLAND & GREAT NORTHERN JOINT RAILWAY
THE NETWORK AT ITS PEAK

now became the terminus of the line for a daily freight train which collected prefabricated housing sections and concrete girders from the factory of Anglian Building Products. This company objected to closure and continued to send substantial volumes of traffic by rail until the 1980s. The exact closure date is not known, but Norfolk County Council was considering acquisition of the trackbed in 1985 and the rails had been lifted by summer 1988.

The Ancestry of the Midland & Great Northern Joint Railway

This table shows the main components of the M & GN and, with the aid of the accompanying map, enables the development of the finished network to be traced. It should be noted that published sources show discrepancies in one or two of the dates.

1. *Midland & Great Northern Joint Railway*
   Act   9 June 1893
   Incorporated   1 July 1893: Eastern & Midlands Railway (2)
   Managed   Norfolk & Suffolk Joint Railway (1a)
   Lines Opened   13 July 1903: Yarmouth–Gorleston North
                     Various minor connecting and avoiding lines

1a. *Norfolk & Suffolk Joint Railway*
   (Managed jointly by the M & GN and the Great Eastern Railway)
   Act   25 July 1898
   Lines Opened   1 July 1898: North Walsham–Mundesley
                     13 July 1903: Lowestoft–Gorleston North
                     2 August 1906: Cromer–Mundesley

2. *Eastern & Midlands Railway*
   Act   18 August 1882
   Incorporated   1 January 1883: Lynn & Fakenham Railway (3)
                     1 January 1883: Yarmouth & North Norfolk Light
                        Railway (4a)
                     1 January 1883: Yarmouth Union Railway (5)
                     1 July 1883: Midland & Eastern Railway (6)
                     1 July 1883: Peterborough, Wisbech & Sutton
                        Bridge Railway (10)
   Lines Opened   5 April 1883: Melton Constable–North Walsham
                     16 June 1887: Melton Constable–Cromer Beach

3. *Lynn & Fakenham Railway*
   Act   13 July 1876
   Lines Opened   6 August 1880: King's Lynn–Fakenham
                     2 December 1882: Fakenham–Norwich

4a. *Yarmouth & North Norfolk Light Railway*
　　Act　　　　　　　　27 May 1878
　　Former Name　　　Great Yarmouth & Stalham Light Railway (4b)
　　Line Opened　　　 13 June 1881: Martham-North Walsham

4b. *Great Yarmouth & Stalham Light Railway*
　　Act　　　　　　　　26 July 1876
　　Line Opened　　　 15 July 1878: Yarmouth–Martham

5. *Yarmouth Union Railway*
　　Act　　　　　　　　26 August 1880
　　Line Opened　　　 15 May 1882: Short link line within Great Yarmouth

6. *Midland & Eastern Railway*
　　(Worked jointly by the Midland Railway and the Great Northern Railway)
　　Act　　　　　　　　23 July 1866
　　Leased　　　　　　 5 July 1866: Norwich & Spalding Railway (9)
　　Incorporated　　　23 July 1866: Lynn & Sutton Bridge Railway (7)
　　　　　　　　　　　23 July 1866: Spalding & Bourne Railway (8)
　　　　　　　　　　　12 July 1877: Norwich & Spalding Railway (9)
　　Lines Opened　　　None

7. *Lynn & Sutton Bridge Railway*
　　Act　　　　　　　　6 August 1861
　　Line Opened　　　 1 March 1865: King's Lynn–Sutton Bridge

8. *Spalding & Bourne Railway*
　　Act　　　　　　　　29 July 1862
　　Line Opened　　　 1 August 1866: Spalding–Bourne

9. *Norwich & Spalding Railway*
　　Act　　　　　　　　4 August 1853
　　Line Opened　　　 3 July 1862: Spalding–Sutton Bridge

10. *Peterborough, Wisbech & Sutton Bridge Railway*
　　Act　　　　　　　　28 July 1863
　　Line Opened　　　 1 August 1866: Peterborough–Wisbech–Sutton
　　　　　　　　　　　Bridge

The Line Today

To set against the M & GN's depressing catalogue of closures, the private North Norfolk Railway reopened the section from Sheringham to Weybourne on 13 July 1975 and has since extended its line to Holt, a total distance of five miles. Cromer to Sheringham (four miles) never closed, although the stark hand of rationalization is everywhere evident. Thus only 5 per cent of the M & GN's route mileage remains intact although, excepting the absence of rails, lonely Melton Constable remains 'a perfect miniature fossil railway town, with little subsequently destroyed as in so many others' (R.S. Joby). William Marriott is commemorated by Marriott's Way, a seven-mile railway path which starts on the outskirts of Norwich, and several other stretches of line have been similarly converted: North Walsham to Aylsham (seven miles), Bengate to Stalham (five miles) and North Walsham to Knapton (one and a half miles). A particularly exciting prospect is the extension of Marriott's Way by the addition of the trackbed from Lenwade to Aylsham via Themelthorpe: this would create a substantial path of approximately twenty miles, connecting at Aylsham with the existing Weaver's Way to North Walsham. Norfolk County Council was negotiating the purchase with British Rail's Property Board in summer 1988. A private company was also hoping to establish a narrow-gauge railway on the remaining ten-mile section from Aylsham to Wroxham. In the meantime, signs of walking along the trackbed suggest that much of BR's Lenwade branch has already become an unofficial trail.

Elsewhere, considerable lengths of M & GN trackbed have been incorporated in road improvement schemes – hardly surprising given the per capita number of cars in the county. Seven miles have been gobbled up west of King's Lynn, another seven between Potter Heigham and Stalham, while four and a half miles have gone into the North Walsham bypass – including the former M & GN railway station, which survived for several years as a Jehovah's Witnesses' chapel. On the whole, however, 'railway motoring' lacks atmosphere and seems unlikely to catch on.

Walk 1 – The Weaver's Way, North Walsham to Aylsham (7 miles)

The Weaver's Way is a long-distance footpath from Cromer to Great Yarmouth via Aylsham, North Walsham and Stalham. Its name commemorates the importance of the weaving industry in this part of Norfolk between the twelfth and eighteenth centuries, although it was in decline by the time the Midland and Great Northern Railway arrived, largely as a result of its failure to adopt new methods – principally the power-loom. This part of the route starts from a small car-park in North Walsham at grid reference 275300. It may be reached most easily by finding the railway station in the town and then following Station Road, which starts opposite. There were originally two stations at North

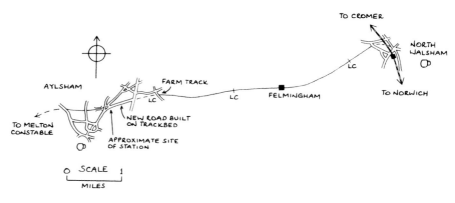

THE WEAVER'S WAY

Walsham which were practically next door to each other; the present-day station, the sole survivor, was provided by the East Norfolk Railway in 1874. The disused line which we are about to follow was constructed by the Eastern & Midlands Railway and opened for traffic on 5 April 1883. It was part of a connection from Melton Constable to North Walsham which enabled through running from King's Lynn and points west to Great Yarmouth.

As the walk leaves North Walsham, look out for the concrete fence-posts on the right-hand side of the formation – reminders of Mr Marriott's concrete shop at Melton Constable. Within half a mile, Tungate is reached and the first of several crossing-keeper's cottages (grid reference 269295), a source of unwelcome expense to the line when it was fighting for its survival. Most of the cottages are of the same pattern, although modern owners have added a variety of extensions, sometimes to unattractive effect. After passing through North Walsham Woods, the line crosses a minor road and arrives at the single platform of Felmingham station (grid reference 251287). The platform is now so overgrown as to be almost unrecognizable, but the small, red-brick station building survives, although unoccupied and boarded up. It is of a very plain design and not a particularly good example of railway architecture, but then economy was the watchword of the M & GN! The small goods yard opposite used to accommodate two sidings for freight traffic, such as it was.

The line now passes into a wide cutting, which accommodates a variety of butterflies: they obviously like the sandy terrain, for they flourish in great numbers. Species include small tortoise-shells, peacocks and fritillaries. Another crossing-keeper's cottage is met at The Meadows (grid reference 236285), followed by an attractive bridge over a tributary of the River Bure (234284). The bridge-spans are made of concrete, which again makes one think of the Melton Constable concrete shop. At the next crossing-keeper's cottage

(214283), the path swings away to the north to avoid a section of trackbed which has been used to accommodate a new road. The diversion is well waymarked and easy to follow, arriving just west of Aylsham North station which stood at grid reference 201279. Anyone who has ever complained about railway punctuality might care to recall that a train was marooned here for five weeks in August 1912 when a freak storm delivered 8 in of rain in twenty-four hours – one-third of the area's annual total in one day. The sheer size of the deluge caused many slips in cuttings and embankments, not to mention washing away a number of bridges and culverts altogether. In several places, railway workers arrived to find rails and sleepers suspended in mid-air above swirling rivers below.

The trackbed can be regained at grid reference 198278 and then followed for another half mile westwards. The most notable feature is a low, metal bridge over the River Bure (197277), popular with schoolchildren practising their fishing skills. This is followed by a road bridge which carries a minor lane to Ingworth. The walker then enters a secluded, wooded cutting but, as the next road bridge is approached, the path swings to the left and joins the B1354 at grid reference 188276: the centre of Aylsham lies half a mile ahead. The trackbed continues west for another half mile until it disappears into a field, but this is not part of the official walk.

This sample of the Weaver's Way passes through a mixture of arable and wooded land which, in the words of the official guide, 'makes up some of the most attractive rural scenery in the county'. The only caveat is that, in places, the trackbed is now very sandy and this rather reduces the walker's pace. Wellington boots would be a sensible precaution in winter as these sections could become rather soggy.

Walk 2 – Marriott's Way, Attlebridge to Hellesdon (7 miles)

This is part of the line built by the Lynn and Fakenham Railway from Fakenham to Norwich: it opened to Lenwade on 1 July 1882, extending to Norwich City on 2 December that year. Marriott's Way actually starts from a bridge over the River Wensum at grid reference 122178, but there is presently no access to it other than via the trackbed; this means that anyone who wishes to view it must walk out and back from the site of Attlebridge station. The station, now a private residence and much altered, is located at grid reference 129176 just off the A1067 Fakenham-Norwich road. A small car-park is provided just to the west of it and refreshments can be obtained from the nearby post office

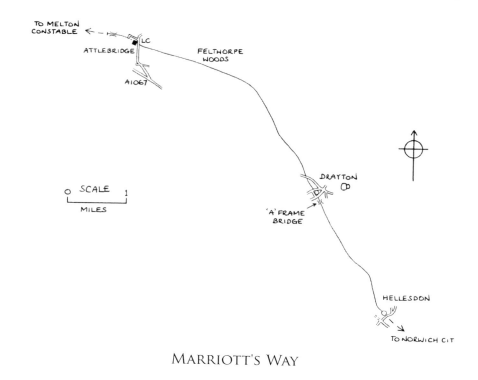

MARRIOTT'S WAY

and stores. A substantial level-crossing gate ensures that no visitors miss the historical connections of the site.

The main walk strikes off in an easterly direction and, after passing through a short cutting, runs along an embankment which offers fine views of the surrounding countryside. A distinctive concrete mile-post (another product from Melton Constable) may be found on the north side of this embankment, measuring forty-four and a half miles from South Lynn station – confirmation, were it needed, that the line was built by the Lynn and Fakenham Railway. A similar post for forty-five and a half miles follows in Felthorpe Woods and this has somehow managed to retain a few traces of paint – white, with the numbers picked out in black. This probably dates from the period when the line was open for freight traffic to Norwich City, for black and white was part of the 'corporate image' introduced by British Rail in 1967. Felthorpe Woods may seem innocent and tranquil enough now, but in the early 1880s they were the scene of a brawl between the foremen of two contractors' spoil trains. Neither would give way to the other, so, in the end, the two men resorted to fisticuffs; the smaller man won and his train was accordingly let through.

As on the Weaver's Way, parts of the trackbed are very sandy and this again reduces the walker's pace, but a pleasant by-product has once again been the creation of a habitat much favoured by butterflies. Given the nature of the terrain, it is hardly surprising that a number of sand and gravel pits are still being worked in the area. As the route descends towards Norwich, the soil becomes increasingly heavy, and gradually bracken, birch and gorse give way to a richer vegetation of trees, shrubs and wild flowers – dogroses, ox-eye daisies and white campion being but three examples. With the onslaught of prairie farming and the wholesale removal of hedges in parts of East Anglia, the borders of railway paths such as this are becoming important habitats for birds and animals in their own right.

On the approach to Drayton, a new residential road crosses the line and many superior new homes can be seen in a style recalling the 'brewer's Tudor' of the 1930s. While it may be fashionable to poke fun at this borrowed style, the properties are far more attractive and varied than on many other modern estates. The A1067 is crossed at grid reference 175139, and shortly after this the site of Drayton station is reached. This originally had a passing loop and five sidings, which made it the largest station between Norwich and Melton Constable. Now, however, it has been transformed into Drayton Industrial Estate and no trace of the railway remains at all. A waymarked diversion takes the walker around this obstruction and back on to the trackbed at grid reference 179133; the waymarking signs are themselves worthy of note, inasmuch as they are made of enamelled metal and bear the colours of the old M & GN livery. It is to be hoped that the council will repair or replace the small number which have been vandalized.

Immediately after regaining the trackbed, the path crosses the River Wensum on a distinctive A-frame girder bridge; this is one of only three surviving in the county, the other examples occurring at Hellesdon and Mile Cross, Norwich. I was interested to note a number of youths practising their abseiling on the north side of the bridge; perhaps they had been turned away from Monsal Viaduct in Derbyshire, where this pursuit is strictly prohibited.

The last two miles of Marriott's Way are very well used, as one might expect from the encroaching urban area which the path now approaches. Dog walkers, blackberry-pickers and young families were met frequently, and it was good to see the route justifying its existence. The views are generally very open, mainly across cornfields which in August are dotted with huge, rolled bales awaiting collection. A small bridge carries the line over the River Tud at grid reference 195107 before reaching the ruins of Hellesdon station. This closed, in advance of the rest of the line, on 15 September 1952, but a small section of the station's platform survives, albeit overgrown and easily missed. A small car-park is provided at grid reference 198101 and this is where the railway path comes to an end. However, across the road, Norwich City Council has provided an attractive riverside walk, which carries on towards the city centre.

There are only three of these unique A-frame bridges in Norfolk, all of them on the M & GN's Norwich branch. This example at Drayton carries Marriott's Way across the River Wensum

Further Explorations

Mention has already been made of other railway paths in the area, the main routes being Bengate to Stalham on the southern part of the Weaver's Way (five miles) and the Paston Way, an entirely new walk on part of the former Mundesley branch. This starts on the outskirts of North Walsham at grid reference 286316 and runs for one and a half miles to Old Hall Street, south of Knapton. The southern part of the Weaver's Way, incidentally, also gives walkers a chance to inspect parts of the disused North Walsham and Dilham Canal, a late and ill-fated construction of 1826. Elsewhere in the county, British Rail has been closing long-surviving freight lines and this increases the scope for future paths. The fate of the disused Lenwade branch has already been discussed; further west, the line from North Elmham to Fakenham has also been abandoned. It is understood that Breckland District Council has acquired part of this for a railway path of its own.

Switching to the subject of preserved rail transport, the North Norfolk Railway is a must for M & GN enthusiasts, for it exists 'by way of tribute to the line's importance in the development of north Norfolk'. It runs from

Sheringham to Holt between April and October each year. More recently, the Wells and Walsingham Light Railway has become established on the northernmost five miles of the former GER branch from Fakenham to Wells-next-the-Sea. This is a narrow-gauge line which runs from Easter to September and features a 1986-built Garratt steam locomotive, which was constructed specially for it; readers will not need reminding that brand new steam locomotives of any gauge are a rarity these days! Finally, it might be worth seeking out the East Anglia Transport Museum at Carlton Colville, outside Lowestoft, which is busy building up a working collection of mechanized street transport spanning the last seventy-five years; the link with rail transport is in the form of trams.

Transport and Facilities

Map:	Ordnance Survey: Landranger Series Sheet 133 (recommended)
	Ordnance Survey's Tourist Map 11 (The Norfolk Broads) should be avoided, as a number of photographs have been superimposed on the map content, thus obliterating much of the detail so important to walkers.
Buses:	NORBIC (Norfolk Bus Information Centre) 4 Guildhall Hill, Norwich, NR2 1JH Telephone: 0845 300 61166
	First Eastern Counties www.firstgroup.com/ukbus/easterncounties/easterncounties Telephone: (Traveline) 0871 200 22 33
Trains:	National Rail Enquiries www.nationalrail.co.uk Telephone: 08457 48 49 50

Norwich and North Walsham are still well served by rail, which is just as well, considering that one railway path starts on the outskirts of Norwich and the other three on the outskirts of North Walsham. Unfortunately, getting back by bus is not so easy. On the face of it, Marriott's Way from Attlebridge to Hellesdon is well served by Norfolk Green service X29 Monday to Saturday. The situation is better at the southern end of the walk, where a where a First Bus service runs from Drayton to Hellesdon (services 28, 29, 9 and 9A).

The Weaver's Way between North Walsham and Aylsham has no parallel bus service at all, so the best approach is to tackle the walk with a friend and place a car at each end. The only possibility using public transport is to travel out and back from Norwich to opposite end points, namely, Norwich–North Walsham–Aylsham–Norwich. North Walsham is best reached by train as the bus service from Norwich is extremely sparse; there is no room in these parts for unnecessary competition. Aylsham has a bus to and from Norwich approximately once per hour (Mondays to Saturdays) with the possibility of a few Sunday journeys if county council support is continued. The other major walk, from Stalham to Bengate (not covered in this chapter), is served by an irregular Sander's Coaches service 6.

As with bus services, so with pubs. In fact, Norfolk was for many years written off by the Campaign for Real Ale as a beer-desert and, if anything, the situation is worse following another decade of brewery rationalization and pub closures. Outside Norwich (an obvious exception), pubs and other facilities can be found in North Walsham, Aylsham and Drayton but, as far as the pubs are concerned, do not expect too much: an almost total lack of competition has encouraged some of them to adopt very mediocre standards.

4

THE SPA TRAIL

HORNCASTLE TO WOODHALL SPA

Introduction

Horncastle and Woodhall Spa both sound like places from a novel. Their names have that ring of familiarity and 'rightness', like Casterbridge and Barchester, but it is a fair bet that they are little known outside Lincolnshire and its bordering counties. Horncastle is the more ancient of the two settlements and stands at the south of the Lincolnshire Wolds, in the approximate centre of a large area made rail-less by Dr Beeching and his successors. The 'castle' in its name is a corruption of the Latin 'castra' (a military camp), which recalls the days in the first century when the Roman Ninth Legion occupied the locality; remains of the Roman walls are still evident in the town. The parish church of St Mary also contains a memorial to Sir Lionel Dymoke, a sixteenth-century ancestor of Sir Henry Dymoke, the first chairman of the Horncastle Railway Company.

Woodhall Spa, by contrast, is a more recent development, but it still has an unusual and colourful history. Its existence as a one-time spa town owes much to the endeavours of a certain John Parkinson, who frittered away a fortune in a forlorn attempt to find coal in the area. It is not known what convinced him that this was a worthwhile undertaking, but the miners he employed smuggled lumps of coal into the bore, only to present them later as evidence that they were nearing a valuable seam. Unfortunately, Parkinson's funds were not unlimited and his project was eventually wound up in the bankruptcy court; it is believed that he ended his days as a turnkey in Lincoln Jail. Many thought that the episode was over when the mineshaft was sealed with a metal cover in 1809, but three years later locals noticed that it had turned a strange colour and that water was overflowing into a ditch in Coalpit Wood. In due course, Thomas Hotchkin, owner of the Woodhall Estate, had a sample of the water analysed and was delighted to find that it contained large quantities of bromine and iodine, which were known to help in the treatment of rheumatism and gout. He accordingly had a small bath-house built on the site in 1830 and appointed a resident doctor. The next step was to build a small hotel and, with this, the foundations of Woodhall Spa had been laid. Nowadays, the history of the spa is told by the town's Cottage Museum – once the home of Johnny Wield, the local Bath chair proprietor. It is instructive to note that Mr Wield's trade has now vanished from Woodhall Spa, as has Sir Henry Dymoke's profession from Horncastle.

History

Horncastle's first chance of joining the growing railway network occurred in 1845, when a line was proposed from Kirkstead to Wainfleet via Horncastle and Spilsby; the underlying idea was to develop a harbour at Wainfleet which could be used for exporting manufactured goods from the Midlands. While this scheme was, and still is, regarded as one of the most sensible made at the time, it foundered due to arguments amongst the various companies involved as to who should control what. As a result, Horncastle had to wait another ten years before the first train finally arrived.

By 1851, the Great Northern Railway had established routes from London to York and from Boston to Lincoln. After the heavy capital expenditure involved, it was keen to find ways of maximizing revenue, and traffic from branch lines was seen as an obvious solution. However, the best it could afford to do for Horncastle was to construct a coal-wharf and warehouse at the head of the Horncastle Canal; goods were delivered by rail to Dogdyke on the Boston–Lincoln line and conveyed thence by canal. In the long term, the GNR hoped to encourage a local company to construct a branch line to the town which it would then lease and operate. In 1853, just such a company was formed. The Horncastle Railway Company aimed to construct a branch from Horncastle to Kirkstead (on the GNR's existing main line) with an intermediate station at the village of Woodhall. By the end of the year, it had agreed terms with its larger neighbour, and a bill was subsequently presented in Parliament for the Horncastle and Kirkstead Junction Railway. Strong opposition was organized by the local canal company but, when it was demonstrated that most of the objectors held shares in the Horncastle Canal, the bill was duly passed; it received the Royal Assent on 10 July 1854.

The company's Act allowed it to raise £48,000 by share capital and £13,000 by borrowing. An optimistic prospectus promised a minimum of three trains per day with one every Sunday, and spoke in generous terms of the principal landowners offering their land at an agricultural price. The projected dividend was 5 per cent, a figure which allowed for the GNR taking half the line's earnings in return for operating it; the Horncastle Canal was then paying an average dividend of 7 per cent, so the directors were highly confident of reaching their target. The prospectus certainly did the trick – by August 1854, three-quarters of the share capital had been taken up. Unfortunately, the winter of 1854/5 was particularly severe and this delayed construction until March 1855, but progress was then very rapid. The whole line was completed within six months, a fact which owed not a little to the undemanding terrain and the general lack of engineering works; in fact, it possessed but a single overbridge near the tiny village of Martin. On the debit side, it also possessed a fair number of level crossings, which were to become a costly and damaging burden a century later.

It would appear that the navvies who constructed the line behaved reasonably well, which must have been a great relief to those local residents who remembered the notorious Bardney riot of 1812. This is worth a mention as it reveals what could happen if things went wrong. The navvies in this case were working on improvements to the River Witham and rioted after a dispute with a local baker. The unfortunate village publicans bore the brunt of their rage, which was expressed by a 'pub-crawl' of excessive proportions: the navvies attended one pub after another, evicting the landlord and then consuming all his beer. The proprietor of the Angel Inn saved himself only by rolling his beer barrels out into the street. Thirteen constables were called out from Horncastle but were quickly seen off; one of them was so badly injured that he died shortly afterwards. The uproar was only brought under control after the Riot Act had been read and the cavalry sent in. When railway and canal historians hint at the turmoil which navvies could bring to a district, this is the sort of conflagration they have in mind.

The official opening of the branch had been planned for 11 August 1855 when the weather intervened again, this time with persistent heavy rain which caused an embankment to settle. As a result, the Railway Inspector, Colonel Wynne, refused to approve it for use, but it was already too late to stop the opening celebrations, which went ahead as planned. Children who participated in the procession through Horncastle were rewarded with a free bun, which was presumably the price of their good behaviour. The contractors rapidly repaired the rain damage so that, when Colonel Wynne revisited the line on 17 August, it was duly approved for use; services began immediately.

The canal company responded by reducing its rates to those charged by the railway, but a spell of severe weather in December resolved the issue prematurely by freezing the canal and suspending all traffic. This encouraged many traders, particularly coal merchants, to switch to the railway much faster than they might have done otherwise. One happy result of this was a 23 per cent reduction in the local price of coal, which conveniently fulfilled one of the promises made in the railway's prospectus. On the other hand, the early dividends were not as great as had been hoped, a few sample years being listed in the table below:

Year	Dividend
1856	1.5%
1857	2.2%
1876	4.1%
1880	3.5%

The increase between 1857 and 1876 may owe a little to the fact that the Horncastle Canal gave up the unequal struggle and closed to traffic in 1871. Thereafter, dividends increased steadily until 9 per cent had been reached by the end of the century and the company even paid 6 per cent throughout the First World War. It was still producing a reasonable return on investment when it became part of the London and North Eastern Railway in 1923, a proud achievement unequalled by any other Lincolnshire branch line. An interesting sidelight on these financial matters is revealed by a dividend draft of 1880, which shows that income tax was then charged at 5d in the pound – a rate of just over two per cent!

Woodhall Spa station, photographed in 1903 at the height of the town's popularity as a spa. The passing loop and second platform to the left were added after 1880 to cope with the increase in traffic. The Broadway is seen to the right

Great Grimsby Borough Council

This photograph, taken in the 1920s, depicts the scene at Horncastle station on the day of the great horse fair. There were four such fairs a year, the first taking place on the second Monday in August. Each lasted a week, and in the early 1920s they were considered to be among 'the largest horse fairs in the kingdom', being 'resorted to by dealers from all parts of England and the continent'. Off the right of the picture were a further two tracks, along with the main platform and station building; there was also another platform situated behind the horse wagons shown here

Great Grimsby Borough Council

The general history of the line is relatively quiet and uneventful. The development which most helped to sustain it was the growth of Woodhall as a spa town, which conveniently replaced business lost by the decline of agriculture in the area. The period from 1880 to 1914 marks the height of Woodhall's popularity as a resort and the railway soon found that the original station was insufficient to cope with the volume of traffic generated. A succession of improvements was carried out between 1888 and 1910, during which the station acquired a passing loop, a second platform, a footbridge, a signal-box, a new waiting room, a booking hall and even a bookshop. Finally in the 1920s, Kirkstead, the junction station on the local main line, was renamed Woodhall junction, as though to acknowledge the town's rise to prominence.

Despite all this, agricultural traffic at Horncastle still had its moments, for the regular and special livestock markets brought a tremendous amount of business to the railway. In 1906, for example, there were some 8,000 sheep in the spring fair and 5,715 of them had been brought in by rail. The photograph above shows a similarly busy scene, this time with horses crowding part of the station yard. However, the regular Thursday sheep fairs were the most important ones and, at their peak, they generated some thirty special trains over the branch in a single day; it even became possible to see as many as seven steam locomotives in Horncastle yard. The demand to move livestock was so great that, at times, the railway had to draft in open wagons, although this expedient was not popular with the platelayers who had first to clean them out with lime.

Passenger traffic at Horncastle also had great peaks during the year, particularly at Easter and bank holidays, although the regular high spot appears to have been Jackson and Son's annual excursion to the coast. In July 1905, for example, this attracted over a thousand passengers and required two separate trains; one of these was fourteen coaches long and probably formed the branch record. Naturally, the line also had its human side, and there are two delightful stories of the wildlife at Horncastle station. The first concerns a pike, who somehow took up residence in the station's water-tower; while the second concerns the toads and frogs who lived in the well of a wagon turntable. All of these creatures were met regularly during the course of routine maintenance and were carefully stored, the pike in a bucket of water, until they could be returned to their homes.

Unfortunately, the line had lived through its best years by the end of the Second World War, when the LNER introduced a basic service of five trains per day; this survived, with only minor modifications, until the end of passenger services in 1954. The story is the familiar one of increasing competition from buses which provided cheaper, more frequent and more convenient services. By 1952, passenger loadings were very light and the passing loop at Woodhall Spa had fallen into disuse. In July that year, the Eastern Region of British Railways proposed withdrawing the passenger service altogether, claiming that Woodhall Spa and Horncastle could be served by adjusting the local bus timetable to provide good connections at Woodhall Junction. A number of local people submitted written objections but, unfortunately, these went astray and BR innocently announced that there was no opposition to its proposals. This produced a minor uproar which soon corrected BR's misunderstanding of the situation.

The protest movement was led by Richard Chatterton, who was then the Clerk of Horncastle Urban District Council. It culminated in a meeting at Nottingham with the East Midlands Transport Users Consultative Committee, where a discrepancy became apparent between the policies of the government and those of the Railway Executive. The government was anxious to develop the country's agricultural resources (and this included preventing the depopulation of rural areas) while the Railway Executive was busy closing rural branch lines on economic grounds. The two policies appeared to be in conflict, and Mr Chatterton made it quite clear that he regarded the modest cost of maintaining the Horncastle passenger service as a legitimate expense, consistent with the government's policy for rural areas. A sub-committee was formed to investigate and report back, which it did in July 1953. The majority report concluded that the Railway Executive should be asked to withdraw its proposals as there was a human side to the question which far outweighed the modest savings on offer. Unfortunately, however, the Railway Executive rejected this advice on the grounds that it had already presented, namely that the cost of providing the service exceeded the revenue it produced and, given legal requirements as to signalling and level crossings, there was no way in which it could be provided more cheaply. The closure notices accordingly went up in July 1954, announcing that the last train would run on Saturday 11 September. On the fateful day, BR provided six carriages hauled by a 4-6-2 tank engine of Great Central origin. Black crape was tied to the door-handles, and Woodhall Spa provided a wreath for the front of the engine. As is so often the way on these occasions, the train was crowded with passengers whose previous neglect had made it the last one.

Despite losing its passenger service, the branch remained open for parcels and freight, principally petrol, coal and agricultural equipment. There were initially two return trips per day but this was reduced to one as the volume of traffic declined. The timetable became very relaxed, the only stipulation appearing to be that the train reached Horncastle before lunchtime; this generous arrangement gave the crews plenty of time to snare rabbits and gather wild mushrooms along the way. Woodhall junction lost the first of its four rail routes on 17 June 1963, when Dr Beeching closed the line to Boston. The lines to Firsby and Lincoln went next, on 5 October 1970, although freight continued from Lincoln to Horncastle for another six months. The end finally came on 6 April 1971, when the last diesel-hauled freight train rumbled out of Horncastle. Today, the once extensive local network has been eradicated altogether: the last survivor was a nine-mile stub from Lincoln to Bardney which remained open into the 1980s to serve a sugar refinery.

The Line Today

After closure, the line remained derelict until 1975, when Lincolnshire County Council purchased most of the Woodhall Spa-Horncastle section from British Rail for £3,800. For some reason, it did not exercise its right to buy the one-mile section through Woodhall Spa Golf Course, although a detour has been provided just to the north of the line. Perhaps this was a gesture of appeasement to local golfers? The rest of the trackbed was duly converted into the Spa Trail, which now forms part of the longer Viking Way, a long-distance footpath from Oakham in Leicestershire to the south side of the Humber Bridge.

Unfortunately, the stations along the branch have not fared at all well. Only the station-house survives at Woodhall junction, although the remarkable cast-iron Gents which once stood on the northbound platform has been preserved in Lincoln at the Museum of Lincolnshire Life. This extraordinarily ornate public convenience was cast at Glasgow in the 1880s. The wildlife artist, David Shepherd, has a similar, though less elaborate, specimen at Cranmore, his preserved railway station in Somerset, which makes one wonder if nineteenth-century Glaswegians had a special factory dedicated to this sort of thing!

Of Woodhall Spa station, hardly a trace remains. the site is marked by a clearing behind the shops where the line once crossed Station Road. Horncastle station fared much better until January 1985, when its new owners cleared the site completely. This was all the more distressing to railway enthusiasts and historians, as the buildings appeared to have survived in reasonable condition. All that remained in August 1988 were two low brick walls (the last vestiges of the platform) and a derelict brick-built shed at the south-west corner of the site. The design of this suggested railway origin although its state suggested imminent collapse.

Apart from the trackbed itself, the only other reminder of the railway's existence is a number of crossing-keeper's dwellings dotted along the route. It is ironic that these should have survived longest, as they are partly to blame for the line's demise. Local people were not to know it in 1954, but the deadly formula of level crossings and staffing costs was to spell disaster for many more rural branch lines.

The Walk (6½ miles)

The site of Horncastle station lies off a sharp curve on the B1191 at grid reference 254694; it is now used as a lorry-park, and inspection may not be a practical proposition during working hours. Most of the site has been flattened in accordance with its new use but, as noted above, the remains of a platform and a brick-built shed were still extant in 1988, though how long this will remain so is anyone's guess. At the south of the site, I found a notice with the familiar British Rail logo, instructing observers to 'keep off'. It looks as if the BR Property Board has managed to leave itself with yet another small enclave miles from the nearest operational line. Still, at least it is a flattened site rather than some lofty crumbling viaduct.

The disused Horncastle Canal lies immediately east of the old railway and, in 1988, a short section of rail was still evident running between the two. This might cause the casual observer some confusion as it lies at right angles to the general alignment of the station; the main platform ran north-south whereas this short length of track runs east-west. The mystery is explained by the fact that a wagon turntable used to stand at the north end of the station platform.

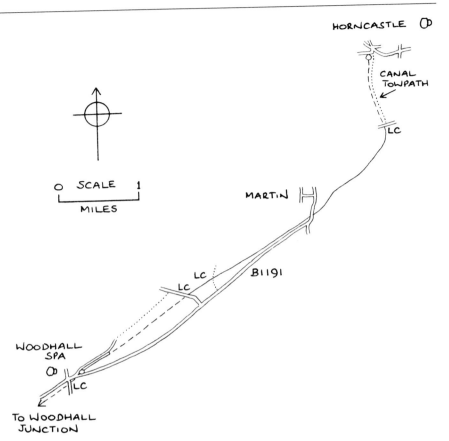

THE SPA TRAIL

This was used for turning wagons through 90° so that they could be led across the road into the warehouse of Harrison's, the corn merchants – a task presumably carried out by the shunting horse which worked the turntable. The 1897 Ordnance Survey map shows this siding running right through the warehouse and out the other side, stopping just a few yards short of the waterway. It looks as if any runaways would have ended up in a watery grave.

The best place to start the Spa Trail is from the north-east corner of the station site, where a footpath leads to the old canal. On reaching this, the walker should turn right (south) and then follow the west bank of the canal to a minor road at grid reference 257680. Along the way, the branch will be seen curving in from the right; unfortunately, this section is now private. On reaching the road, the walker should turn right and then immediately left to join the trackbed proper. A large sign confirms that this is indeed the Spa Trail and an information board gives details of farming in the area. Were further confirmation required, a neatly restored crossing-keeper's cottage adorns the site. This is the first of several on the branch and its owners have understandably decided to conceal the gloomy purple-black brickwork with white paint; its fellows have not been so lucky. The porch and door at the northern gable-end have also been removed and replaced with a window, which suggests that they were troubled by chilling north winds. The same alteration has been made to other cottages on the line, but this remedy would not have been permitted in the railway's heyday. Early regulations forbade staff the pleasures of singing and whistling while at work, and they were even required to salute passing trains; such a company would hardly tolerate structural alterations to its property!

The old canal keeps the railway company for just over another mile but then turns away to the south, weaving a leisurely course to Coningsby and Dogdyke where it joins the River Witham. Its locks have been turned into weirs and it is now nothing more than a drainage channel for the surrounding land, which is host to agriculture of a particularly efficient and mechanized kind. Conservationists are concerned about the growth of prairie farming with its associated hedgerow destruction, but one local farmer admitted candidly that modern fertilizers replace anything the wind blows away. Of course, they cannot replace habitats but the main argument is a purely financial one: hedgerows occupy land which could be used to produce more crops and their retention therefore has a price.

Moles are much in evidence on the approach to the bridge south of Martin village (grid reference 242662) and their numerous hillocks of neatly turned soil become difficult to avoid. There is also an old concrete gangers' hut on this section, though many of its concrete side-panels have fallen (or been pushed) out, giving it a very skeletal appearance. Beyond the bridge at Martin, the character of the line changes dramatically from prairie to woodland, and the next information board describes how nature gradually reclaims her own. Were it not for the county council's active management, the southern part of the line would rapidly end up as a wild wood of oak and ash.

A minor road is reached at Martin Moor (grid reference 217647), where a railway cottage in the now familiar style reveals the site of another level crossing. The walker should turn right here and proceed north-west for a quarter of a mile until a bridleway is met on the left at grid reference 213648. Fortunately, the waymarking hereabouts is quite adequate, and the route is picked out by a number of signs which carry the symbol of a yellow Viking's helmet: these denote the Viking Way, of which the Spa Trail forms a minor part. On reaching the bridleway, the walker should turn left and proceed across the northern reaches of Woodhall Spa Golf Course.

Here, alas, the waymarking is poor, the result of various signs having been

There is only one bridge on the Spa Trail and that carries the B1191 over the line. The authorities obviously expect bad weather, for they have installed a picnic table beneath it

uprooted. It would be interesting to know who is responsible for this – hopefully not the golfers themselves. The walker should follow the bridleway through small pockets of woodland and across some of the greens, keeping to the obvious path ahead of him in case of doubt. There are plenty of signs declaring where the path does not go, so its course can usually be deduced by applying a little bit of inverted logic. At grid reference 202638, the bridleway passes a large property on the left, beyond which it becomes an access road. The Viking Way follows this to the centre of Woodhall Spa, but the Spa Trail diverges to the south at grid reference 201637 to regain the trackbed, which may now be followed to the site of the old station (194632).

As noted earlier, the station buildings have been completely demolished, but the large vacant site to the north of Station Road makes it clear where they once stood. The level crossing to the west must have been extremely unpopular with motorists, their delays spun out by southbound trains waiting at the station to pick up and set down passengers. The trackbed beyond now accommodates Clarence Road, where a number of long, thin bungalows reveal the constraints the nineteenth-century railway managed to impose on some twentieth-century architect. When I visited, a local resident was busy cutting up railway sleepers on a piece of waste ground – further evidence of what once passed his door.

Another crossing-keeper's cottage stands at grid reference 192630, and beyond this the empty trackbed continues for another one and a half miles to Woodhall Junction; but this is neither part of the Spa Trail nor a public right of way. Opposite the cottage there is a small park containing a plaque which recalls that the site was donated to the community after the hotel which stood there was destroyed by enemy action in 1943. This is a stark reminder that the RAF bomber squadrons stationed nearby during the last war made this rather quiet and out of the way rural area a prime target for the Luftwaffe. Not for nothing was Lincolnshire known as 'bomber county'.

In general, the Spa Trail makes a very pleasant rural walk, the only regrettable thing being the lack of railway relics; but this is hardly surprising considering that its progressive run-down and closure began as early as 1955. The wonder of it is that freight services survived as long as 1971.

Further Explorations

Lincolnshire is not a county well endowed with railway footpaths: this could reflect a lack of interest in official circles, or perhaps a feeling that the flat landscape which characterized many of the lines would not allow for particularly interesting paths. In either case, this is regrettable as it ignores a number of powerful arguments. Apart from the inherent historical interest which will always appeal to a few, railway paths enable local authorities to get pedestrians and cyclists off the roads, and to offer disabled people easy access to the countryside.

The very flatness of the lines has, indeed, been a problem. While this feature was welcomed by the companies which constructed them, it has been equally welcomed by those farm managers who have removed them – an easy task, as a brief study of the local Ordnance Survey map will show. The line from Woodhall Spa to Firsby reveals all too clearly how the route has been fragmented and, in some places, totally eradicated. The basic need is for quick, decisive action when British Rail offers to sell a disused trackbed to the local authority. Many chances have been lost forever, but two still remain. The lines from Spalding to March and from Grimsby to Louth are both recent closures and could conceivably be put to some worthwhile public use. A local charity has

Louth station viewed from the former station approach. Building materials in the foreground indicate that salvation may be at hand

already organized a sponsored walk over the Louth line, which reveals that there is both interest and social value in preserving the route as a traffic-free thoroughfare.

Mention of the Louth line naturally raises the issue of Louth station, which local people will know was the subject of controversy, proposal and counterproposal for many years. The basic problem was that of a fine building neglected, vandalized and allowed to rot, until it became unsafe and unusable. In May 1988, the whole sorry tale moved several steps nearer to a satisfactory conclusion. The owners, Louth Station Estates, applied to demolish it in order to build eleven new homes on the site, but their proposals were rejected at an enquiry. In his findings the inspector, Anthony Bingham, made the following judgement: 'It is a building which has been exquisitely designed, with the façade presenting a fine composition which still stands largely in its original form'. Hopefully, that façade can now be preserved, so that the station will again be a source of pride instead of embarrassment to the town.

Unfortunately, these considerations – interesting though they may be – do not offer much in the way of official walks for those with an interest in industrial archaeology and, regrettably, there is not much to offer. Four miles of the trackbed from Woodhall Spa to Southrey (part of the GNR main line to

Lincoln) are used as a footpath, but its status is not known: it could be official but it could just as easily be private land. The usual solution, of turning to the waterways, is itself unreliable in this case, as many of them do not have towpaths (and there is no reason why they should, for many of them were constructed primarily as part of an irrigation system). The only exception of any note is the Horncastle Canal from Coningsby to Dogdyke, followed by the River Witham from Dogdyke towards Boston. Anyone who attempts this route will at least have the satisfaction of knowing that, south of Dogdyke, the opposite bank of the river carries the abandoned line from Woodhall Spa to Boston. In the end, however, the simplest solution might be to devote any remaining time and energy to lobbying the county council for more railway paths.

Transport and Facilities

| Map: | Ordnance Survey, Landranger Series Sheet 122 (recommended) |

Buses: Brylaine Travel
291 London Road, Boston, Lincolnshire
Telephone: 01205 364 087

Stagecoach Lincolnshire
www.stagecoach.com/lincolnshire
Telephone: (Traveline) 0871 200 22 33

Trains: National Rail Enquiries
www.nationalrail.co.uk
Telephone: 08457 48 49 50

It must be said that public transport in this area is not good and that the easiest way to get around is by car. As far as the Spa Trail is concerned, the ideal solution is to cajole a car-driving friend into taking some exercise with you. Drive both cars to one end; park the first, drive to the opposite end in the other, and then walk back. Those who insist on using public transport are made of sterner stuff. They must also be long-suffering, patient and prepared to spend a lot of time on the telephone.

The area as a whole is totally bereft of railways, the nearest useful stations being Lincoln (for Horncastle) and Boston (for Woodhall Spa). Both are well served, although trains to Boston are few and far between on a Sunday. The most useful bus routes are listed below, but it must be understood that they are liable to change at short notice; there is not a great deal of revenue to sustain the various competing operators. The quickest way to get an up-to-date review of the situation is to see the Stagecoach Lincolnshire website (www.stagecoachbus.com/lincolnshire) or ring Traveline on 0871 200 22 33.

a. *Lincoln–Horncastle–Skegness*

    Mondays to Saturdays
    Operator: Stagecoach Lincolnshire (route 6)
    Frequency: Hourly

    Sundays
    Operator: Stagecoach Lincolnshire (route 6)
    Frequency: 5 journeys per day

    Note that this level of service may be reduced during the winter period.

b. *Harncastle–Woodhall Spa*

    Operator: Translinc (Connect Dial a Bus)
    Telephone: 0845 234 3344

c. *Boston–Woodhall Spa*

    Mondays to Saturdays Only
    Operator: Brylaine Travel
    Frequency: 12 journeys per day

As far as other facilities are concerned, the obvious centres are Horncastle and Woodhall Spa. There is precious little in between other than the solitary picnic table beneath the bridge at Martin! However, the two towns make up for this with a reasonable provision of shops, tea-rooms and pubs. A number of the big East Midlands brewers are represented in the area, the only independent brewery in Lincolnshire being Bateman's of Wainfleet. It is sad to relate that even this company had an agonizing fight for survival in 1987 but, happily, it pulled through and the company's products are still worth seeking out. This is what Nicholson's *Real Ale Guide to the Waterways* had to say on the subject in 1976: 'The Salem Brewery is a landmark in the town of Wainfleet, as is the Bateman's slogan in Lincolnshire – "Good Honest Ales". Bateman's have been brewing now for over 100 years as a family company and own more than 100 public houses and hotels. One cannot speak too highly of the quality of their real draught beer . . .' It is a credit to George Bateman and his family that this generous compliment still holds true today.

5
THE HORNSEA RAIL TRAIL
HULL TO HORNSEA

Introduction

Prime Minister Edward Heath created the new county of Humberside in 1974 from parts of Lincolnshire and the old East Riding of Yorkshire: with it, he also created a long-term bone of contention. North of the Humber particularly, people still regard themselves as Yorkshire folk rather than 'Humbersiders'. The unfortunate county council thus has something of an image problem, as it represents a concept which a good number of local people simply do not want!

Alas for those displaced Yorkshire men and women, Humberside seems likely to stay. On the plus side, it possesses some delightful countryside, particularly in the Wolds, a range of hills which sweep down in a huge arc from Flamborough Head to the Wash. It also possesses some extremely helpful council staff who seem genuinely committed to the reuse of abandoned railways: their excellent route guides are probably the best produced anywhere in the country. While the next chapter deals with a walk through the Wolds, this one takes a bracing march across the coastal plain, which stretches from Bridlington to Spurn Head. The southern part of this area is known as Holderness: it is a quiet and gentle landscape which is relatively undiscovered, a backwater of tiny villages, winding lanes, irrigation channels and obscure little resorts that are hardly known to the outside world.

In the nineteenth century, two fully independent railway companies saw commercial possibilities in developing two of these resorts and duly constructed branch lines, first to Withernsea, and then to Hornsea. Poor little Withernsea hardly existed before the railway selected it for seaside fame: ten miles of coastline from Tunstall to Easington were carefully surveyed before the fateful decision was made. The 1851 census recorded just 109 residents, while a contemporary writer described it as nothing more than 'a handful of houses with a single shop'. At least Hornsea had something to start with, a fact which caused the town's Victorian residents to look down on its then modern neighbour.

The whole of the Hornsea branch is now an official railway walk and, as the rambler strides along the empty trackbed, the remoteness of the Holderness countryside is all too evident. In places, it seems remarkable that it was ever crossed by a double-track railway. Still, the Victorians were optimistic folk and their line to Hornsea managed a useful existence of just over a hundred years. The landscape was quiet before the railway came and now it is quiet once again.

History

Hornsea's first chance of joining the railway network occurred in 1846, when an Act was passed authorising a branch to the town from Arram on the existing Hull-Bridlington line. Unfortunately, this was to have been constructed by George Hudson's York and North Midland Railway and, following Hudson's downfall in 1849, it was never built. In fact, one of the Committees of Investigation which looked into the affairs of the company found that its branch lines were a major cause of low dividends. It may not have been much consolation to the folk of Hornsea, but seven other projected Y & NM branch lines were suspended or scrapped at the same time. Holderness thus remained without modern communications until Anthony Bannister's Hull and Holderness Railway Company opened its branch line to Withernsea on 26 June 1854. This was a most ambitious undertaking, for despite the modest twenty miles of its route, it was a fully independent company with its own locomotives, rolling stock and livery. Unfortunately, it was not a large enough unit to function economically and the common pattern of lease to a mighty neighbour, followed by inevitable takeover, occurred in 1860 and 1862 respectively, the mighty neighbour in this case being the North Eastern Railway.

The relative failure of the Hull and Holderness Railway did not go unnoticed in Hornsea, for when new proposals for a branch line to the town were formulated, they included provision for it to be worked by the NER from the outset. The main instigator of the new scheme was one Joseph Armytage Wade, a Hornsea resident and Hull timber merchant. He and his associates were convinced of Hornsea's potential both for residential development and as a popular Victorian watering place – a role which, in the fullness of time, Hornsea proved singularly unwilling to accept. The Hull and Hornsea Railway Company was duly formed in 1861 and obtained an Act for the construction of its line on 30 June 1862. Two rival schemes both failed to reach parliament, so the Hornsea Bill met with no opposition, a most fortunate state of affairs which resulted in the company's legal and parliamentary expenses totalling a modest £1,740 – a real bargain price by the standards of the day. The Act authorized construction of a thirteen-mile branch line from Hornsea to Wilmington, on the outskirts of Hull. Share capital was set at £70,000 with borrowing powers of

£23,000. As might be expected, the Act also granted powers for the company to enter into working or traffic arrangements with the NER.

Mr Wade turned the first sod at Hornsea on 8 October 1862 with a 'polished electro-plated steel shovel'; this fascinating detail must originate from a contemporary newspaper report. The occasion was attended by the usual celebrations and euphoria, but they could not be maintained in the face of a succession of problems which soon placed the company in serious financial difficulty. The ground at Hornsea Bridge was discovered to be unsound and the viaduct there had to be rebuilt; similar problems afflicted the embankments in the area. This was followed by an unpleasant incident in which Anthony Bannister, one of the shareholders in the company, claimed that Joseph Wade was making Hudson-like profits out of the project by buying land and materials personally and then selling them back to the company at inflated prices; one cannot help wondering if this accusation was motivated out of jealousy or whether it was the result of an excessive zeal to steer the company away from the fate of his own Hull and Holderness Railway. As if these difficulties were not enough, the company's line was then given a most rigorous examination by the

The train for Hull awaits departure from Hornsea Town station in 1952. The overall roof, just visible in the distance, has now been demolished

N.E. Stead Collection

railway inspector, Captain Rich. Amongst other things, he found that various level-crossing gates were below standard and that the junction at Wilmington with the existing Victoria Docks branch was not in the exact location specified by the company's Act. To cap it all, he then fell into the Sutton Drain (a large irrigation channel) while examining a bridge, an incident which did nothing to improve his temper, although it did provide the troubled directors with a little light relief.

The contractors hurriedly corrected the various imperfections specified by Captain Rich, with the result that government permission for the opening was finally obtained late on 26 March 1864, Easter Saturday. An official opening was promptly arranged for Easter Monday, when, to mark the occasion, a sixteen-coach special left a hastily decorated Wilmington station. On arrival at Hornsea, the train was greeted by a procession, the firing of cannon and a celebration tea, provided at the personal expense of Mr Wade. The inaugural speech emphasized again the need to attract visitors to the town but, once again, Hornsea turned a deaf ear. Only Mr Wade seemed moved by the exhortation, for he soon provided the town with a pier.

The line then settled down to its role of serving the local community.

Engine No. 6776 arrives at Swine station with a Hornsea-Hull passenger service in 1955

N.E. Stead Collection

Initially, trains terminated at Wilmington, pending doubling of the Victoria Docks branch into Hull Paragon; this was duly completed, and Hornsea trains began to use the city's principal station with effect from 1 July 1864. Hornsea trains started by heading west from Hull but then negotiated a U-turn to the north which brought them to the first station at Botanic Gardens. This was followed by further stops at Stepney and Wilmington, both on the Victoria Docks branch, before trains turned north-east on to the branch proper. It is no exaggeration to say that this was littered with stations, for the Hornsea company provided a halt at practically every road-crossing, a policy which created considerable confusion with station names. Initially at least, the stations were called Sutton-on-Hull, Swine, Skirlaugh, Ellerby, Burton Constable, Whitedale, Sigglesthorne, Goxhill, Hornsea Bridge and Hornsea Town. The majority were provided with substantial station houses of a uniform pattern, while a splendid terminus was constructed at Hornsea Town, complete with a five-pillar portico similar to that at BR's existing Whitby station. To judge from contemporary photographs, the line was initially single track, although the NER had doubled it by 1908.

Unfortunately, the cost of constructing the line exceeded the estimates by some 75 per cent, and early traffic revenue fell below expectations. As a result, shareholders' meetings were apt to become stormy affairs and the directors were soon forced into the only feasible escape route – an approach to the North Eastern Railway with a view to amalgamation. While negotiations to this effect were still going on, an aggrieved creditor brought an action against the company and forced most of its station equipment to be sold by auction. The sale took place on 4 January 1866, with station furniture, fittings and even telegraph equipment coming under the hammer. Fortunately, most of the lots were purchased by an individual acting on the company's behalf, which meant that it could continue to use them and avoid more serious embarrassment. The merger with the NER duly took place by an Act dated 16 July 1866. This required the NER to keep a separate account of Hornsea revenue: after working expenses and interest charges had been paid, any balance remaining was to be remitted to Hornsea shareholders. The Act also allowed Hornsea shares to be exchanged for NER 4 per cent guaranteed stock at any time.

The most singular feature of the line's subsequent history concerns its many stations. Ellerby was closed to passengers in 1902 as the NER considered that the immediate vicinity was well enough served with stations three-quarters of a mile to the south at Skirlaugh and three-quarters of a mile to the north at Burton Constable. However, it retained its platform and stayed open for goods as Ellerby West Siding. In 1922, the company suddenly became aware that Burton Constable invited confusion with Constable Burton on its Wensleydale branch and duly renamed the offending station Ellerby, thus reviving a name which had lain dormant for twenty years and effectively moving Ellerby station three-quarters of a mile to the north.

The situation at Goxhill was even more bizarre. For a start, the village consisted of little more than a church. Moreover, it took the NER a long time to wake up to the fact that there was another Goxhill in the area, on the Great Central's line to Barton-on-Humber. After forty years of confusion, Goxhill was accordingly renamed Wassand after a local hall; needless to say, Wassand Hall was substantially further from the station than the tiny village of Goxhill. Services here were extremely spartan to say the least, for the station had but one train per week, which was provided for the benefit of shoppers. The London and North Eastern Railway perpetuated this arrangement until 1953, when Wassand and its single siding were both closed. Some railway historians, such as C.T. Goode, doubt that they ever really opened!

The main emphasis on the branch was always on passenger traffic and, for much of its history, a goods service was provided on alternate days only. When absent from the Hornsea branch, this train could normally be found working an identical service to Withernsea. Sometimes, however, the volume of freight was sufficient to warrant crews splitting the train in two at Whitedale and taking it into Hornsea in two separate runs; a stiff 1 in 44 gradient near Hornsea Bridge necessitated this manoeuvre. One unusual but typical feature of NER operation was that station-masters were expected to trade as local coal merchants. They would rent coal drops, books, scales and shovels from the company and retail coal, which was delivered in wagons with bottom-opening doors. The profit on this trade in the 1950s was ten shillings (50p) per ton, before rental and hire charges, which must have been a welcome addition to the station-master's wages – provided there was sufficient local business.

Passenger services developed to the point where, by 1914, there were thirteen workings in each direction. These included an 8.50 a.m. express from Hornsea which covered the 15 miles to Hull in just 28 minutes; this was balanced by a return working which left Hull at 5.18 p.m. but made conditional stops at Sutton and Hornsea Bridge. There were also two return trips on Sundays, which catered for the growing number of day-trippers. The First World War caused predictable reductions, but these were quickly reversed after 1918. In fact, the inter-war period can be regarded as the line's heyday, with the LNER introducing regular interval services on 8 April 1929; similar improvements were made on the lines to Brough, Beverley and Withernsea as part of the company's drive to encourage and develop Hull-bound suburban and commuter traffic.

During the Second World War, the passenger service was reduced to nine journeys each way and Sentinel steam railcars took over the two Sunday workings; a number of these units congregated from time to time at Botanic Gardens, one of the city's large steam sheds. By the 1950s, however, the service had crept back to twelve weekday trains with four Sunday workings, including an express which conveyed day-trippers from Hull. By now, however, competition from buses, lorries and private cars was beginning to bite, and British

Railways had to introduce a number of economy measures in order to reduce costs. As noted above, Wassand was closed in 1953, although the level of service was so spartan that the station might just as well never have been built. Skirlaugh suffered the same fate on 6 May 1957. It was badly sited anyway, being some two miles from the village it was supposed to serve, and shared its station-master with Ellerby, which was always far busier. Subsequently, all stations between Hull and Hornsea became unstaffed with the introduction of diesel multiple units on which the guards issued and collected tickets.

Despite these economies, the timetable introduced on 10 September 1962 still offered an extremely good service with nine trains in each direction every weekday and five every Sunday, although the Sunday workings were restricted to the summer months only. The commuter trains even offered limited first-class accommodation. This, then, was the state of affairs when a certain gentleman from ICI intervened. The county council guide concludes the story with a neat touch of irony: '. . . the line continued to lose money. Closure inevitably drew nearer. This came when the good Dr Beeching discovered an interest in rural branch lines and promptly closed them! The last train to Hornsea ran one cold wet day on 19 October 1964.' The railway had never managed to 'Brightonize' the town and, for the sake of those who love unspoilt and out-of-the-way places, that is probably just as well.

The Line Today

Following the line's closure, British Rail removed the rails and demolished a number of bridges, notably those at Sutton and Ellerby over the Holderness Drain and Lambwath Stream respectively. The future of the route then became a subject of speculation and uncertainty. This was resolved in 1971 when the former East Riding County Council purchased the trackbed with a view to converting the section from Hull to Skirlaugh into a railway walk and the section from Skirlaugh to Hornsea into a new road. Fortunately, the road part of the scheme was abandoned in 1974 when the Heath administration reorganized local government and created the new county of Humberside; Humberside County Council soon decided that it wanted to keep the whole of the route for recreational use.

The ballast has now been removed and a variety of new surfaces provided. The section from Wilmington to the Holderness Drain at Sutton-on-Hull has been tarmacked, as befits a path in the heavily populated suburbs of Hull. The Holderness Drain has been spanned by a new bridlepath bridge of timber construction, as has the Lambwath Stream further north. The section from the Holderness Drain to Ellerby has a 'split' surface, with rough gravel on one side and consolidated ash on the other; while the final section from Ellerby to

Hornsea uses consolidated ash alone. Loose bits of gravel on the middle section can be quite uncomfortable underfoot, so it is a relief to leave it. In the long term, the council intends to provide a proper cycle track along the whole length of the line, and a small section has already been laid north of Sigglesthorne station, where a newly constructed detour climbs the east side of a cutting to avoid the boggy cutting floor. This appears to have been built according to the principles developed by Sustrans Ltd and, if the whole of the line is eventually treated in this way, it will make a fine facility for local walkers, cyclists and wheelchair users. In the meantime, make sure that you wear a pair of thick-soled shoes – I didn't, and paid for it!

Miraculously, very few stations and level-crossing gatehouses have disappeared, the only exceptions being Sutton, Skirlaugh and Hornsea Bridge. The council has taken the opportunity to create a small car-park and picnic area at Skirlaugh, with more landscaping, tree planting and picnic areas to follow elsewhere, notably at Swine, Ellerby and Sigglesthorne. Apart from the county, the route involves three other local authorities, namely Hull City Council, Beverley Borough Council and Holderness Borough Council; due to its highly quirky boundary, the Beverley authority gets off very lightly with just over five hundred yards of trackbed sandwiched between the other two. A variety of other groups are involved in monitoring and caring for the route, including conservation groups and local schools; the latter is a particularly welcome development. The whole path has the appearance of an attractive, well managed and well thought-out public amenity; it reflects credit on all those involved.

The Walk (15 miles)

These notes direct the walker from Hull Paragon to Hornsea Town. I had expected that the city would gradually give way to the country, but in practice this was not the case: the city stops abruptly at Sutton-on-Hull, where the change from urban to rural is made in about a hundred yards. No matter, tackling the walk in this direction keeps the afternoon sun behind you and ensures that you are going downhill, albeit ever so slightly. Hull Paragon is just 16 ft higher than Hornsea Town, a reflection on the gentle terrain which the route traverses.

Trains arrive at Hull Paragon facing east. The station's name is unique among British stations and is derived from Paragon Square, in which it stands. There are three exits from the station – left, right and straight ahead. Left leads to the bus station; right leads to the parcels office (the original station entrance and well worth a look); while straight ahead leads into Paragon Square. This is the

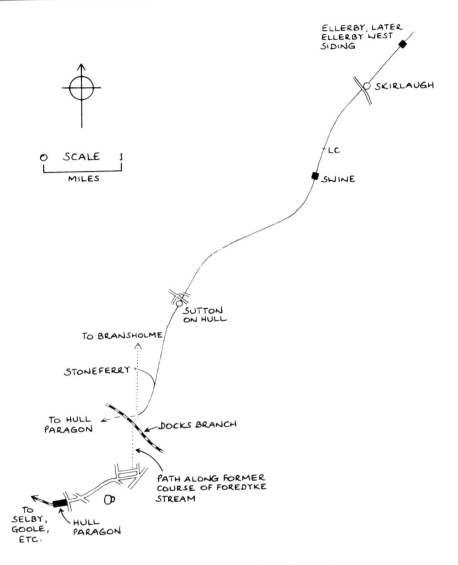

ELLERBY, LATER
ELLERBY WEST
SIDING

SKIRLAUGH

LC

SWINE

SUTTON
ON HULL

TO BRANSHOLME

STONEFERRY

TO HULL
PARAGON

DOCKS BRANCH

PATH ALONG FORMER
COURSE OF FOREDYKE
STREAM

TO
SELBY,
GOOLE,
ETC.

HULL
PARAGON

SCALE

MILES

HULL TO ELLERBY WEST SIDING

exit to take. It is just over a mile to the start of the path and marvellously simple to get there: basically, it is a straight walk as far as the other side of the River Hull, followed by a left and a right turn in quick succession. The details are as follows.

Cross over Paragon Square into Jameson Street and follow this into George Street. At the end of George Street (marked by the Colleges of Further and Higher Education), bear slightly right and cross over the River Hull by a substantial lift bridge. This is painted bright blue so it is difficult to miss. A few tugs and barges can normally be seen to the north of the bridge, proving that commercial traffic on the river is still alive. Having crossed the bridge, take the second left into New Cleveland Street and then first right into Spyvee Street: the path begins at the far end of Spyvee Street on the left-hand side, opposite Holborn Street (grid reference 106294). It is clearly signposted as a cycle path but unfortunately no one has had the foresight to add a notice which says where it goes!

As far as we are concerned, Hull has now been negotiated; from here on, it is a straightforward walk to the north. The cycle path meets most local roads on the level, and keen-eyed observers will notice that most of these junctions are marked with a pair of redundant bridge parapets. The obvious inference is that a railway ran here, in a cutting which has now been filled in. For once, this assumption is entirely wrong, for we are in fact following the course of an abandoned agricultural drain. This was the Foredyke Stream, which once drained much of Holderness and ran into the River Hull near the lift bridge we have just crossed; its course became disused when major drainage improvements were carried out in this part of Hull.

The path follows a course between terraces and large Victorian factories before reaching a railway bridge at grid reference 106304; this conveys the present-day freight line from Springbank to the docks. Having passed under it, the walker should turn right, on to the start of the Hornsea trackbed proper. Take care not to miss this turning, for the cycle path along the Foredyke Stream is by far the more obvious route. From here this heads off due north and finally loses itself in Bransholme, the largest council estate in Europe. Wilmington station stood about half a mile west of this point but is not part of the walk.

The next three miles of the path are tarmacked, but it still possesses the appearance of an old railway, starting out through a corridor of bushes on a slight embankment which overlooks the gardens backing on to it. Reckitt and Colman's sports ground is on the left, while the factory's founder (one presumes) is commemorated by James Reckitt Avenue on the right. At grid reference 111311, the line crosses a busy residential road, after which the former goods branch to Stoneferry can be seen curving off to the left; this can be followed for about a third of a mile.

The station at Sutton-on-Hull used to stand by the bridge at grid reference 116331 but has long been demolished. In its heyday, it possessed two platforms and a collection of rather insubstantial buildings, several of which included a lot of timber in their construction: no wonder so little has survived! Still, the attractive bridge remains intact and the main cross-beam carries details of its construction in raised lettering:

1863
Close Ayre & Nicholson
Phoenix Foundry
York

S & T Crawshaw   G Coulthard
Contractors   Engineer

The next half-mile is characterized by modern housing and, while the architecture is quite acceptable, the sheer number of similar properties and the lack of trees creates a very monotonous effect. It is a relief when the housing suddenly stops at grid reference 121338; it is bounded by a minor stream which must be the limit of development in the current local authority plan. As mentioned above, the end comes with practically no warning – suddenly the vista ahead is one of undulating fields which, in summer, are full of waist-high swaying wheat. In late August, large billows of purple smoke can be seen on the skyline as local farmers burn the stubble. When I was there, two fire-engines were driving away from the trackbed, having extinguished a blaze which may well have been started by local children. Burning cinders had carried this into an adjoining field which had not yet been harvested; as a result, large pools of blackened wheat disfigured the crop.

The Holderness Drain is crossed by a new bridleway bridge at grid reference 126342 and the remaining ten miles to Hornsea are 'pure countryside'. Having studied the map and a number of local histories, I anticipated that the landscape would be flat and rather uninteresting, but this is not the case. Rather, it undulates gently, offering views of the rising Wolds in the west. The spires of distant village churches often punctuate the skyline, while most of the characteristic gatehouses and station buildings can be seen long before they are reached, a feature of the walk which heightens the sensation of being a pedestrianized train driver.

The first surviving station building is met at Swine (grid reference 143356), but the owners must be rather sensitive to walkers, for a large fence now barricades them from the path; perhaps, being somewhat close to Hull, they are troubled by invasions of privacy. Swine may be regarded as a rather unfortunate name for a station but the railway had little choice, for the larger village to the east is Coniston and that name had already been claimed by the village at the head of Coniston Water in the Lake District. The LNER may have boasted that Hornsea was 'Lakeland by the sea', but any holidaymaker expecting Coniston in Lancashire would have been sorely disappointed had he somehow arrived at Coniston in the East Riding!

Stations and gatehouses now come thick and fast. First is a gatehouse near Kelwell Farm (grid reference 145362) followed by Skirlaugh station (154375), where the line crosses the A165 from Hull to Bridlington. The principal

The original Ellerby station, which closed to passengers as early as 1902. It stayed open for good as Ellerby West Siding but twenty years later Burton Constable, the next station up the line, was renamed Ellerby. As if the station naming on the Hornsea branch was not confusing enough, most of the buildings were identical as well. As a result, the modern rambler can be forgiven for wondering sometimes exactly where he is

Hull-Hornsea bus route (number 240) uses this particular stretch of road, so it is a good spot to gain access to the trackbed by public transport. A small car-park and picnic area provide other useful facilities for the modern visitor. While the station building has long been demolished, the platforms survive along with the former coal yard, although oak, ash and sycamore are rapidly colonizing the area. A glance at the map reveals that the villagers of North and South Skirlaugh had to walk nearly two miles to reach their station. The council guide makes the obvious point – 'No wonder they preferred the bus!'

The line now passes below Dowthorpe Hall before reaching the original Ellerby station at grid reference 162384. Like Goxhill, this had a very spartan service for it only opened on market days; the North Eastern Railway closed it to passengers in 1902, transferring the name twenty years later to the next station at grid reference 168394. This was originally named Burton Constable after a hall nearly three miles away; once again, nineteenth-century rail users were expected to be fit! While the trackbed can be followed straight through the former platforms and over an infilled bridge, it is worth leaving the path by the road to the former yard. Not only does this lead to the Railway Inn, a handy

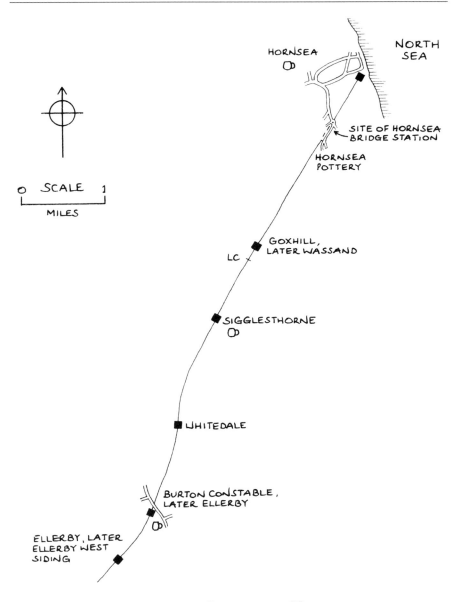

NORTH SEA

HORNSEA

SITE OF HORNSEA
BRIDGE STATION

HORNSEA
POTTERY

SCALE
0   1

MILES

GOXHILL,
LATER WASSAND
LC

SIGGLESTHORNE

WHITEDALE

BURTON CONSTABLE,
LATER ELLERBY

ELLERBY, LATER
ELLERBY WEST
SIDING

ELLERBY WEST SIDING TO HORNSEA

A general view of facilities on the north-bound platform of Whitedale station. The building here is slightly larger than others on the line, which is unusual considering that the surrounding countryside is so devoid of population that the station name was taken from a local farm. The superior provision was intended to impress the Bethall family of nearby Rise Hall, who were even provided with their own separate waiting room

place for refreshments, it also passes a local residence which boasts two of the old station lamps and a nameboard in its back garden; the nameboard proclaims 'Ellerby', so it is obviously from 1922 or later. Incidentally, readers can be forgiven if they are beginning to find the station names on this line a little bewildering!

The path now enters a deep and cool cutting before alighting on the embankment which once led to the viaduct over the Lambwath Stream. Considering the relative flatness of the terrain, this embankment is remarkably high and it is quite a climb down to the new bridleway bridge which now crosses the stream. An attractive brick-built bridge then carries the line over a farm track before reaching Whitedale station at grid reference 173409. Here, the station naming has reached new heights of eccentricity. The nearest village of any size is Withernwick, one and a half miles to the east, but perhaps this name was avoided in order to prevent confusion with Withernsea at the end of the neighbouring coastal branch. In the end, the railway plumped for the name of a local farm. The station survives in good condition and is notable for retaining a timber shelter on the southbound platform, together with the coal-drops in the former goods yard. Two waiting-rooms were provided here, one for the Bethall family of nearby Rise Hall, the other for the ordinary folk, from whom the Bethalls evidently had to be segregated!

Sigglesthorne comes next, one and a half miles later (grid reference 180431). The obvious name for this would have been Hatfield, for it is sandwiched between the villages of Great and Little Hatfield, which are half a mile to the east and west respectively. Unfortunately, there was already a well known Hatfield on the Great Northern's main line from King's Cross, so Sigglesthorne was chosen instead – a village three miles to the north-west. The platforms here were staggered on opposite sides of the road, as at Swine. Both still survive, the southbound platform sporting a railway-style bench, with the letters 'A FIELD' screwed on to the uppermost slat; the letters 'H' and 'T' are missing. Is this an original or a 'foreign' import? In August 1989, the station building was unoccupied and offered for sale by a local estate agent at £60,000. The specification stated that it was 'in need of modernisation', which was at least honest. The slate roof was in good condition, but local vandals had started on the ground floor windows, several of which were broken. I hope that a return visit will find the station in more caring hands; it could make a characterful and attractive family home. Like Whitedale, it still has a set of coal-drops in the old station yard.

By the time Goxhill crossing is reached (grid reference 187443), a white-painted water-tower on the outskirts of Hornsea has come into view to the north-east; this remains a distinctive feature for the next mile. Goxhill (later Wassand) station is passed at grid reference 188446, a most attractive site, with the area between the platforms laid to lawn; if the station owners were responsible for this improvement, it is very commendable. The line now follows a ruler-straight course to its terminus by the sea, oncoming walkers and cyclists first appearing as tiny spots below the horizon. A brick overbridge is passed at grid reference 197460, but a short distance later the trackbed is blocked by garden extensions (200465). The attractive Hornsea Mere lies just to the west of this section, and in the evening the air is filled with the raucous cries of wildfowl roosting for the night.

On reaching the garden extensions, the walker should turn right to gain access to Marlborough Avenue. The path continues downhill to the left, along Marlborough Avenue, but it is worth mentioning that a right turn at this point leads to Hornsea Pottery. It is the pottery for which Hornsea is probably now most famous: tours of the factory are free and there is an extensive factory shop, reputedly the largest in the north-east. Anyone who has visited the Wedgwood factory at Barlaston will be pleased to observe that the prices here are nowhere near so formidable, although Hornsea produces some elegant designs in a variety of fine materials and finishes. Mention has been made elsewhere of some of the unusual scenes encountered in researching this series, but few can equal that of the two full-blooded American tourists at Barlaston who wished to buy a

£1,000 gold-leaf dinner-service; they were particularly concerned about its performance in their dishwasher. It seemed rather like restoring an oil-painting by putting it through the washing-machine and, thanks to MacDonald's, the incongruous image of Wedgwood plates bearing burgers and chips to the table sprung readily to mind.

The railway reappears on the left about half way down Marlborough Avenue, this time astride the embankment which once led to Hornsea Bridge station. The buildings for this were at road level, with slopes up to the platforms, but British Rail cleared the site shortly after closure. The viaduct over the B1242 to Withernsea has also long been swept away. The only facility of any real use to the railway rambler now is Marlborough Stores, which stays open until 10 p.m. daily; this is a good place to obtain refreshments after the long walk, or to stock up if going in the other direction. At the end of Marlborough Avenue, the railway embankment has been graded back to make way for a new roundabout, but the trackbed can be regained on the other side. It is then three-quarters of a mile to the final station at Hornsea Town, which, despite its name, is nearer the beach than the town. The building here is the finest on the line and well repays a visit: it has just been restored after years of neglect. In its new guise, it is Station Mews and the residents now hang their laundry out to dry at what used to be the front, overlooking the one-time station approach. Those who knew the building in the past may be a little surprised to see it turned about thus but, no matter, it has been preserved, and very sympathetically. The elegant and substantial station house at the north end of the building is also worth a look.

Hornsea Police Station stands beyond the old railway terminus, on the site of the former turntable: this was removed years ago and replaced with a new one at the Hull end. The open space to the right accommodates Hornsea Market, which is held during the summer months on Wednesdays and Sundays. Beyond the police station, the road swings round to the promenade and beach. The council guide, which is written with great zest and humour, offers an apt quote with which to conclude: 'You are now at the seaside, so it's boots off for a refreshing paddle in the briny. Well done!' Remember that you could be in for a shock if you don't check the temperature first. Finally, if you have the energy, do explore the rest of Hornsea. It was always considered to be more elegant and refined than Withernsea, and much of its old-fashioned charm has survived intact.

Further Explorations

I have suggested earlier that Holderness is rather out of the way: it would not, therefore, be entirely surprising if the Hornsea Rail Trail was the only railway path in it. Happily, that is not the case for, in accordance with its interest in the reclamation of abandoned railways, the county council has also converted five miles of the Withernsea branch, from Hull to Keyingham. It is positively interested in developing this further, and in 1988 put in a bid to British Rail's Property Board for the next five miles to Winestead. Apart from this, the immediate area offers little else to interest the industrial archaeologist, although there are some extensive walks along the coast. The many walks and facilities which are to be found a little further afield are, in fact, closer to the Hudson Way, which runs from Market Weighton to Beverley. These are accordingly described fully at the end of the next chapter.

Transport and Facilities

Map: Ordnance Survey: Landranger Series Sheet 107 (recommended)

Buses: East Yorkshire Motor Services Ltd
             The Travel Office, Ferensway Coach Station, Hull, Humberside
             Telephone: 01482 325679
             http://www.eyms.co.uk/

             Stagecoach Hull
             www.stagecoachbus.com/hull
             Telephone: (Traveline) 0871 200 22 33

             Alpha Taxis
             39 Ladygate, Beverley, Humberside, HU17 8BH
             Telephone: 01482 881 461

Trains: National Rail Enquiries
             www.nationalrail.co.uk
             Telephone: 08457 48 49 50

The two railheads with buses to Hornsea are Beverley and Hull, although Hull will be the preferred choice for the majority of walkers. Beverley is on British Rail's line from Hull to Scarborough and enjoys an intensive local service from Hull, with about half the trains continuing on to Bridlington or Scarborough. Hull enjoys good services from Manchester and Sheffield, with a small number of inter-city services from further afield. Students of the British Rail passenger timetable may notice that the service from Sheffield occasionally carries a footnote about 'a maritime accident involving the railway bridge over the River Ouse at Goole'. This generally means that another ship has crashed into it. In the past, some of these accidents have been so severe that British Rail has been forced to examine the possibility of closing the bridge entirely, along with the line which runs over it. Local railway managers must have been appalled when it was hit again so recently after extensive repairs.

As far as buses are concerned, there is a very good service between Hull and Hornsea. There are some eighteen buses per day in each direction from Monday to Saturday with about half that number on Sunday. The operators are East Yorkshire Motor Services, but their competition creates a rather odd timetable inasmuch as a number of 'rival' journeys commence within ten minutes of each other or even simultaneously. There are several routes to choose from but, excepting route 240 at Skirlaugh station, only the infrequent ones venture close to the old railway: the best alternative points of contact are Ellerby (the Railway Inn), Whitedale and Great Hatfield.

Buses between Beverley and Hornsea are provided by East Yorkshire with the exception of a solitary evening journey which is operated by Alpha Taxis – presumably with a minibus. This relies on financial support from the county council and may prove to be less than permanent. In all, there are seven buses per day in each direction from Monday to Saturday. A third possibility worth mentioning is that of catching a bus from Hull to Sutton, which conveniently skips the urban section of the walk. There are plenty of buses to Sutton, most of them bound for the huge council estate at Bransholme. It will also help to remind walkers that the bus station in Hull is right next door to Paragon station – what could be more convenient?

Beyond Sutton, few bus routes come close to the old railway and unfortunately the same applies to pubs. The only exceptions are the Railway Inn at Ellerby, which is equipped with a good selection of railway prints and memorabilia, and the Wrygarth Inn at Great Hatfield, which is about 250 yards east of Sigglesthorne station. In Hull and Hornsea, of course, there are plenty of pubs and facilities generally. As one might expect, beers in the area come from established Yorkshire breweries such as Tetley's, John Smith's and Stone's; the pity is that these once proud Yorkshire companies are all now part of vast national combines. Only in Hull is there any real chance of discovering a few outlets for some of the county's surviving independent brewers.

6

THE HUDSON WAY

MARKET WEIGHTON TO BEVERLEY

Introduction

The Hudson Way commemorates the career of George Hudson, who was largely responsible for ensuring that York became the major railway centre it is today. As Hudson's activities were largely centred on that city, the next chapter (which deals with part of the East Coast main line through York) is a more appropriate place to take a closer look at his career and downfall; it will suffice here to say that he built up a huge empire and personal fortune by keeping 'everything except his accounts'. When it came, his downfall was swift, and the city rapidly set about eradicating all trace of his memory: his statue was removed and Hudson Street suddenly became the anonymous Railway Street. Since the 1960s, a reappraisal of his work and influence has rehabilitated him enough for Hudson Street to reappear on the city's street map, and British Rail's new administrative building was even named Hudson House.

The railway path which bears his name uses part of a former line from York to Beverley and is considered to be the most attractive in Humberside. By a strange irony, Hudson never got around to building the section now owned by the council although he certainly intended to; his fall from grace (and a certain Lord Hotham, of whom more later) intervened before the work could be completed. Nowadays, the route is a quiet by-way amongst gently rolling hills, although a dip into history reveals that the land through which it was cut is not without past significance. The tiny village of Goodmanham, for example, was once an early cradle of Christianity, while the remains of castles – often nothing more than a moat and a mound – recall the days of the Knights Templar and the crusades. The walk starts at Market Weighton, which was once the hub of separate lines to York, Driffield, Beverley and Selby. The residents of the town must have been utterly dumbstruck when every single line was closed. To lose one or two might have been forgiveable, but to lose them all smacked of disaster – or official sabotage, and there are a few locals who still suspect that. Whatever the truth might be, there is no disputing the fact that Market Weighton is one of the worst railway graveyards in the country. As such, it is in company with places like Consett and Halwill junction, that remarkable station in the depths of the Devon countryside known only to railway enthusiasts and summer holidaymakers.

History

The line from York to Beverley was opened in two stages, from York to Market Weighton and, eighteen years later, from Market Weighton to Beverley. Thanks to George Hudson's involvement, its history is not without a good measure of complexity and confusion. The difficulty of unravelling his business affairs is perfectly illustrated by the fact that different historians give quite different accounts of events leading up to its construction and opening. What is certain is that by 1845, Hudson had created a monopoly on routes to Hull with his York and North Midland Railway. However, other companies were attracted by the lucrative Hull traffic and sought to break this monopoly by constructing independent lines to the port. In 1845, for example, the Hull and Selby Railway began surveying a route from York to Beverley, when Hudson intervened by taking out a 100 per cent lease on the company. The Manchester and Leeds Railway then entered the fray by promoting a separate York, Hull and East and West Yorkshire Railway. Hudson's success in thwarting this new interloper was more limited: he managed to block its route by buying Londesborough Park and 12,000 acres from the Duke of Devonshire but, against this, he had to share the lease on the Hull and Selby Railway and ended up with a commitment to build the York to Beverley line himself.

The York and North Midland Railway accordingly presented a bill to Parliament for the new line on 30 April 1846. This was passed in a mere seven weeks, and by mid August the company was staking out the line from York to Market Weighton. Whatever else may be said about Hudson, he certainly knew how to get things done. He set 30 September 1847 as the deadline for opening this section and had trains running on 3 October, just three days later than planned. However, the railway did not progress beyond Market Weighton at this stage because Lord Hotham of Dalton Holme, through whose estate the line would pass, imposed conditions 'such that the venture would not have been worthwhile' (Y & NM directors). The company recognized that the extension to Beverley was essential in order for the traffic potential of the line to be realized, and, on 13 July 1849, obtained powers to construct it by a different route. Unfortunately, the famous Committee of Investigation had revealed Hudson's financial methods to the company's shareholders the day before and, amidst the ensuing uproar and litigation, these powers were never acted upon and lapsed.

A return excursion from Bridlington to Leeds passes the junction for the Beverley line at Market Weighton East in July 1961

N.E. Stead Collection

The branch from York to Market Weighton thus remained 'a most beautifully made line, but unfortunately without passengers to travel on it'. Beverley townsfolk requested the directors of the Y & NM to complete the missing link in 1850 and 1851, but the company must have been in considerable disarray after the Hudson fiasco. They pleaded first that the line would be of no public use, then that they had no capital with which to construct it, and finally that their powers of compulsory purchase had lapsed. The company subsequently disappeared from the scene on 31 July 1854, when it became part of the new North Eastern Railway.

The NER soon found itself besieged with requests to complete the Beverley extension and, in 1860, decided to proceed with the project, despite Lord Hotham's stringent conditions. It also decided to acquire land by agreement rather than compulsory purchase and, although rather time-consuming, this did prove a generally successful policy. An Act of Parliament authorizing construction of the line was passed at the end of June 1862, and work commenced in September. However, the eleven miles from Market Weighton to Beverley still took three years to complete, due partly to the difficult Wolds terrain and partly to recurring problems with Lord Hotham. The railway wanted to site a station at Goodmanham, which at least had the virtue of being a village; Lord Hotham, alas, insisted that the company build a station at its own expense at Kipling Cotes. This was intended nominally to serve his estate and racecourse, but it was not particularly convenient for either. In practice, it served nothing but a few farms and was a notoriously poor commercial proposition. Lord Hotham also insisted that no trains should run through his estate on Sundays, a stipulation which was complied with right until the very end, excepting only a small amount of diversionary traffic routed over the line during engineering work and emergencies.

The Beverley extension finally opened to traffic on 1 May 1865. It was initially single track and, apart from Kipling Cotes, the only other intermediate station was the delightfully named Cherry Burton. However, the extension completed a valuable link from York to Hull, and traffic developed steadily to the point where the track had to be doubled. This work was completed in 1889 and meant that the whole forty-two miles from York to Hull were laid to double track.

For most of its life, the history of the line was uneventful. On the run from York to Market Weighton, the maximum speed was 70 mph, although this was reduced to 60 as the line climbed through the Wolds to Beverley. The worst gradient on the extension was 1 in 151, but this was nothing compared with some of the tortuous climbs on the line from Scarborough to Whitby. The initial service was four trains per day from York to Hull, with three in the reverse direction; for some reason, unbalanced workings remained a feature of the line for many years. Services gradually improved until, by 1910, eight trains were provided in each direction with two expresses. The two world wars produced predictable curtailments and economies, but eight trains each way remained the norm until 1960.

Commuter traffic developed at the two ends of the line, and Pocklington (north-west of Market Weighton) did well with pupils attending the school there. British Railways obviously valued this business, for they retimed trains for the school's convenience on several occasions during the 1950s. Earlier in the line's history, the LNER attempted to develop through traffic by providing a connection at York with the northbound 'Flying Scotsman', and this was followed by a subsequent Humber-Tyne restaurant-car express. This made a return trip from Hull to Newcastle and was the line's most prestigious service.

A number of experimental trains worked on the route, the first being a petrol-electric railcar, which ran between York and Pocklington in 1925. This was followed in 1931/2 by the unique Kitson-Still steam-diesel locomotive, which worked a number of freight services over the line. The Kitson-Still engine was privately built and started on steam power, which it used until a speed of 6 mph had been attained; it then switched to diesel, although both forms of traction could be used when extra power was required on gradients. A third unusual vehicle was the diesel-electric railcar, *Lady Hamilton,* but this

Pocklington was one of the major intermediate stations on the double-track branch from York to Beverley. The grand scale of the station is clearly evident in this photograph. Since closure the building has been acquired by the local independent school and the train shed 'boxed in' to form a magnificent sports hall and event centre

H.G.W Household

proved so unreliable in 1933/4 that it frequently had to be replaced by a steam locomotive and two elderly NER bogie-coaches.

The main historical narrative can be picked up in 1945, when both track and locomotives were in a run-down state after six years of austerity and war effort. Although a good service was restored, the damage that Britain's railways had suffered was revealed by schedules which were considerably slacker than those of 1939. The immediate results of this were nationalization in 1948 and the Modernisation Plan of the 1950s, which saw diesel multiple units introduced on most passenger services in 1957. In January 1959, the stations on the line were rationalized, and those with low ticket sales (including Cherry Burton) closed to passengers. This was seen generally as nothing more than cutting out the dead wood, and any fears that might have arisen were allayed in 1960 when the new timetable increased passenger workings to nine each way. This was the best service the line had ever had: while the new DMUs did not better the timings of the old expresses, they observed more stops and attained similar speeds. What the casual timetable-reader might not have known was that a major scheme to modernize the whole line had just been authorized. Under this, the entire route from York to Beverley would be reduced to single track; all but three signal-boxes would be closed; most of the twenty-three level crossings would be replaced with automatic barriers; and colour-light signalling would be installed throughout. Final approval was given to this in January 1961 and deliveries of materials were soon being made to a huge store at Pocklington.

While all this was in progress, the Beeching Report was published in 1963. This now infamous document singled out the line from York to Beverley as a prime candidate for closure. Dr Beeching's figures showed that the line was making an operating profit of £6,000 per annum but, when certain 'terminal expenses' were added, this was reduced to a deficit of just over £17,000. Additionally, he claimed that closure would save £43,300 in track and signalling costs. Reading some of the histories of the route, it becomes quite obvious that there is still considerable anger over its closure. Stephen Chapman, whose book, *Hudson's Way*, gives the most detailed account of its history, concludes that 'when the figures are fully examined it becomes clear that a line with huge potential for traffic development and economic operation was being closed to save peanuts'. Opportunities for staff savings and freight development were apparently ignored, and there were accusations about the credibility of BR's figures and accounting methods. The row was still continuing at full pitch when there was a change of government in 1964. Harold Wilson's Minister of Transport, Barbara Castle, announced that the Beeching closures would be halted until a full investigation had been carried out, but she sanctioned closure of the York-Beverley line shortly afterwards. The closure date was set initially for 8 October 1965, but had to be deferred to 29 November to allow local bus operators extra time to prepare for the replacement services they would have to run. The remaining freight facilities were withdrawn on 1 November 1965, the last passenger trains running at the end of the month on Saturday 27 November. The final day was attended by heavy falls of snow, and all locomotive-hauled services were worked by steam, perhaps as a precaution against the failure of diesel locomotives in the bad weather. The last train was the 9.42 p.m. from York, a packed six-car DMU; its passage through Pocklington was marked by detonators placed on the rails.

It might have been expected that the track and materials would be removed shortly afterwards, but this was not the case. Gas and oil had recently been discovered in the North Sea and this kept alive a faint glimmer of hope that the line might be reopened, if only for freight. In January 1966, the line was accordingly reduced to single track, and all sidings were removed for scrap. Unfortunately, the now deserted railway buildings began to attract the unwelcome attention of vandals and many of them became dangerous as a result; the worst examples were therefore demolished in 1968. The remaining single track was used for training the operators of track-maintenance machines, which were being widely introduced at the time. The end finally came on 15 January 1969, when the Eastern Region of British Rail finally approved recovery of all remaining assets on the line, then valued at £88,200. North Sea oil was not to travel via Market Weighton after all.

The Line Today

The rails were removed shortly after BR's decision to recover the track; they were reused on the slow lines of the East Coast main line around Thirsk. Fortunately, however, the route was not allowed to moulder away for years on end: the former East Riding County Council soon recognized its potential as a recreational route and, in 1971, purchased the entire trackbed from Market Weighton to Beverley. Despite this, it appears that no conversion work was carried out at this time, for in January 1978 a correspondent to the *Hull Daily Mail* suggested that a steam railway and footpath could be created between Market Weighton and Beverley, particularly as a station and engine shed still survived at Market Weighton. Perhaps the writer was not familiar with the then decrepit state of the old railway buildings in the town: the main station had once been an impressive structure with an attractive portico, but vandalism and years of neglect had taken their toll. Carelessly reversing motor vehicles had also cracked the sandstone pillars of the portico, with the unfortunate result that its roof had been dislodged. It therefore came as no surprise when, in 1979, British Rail cleared the site completely, prior to selling it to North Wolds Borough Council for housing development at a cost of just over £373,000. At the start of the decade, Pocklington Rural District Council had baulked at a price of £40,000; what a bargain that original price now seemed! Further along the line, Kipling Cotes station was purchased privately and became Grannie's Attic antiques shop. This employment was not entirely out of character with its previous use, for after the withdrawal of full-time staff, the railway had used it to store artefacts destined for the York Railway Museum. Cherry Burton station was also sold and became a private residence.

In 1983, Humberside County Council finally converted the trackbed into a railway walk and nature trail, and named it 'The Hudson Way'. The conversion work involved clearing undergrowth, improving the surface, providing access points and, in a few locations, removing unwanted bridges. The embankments approaching several of these have been graded back to create safe and easy crossings for horseriders and cyclists, but this work is by no means complete; a number of difficult crossings still remain and users other than walkers use them at their own risk. Notwithstanding this, many improvements have been made already and more are planned as funds become available.

A glance at the map shows that the area possesses a large number of country halls, many of which are associated with established titles. One result of this is that the rural parts of the county can seem, even now, to possess a slightly feudal atmosphere, recalling the days of Lord Hotham and his battles with the North Eastern Railway. Indeed, when the county council was creating one of its railway paths, an estate manager wrote, advising that 'his lordship would like to know what steps will be taken to prevent your invitees escaping on to his land'. I am not aware of the council's reply, but at least walkers can use the Hudson Way on Sundays – something which the old North Eastern never achieved!

The Walk (11 miles)

The walk begins at the site of the former Market Weighton station (grid reference 878420). From the centre of the town, walkers should take the lane to Londesborough and look out for Hall Road on the right; this leads to a gate which marks the start of the route.

Market Weighton is a small but ancient settlement with no obvious claim to fame other than the fact that William Bradley, England's tallest man, was one of its residents. Mr Robert Stephenson, a local farmer, has lived in the area all his life and has some interesting anecdotes to tell about the town and its former railway. He also possesses a detailed surveyor's map dating from 1848, which shows all the buildings in the town and outlying area, together with the names of their owners and occupiers. William Bradley's house is clearly shown (with an extra tall door!), as is the residence of 'George Hudson Esq., M.P.'. What is noticeable is the large number of properties which Hudson owned in the town – he obviously thought it wise to invest a good part of his fortune in property. In more recent times, Mr Stephenson worked as a nurseryman within sight of the station. He can remember one occasion when a shunting engine was derailed by an absent-minded signalman who, engrossed in conversation with the driver, failed to notice that half the locomotive had already crossed the points. He also relates with glee the story of the policeman's son, 'Chuffer', who was 'a bit short in the head' but could imitate the whistle of an approaching train. This performance was once carried out under Market Weighton West signal-box with the result that the signalman mistakenly closed the gates.

Returning to the walk proper: the path soon leads through the site of the old goods yard and out into open country. The general appearance of the area is very similar to the Downs in Sussex: cereal crops are much in evidence, together with a smaller amount of dairy farming, and horses can sometimes be seen grazing in nearby fields. The horse breeding is probably on a serious basis, with racecourses at York, Beverley and Kipling Cotes.

The line soon passes below the little village of Goodmanham, which the North Eastern Railway had wanted to serve with a station; unfortunately for the

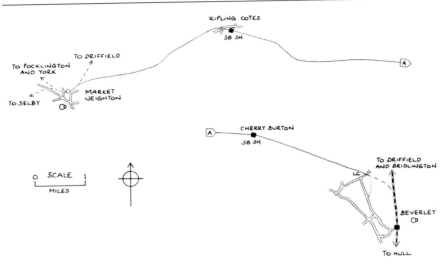

THE HUDSON WAY

villagers, the powerful influence of Lord Hotham dashed any such hopes, and those who wished to use the railway had to walk into Market Weighton. Goodmanham now is little more than a sleepy village, but in the seventh century it was a major religious centre and the site where King Edwin of Northumbria was converted to Christianity. He subsequently built a simple shrine at York, on the site of what is now the magnificent minster.

A couple of overbridges have been removed between Market Weighton and Kipling Cotes, but a real gem remains just west of Kipling Cotes station at grid reference 926440. It is best viewed from the road rather than the trackbed, which does not reveal its full size and grandeur. The walker cannot fail to be impressed by its height and the large, brick abutments, which are in marked contrast to the tiny lane which it spans. Kipling Cotes station is also a real find, as a complete set of railway buildings survives there: the signal-box, goods shed, station building and shelter on the westbound platform are all completely intact. The provision of a signal-box may surprise anyone familiar only with the spartan railways of today, but all of the stations on the line originally possessed busy goods yards, which, in some cases, outlived the passenger services. Kipling Cotes, for example, possessed a set of coal-drops to the north of the goods shed and a quarry siding at the east end of the station. Nowadays, walkers are asked to keep off the platforms as they are a conservation area, but I could not help wondering if this simply meant that they needed repairing; it certainly looked like it. On the westbound platform, a stone statuette stood by the platform edge as though waiting for a train which would never come; it conjured up the image of an ever-patient passenger petrified by the long wait.

This fine brick bridge is situated immediately west of Kipling Cotes station

Continuing east, there are attractive views across the Wolds, which are golden with wheat in summer. A small amount of tree planting has taken place beyond the station, but this is not a feature of the line generally: what trees there are have grown naturally and this enables the walker to enjoy the surrounding views uninterrupted. The line then enters the deep Gardham Cutting (grid reference 937437), which is now an important wildlife habitat; the British Trust for Conservation Volunteers has been carrying out a study of the regeneration of its banks. It is ironic that railways like this, which were once regarded as intrusive scars on the landscape, are now valued as havens for species which intensive farming has driven from the surrounding countryside.

The tall, narrow spire of South Dalton Church then comes into view to the north, after which the path passes below Etton and plunges into a small wood before reaching the site of Cherry Burton station (grid reference 993427). Anyone who studies the map will see that the siting of this station was not at all convenient: had it been situated half a mile to the west, it would have been equidistant between the villages of Etton and Cherry Burton and, incidentally, closer to both. Its poor location must account for its premature closure to passengers on 5 January 1959; it is interesting how decisions taken in the nineteenth century often influenced those taken in the twentieth.

Cherry Burton signal-box. Signal-boxes do not readily lend themselves to any form of reuse, so it is not suprising that this example is in an advanced state of decay

Immediately before reaching the station, a bridge over the B1248 Beverley-Malton road has been removed and the walker must climb down to and up from the road. Steps have been provided but the crossing is rather awkward due to poor visibility. However, immediately east of the crossing the walker finds himself between the two platforms of another perfectly intact disused railway station, just like Kipling Cotes. The main station building is privately occupied and the owners have even preserved the timber lamp-room, which now has a greenhouse grafted on to it. An attractive weighbridge office has also been preserved, while the station goods shed is in use as commercial premises. The signal-box, however, stands utterly forlorn and derelict at the north-east corner of the site. How much longer it can survive in this state is a matter of conjecture.

Beyond Cherry Burton, the landscape rapidly levels out as the coastal plain is approached, but the line remains slightly elevated and thus still offers good views, particularly of Beverley away to the south-east; this is instantly recognizable by the distinctive towers of its minster. Before Beverley, however, the line passes below Leconfield Aerodrome which, despite a chequered history, is still the home of the 202 Search and Rescue Helicopter Squadron. It was built in the 1930s as RAF Leconfield and, during the war, housed fighter squadrons of Spitfires and Hurricanes followed by bomber squadrons of Blenheims and Halifaxes. In 1977, it passed to the army and was renamed Normandy Barracks; as such, it now houses the Army School of Mechanical Transport. Airfields are quite common throughout the area, which is hardly surprising since it is on the east coast – the natural place to locate airborne resources during the war. Many of the airfields have closed since 1945, but a few remain open, as the occasional jet roaring overhead at low altitude demonstrates!

The official railway path ends at the site of Pighill level crossing (grid reference 029414), although dedicated explorers might care to continue along the remaining three-quarters of a mile to the junction with the Beverley-Driffield line. I did not have time to investigate this final leg of the route, so please turn back if there is obviously no public access. Those who are tired and thirsty after the eleven miles of the walk should turn right at Pighill crossing and then first left to reach the centre of Beverley which is just over a mile away. If time is pressing (or you are simply desperate to anaesthetize your aching limbs), the nearest pub is the Molescroft Inn at grid reference 020408; this is an attractive Mansfield house which serves good food.

All in all, the Hudson Way is a most attractive and well executed railway walk. One of its delights is that reclamation work and the hand of officialdom are not obvious, which encourages walkers to feel that they are exploring a forgotten and undiscovered place. Anyone who has grappled with the choking undergrowth of a truly forgotten and undiscovered trackbed will realize that this is nothing more than a carefully cultivated illusion but, for all that, the walk remains an enjoyable and highly recommended discovery.

Further Explorations

Humberside is a county with a distinct interest in the reclamation of abandoned railways. Apart from the Hudson Way, the Hornsea Rail Trail and part of the branch line to Withernsea, it is also interested in converting a large part of the former line from Market Weighton to Selby. Plans have been proposed for a new path from Market Weighton to the River Derwent at Bubwith, which would place Market Weighton in the middle of a continuous twenty-three mile walk built entirely on abandoned railways. Only time will tell if this scheme is implemented, but it would certainly give Humberside a railway path to rival some of the best in the north. Outside the immediate area, the routes from York to Selby and from Scarborough to Whitby (both covered in this volume) are within easy access, while, south of the Humber, the abandoned line from Grimsby to Louth offers possibilities, as discussed at the end of Chapter 4.

Humberside generally contains a good number of canals (several of them disused) and irrigation drains, many of which are themselves the size of a canal. The county's waterways suffered terribly when the railways were being built, for the railway promoters were almost paranoid about competition and bought the canals up, before leaving them to rot. The now derelict Market Weighton Canal is a good case in point. It was purchased by the York and North Midland Railway in 1846 and passed to the new North Eastern Railway in 1854. However, the NER refused to assist with dredging in 1888, and by 1896 a commercial user was complaining that he could no longer reach Market Weighton due to the high level of mud. The local authorities became involved when stagnant water began to pose a health hazard, with the result that the top end of the navigation was closed to all traffic in 1900.

Not all of the canals were quite so unlucky, however, for the Pocklington Canal has enjoyed a remarkable revival in recent years. Like the Market Weighton Canal, it was acquired by the Y & NM during the course of constructing the line from York and suffered the consequences of a similar neglect. It was closed to commercial traffic in 1932 and to pleasure traffic in 1934, but in 1969 the Pocklington Canal Amenity Society set about restoring the waterway for pleasure craft. This restoration is now complete and a stroll along the tow-path is made the more memorable by a number of brightly-painted traditional canal-craft. The county's waterways generally offer many opportunities for attractive country walks, particularly to the east of the railway line from Beverley to Driffield.

The area is not well endowed with preserved railways although, to the north, British Rail has occasionally provided a number of summer steam specials on the line from York to Scarborough. There are also plans to create a preserved railway along all or part of the Grimsby-Louth line but, as noted in Chapter 4, the future use of this route is unfortunately clouded in uncertainty at the moment.

Beverley houses the Museum of Army Transport, which features a number of railway exhibits, including an ungodly contraption designed for destroying railway lines. Mr Stephenson of Market Weighton gave me a graphic description of how this operated, with that characteristic note of mischief which is his trademark. It is a good job that Dr Beeching was not acquainted with the machine, otherwise he might have attached it to the rear of an inspection train and disposed of unwanted lines simply by travelling over them!

Transport and Facilities

Maps: Ordnance Survey: Landranger Series Sheets 106 and 107 (recommended)

Buses: East Yorkshire Motor Services Ltd
The Travel Office, Ferensway Coach Station, Hull, Humberside
Telephone: 01482 325679
http://www.eyms.co.uk/

Trains: National Rail Enquiries
www.nationalrail.co.uk
Telephone: 08457 48 49 50

Since the closure of the Selby-Driffield and York-Beverley lines, Market Weighton has stood forlornly in the middle of a large 'railway-desert' between the East Coast main line and the Hull-Scarborough branch. Beverley is the most convenient local station and enjoys an excellent service of some forty trains per day to and from Hull, about half of them continuing to Bridlington or Scarborough. For some years, the trains ran from Monday to Saturday only. In 1989, however, British Rail introduced an experimental Sunday service. If this proves as successful as similar experiments elsewhere, it should become an established feature.

As far as buses are concerned, the most useful service is number X46/X47, operated by East Yorkshire Motor Services. This runs from Hull to York via Beverley, Market Weighton and Pocklington. At the time of writing, there were fifteen buses daily from Monday to Saturday, with three on Sunday. A few extra workings covered only part of the route, generally from Hull or Beverley to Pocklington. This provision is remarkably similar to that offered by the former railway but, unfortunately, the end-to-end journey time has stretched out to 1 hour 50 minutes. Given this pattern of public transport, the best way to tackle the Hudson Way is to travel to Beverley, take a bus out to Market Weighton and then walk back.

As for refreshments, there are plenty of pubs and other facilities in Beverley and Market Weighton, but they are rather thin on the ground elsewhere on the route. The most convenient place is Grannie's Attic, the former Kipling Cotes station, which sells teas and soft drinks. Just east of Market Weighton, the Goodmanham Arms in the village of that name is worth a visit, although the county council's guide notes that outsiders 'may have trouble understanding the landlord's broad East Yorkshire dialect'! Other useful pubs are situated at Etton and Cherry Burton. Most of the Yorkshire brewers (Tetley, Ward, Darley, Theakston, the Smith brothers and all) are well represented in the area, together with Cameron's of Hartlepool, who in 1986 acquired a large number of pubs which formerly belonged to the North Country Brewery of Hull.

7
THE VALE OF YORK
BISHOPTHORPE TO RICCALL

Introduction

Passengers travelling over the East Coast main line between Doncaster and York in the late 1970s would have been rather surprised had anyone told them that, within a decade, one third of the route would be closed; yet this is precisely what has happened. The section affected lies between Selby and York. Selby was always an easy place to spot on the old main line because trains had to slow down dramatically to negotiate Selby swing bridge; as a result, they passed through the town's station slow enough for passengers to read the nameboards. Most other wayside stations (not that there were many of them left) disappeared as a mere blip.

The reason for this extraordinary turn of events lies in coal mining, for the old main line sat right on top of Selby coalfield. High speed running was clearly impractical with the National Coal Board tunnelling away below ground, for any subsidence could have had fatal effects with trains running regularly at 125 mph. Fortunately, the value of the coal reserves was such that the Coal Board agreed to finance the construction of a new line to the west of the coalfield, and this opened to traffic in September 1983. From British Rail's point of view, this removed the long-standing speed restriction at Selby and bypassed the irksome swing bridge by a good four miles. In its time, this and a second swing bridge at Naburn had been unwelcome obstructions – especially on hot summer days. When open for river traffic, the Selby bridge expanded so much in the heat of the sun that it could not be manoeuvred back into place for rail traffic; the only solution was to hose it down with cold water to reverse the effect. Too bad if an East Coast express happened to come along at the same time!

From the walker's point of view, the upshot of all this is that he can now stroll along seven miles of what used to be Britain's premier main line. With its gentle gradients and imperceptible curves, it still looks very much the part; it also has a history to match. Long before the advent of High Speed Trains, steam locomotives of the Great Northern Railway thundered this way in the summers of 1888 and 1895, racing the companies of the West Coast main line to Edinburgh and Aberdeen. The Great Race to the North is now no more than a memory, but, thanks to the Coal Board, part of the old racing ground is now available for the less strenuous pursuits of walking, jogging and cycling.

History

The first railway from York was promoted in 1835, prompted by developments to the south. The North Midland Railway was formed in September that year, with the object of constructing a line from Leeds to Derby; at Derby, it would connect with the Midland Counties Railway to reach Birmingham; and at Birmingham, it would connect with the London and Birmingham Railway to reach London (Euston Square). If a line could be constructed from York to connect with the North Midland Railway, the city would have access to both Leeds and London without the expense of having to build independent lines. As a result, the York and North Midland Railway was formed at a meeting in York Guildhall on 13 October 1835, and George Hudson, destined to become the famous 'railway king', was elected its first chairman. The company's Act followed quickly, on 21 June 1836, authorizing the construction of a line from Tanner Row, York, to Altofts, north of Normanton, with various branches and connections to the Leeds and Selby Railway, which it would cross just south of Church Fenton. The completed line opened on 1 July 1840, the same day as the opening of the North Midland Railway from Leeds to Derby. This enabled the citizens of York to travel to London by train for the first time, although the route was hardly direct. They also needed considerable stamina, for the fastest journey time was 9 hours 45 minutes. As if this were not enough, the motion of the four-wheeled carriages was similar to that of a ship in rough seas, with similar bilious results.

The first part of the York and North Midland Railway had opened somewhat earlier, on 29 May 1839, attended by celebrations on a grand scale. A temporary station was provided outside the city walls on this occasion, but by the time the first permanent station opened in January 1841 these had been breached by a 70 ft arch, through which trains merrily chuffed to their new terminus. If such a development were attempted nowadays, it is quite likely that the whole nation would rise in uproar, but aesthetic considerations then were swept aside on the basis of the benefits which the railway would bring. This assumption was fully justified, for York soon became a major railway centre with lines opening to Darlington in 1841, to Malton and Scarborough in 1845, to Market Weighton in 1847 and to Knaresborough in 1848. Before long, the worst service was the circuitous route to London. By then, George Hudson had become the chairman of a great number of railway companies: he had made a personal fortune out of building and taking over railways, and his shareholders enjoyed substantial dividends in the order of 10 per cent per annum. However, he had made many enemies, and they were given a chance to strike when he created a more direct route from York to London. The background to this is rather complex and requires some explanation.

In 1847, the Great Northern Railway was forging north from Doncaster with the aim of making an end-on connection at Askern with a local company's branch line from Knottingley. The Great Northern was dedicated to creating a major north-south trunk line, an aim which should have been anathema to Hudson, with his various chairmanships and business interests. He recognized, however, that the creation of an East Coast main line could not be resisted forever and, as far as York was concerned, it would make a lot more sense than the present quirky route to Euston. He decided, therefore, that it would be far better to bring the Great Northern into his web than spend pointless energy fighting it. As Knottingley was barely three miles from the original York and North Midland line (York-Normanton), Hudson decided to construct a short line from Burton Salmon to Knottingley, which would enable him to 'tap into' the Great Northern project. An Act of 1847 provided him with the necessary powers and, at the end of 1848, he negotiated an agreement with Edmund Denison, chairman of the Great Northern: in return for the GNR abandoning its intention to construct an independent line from Askern to York, the York and North Midland would grant running powers from Knottingley to York. The arrangement also provided Hudson's company with a more than reasonable level of remuneration. However, as far as his shareholders were concerned, he had sold out to the enemy: he had willingly surrendered a significant proportion of their traffic to the Great Northern. The consequences were catastrophic – the 'injured' companies ganged up against the Y & NM to deprive it of traffic, and a Committee of Investigation revealed how Hudson's accounts had been manipulated to make everything look sweetness and light. By the end of 1849, he had resigned all his chairmanships and disappeared from the railway scene altogether. The ultimate effect was to show his personal profits, and the dividends declared by his companies, as having been founded on sharp practice. The connecting line from Burton Salmon to Knottingley opened in April 1850, when the worst of the furore was over. The first GNR through train from London ran over the route on 8 August 1850, but it arrived in York without ceremony: the memory of Hudson's treachery was still too recent. Despite this, something resembling the present day East Coast main line had been brought into existence although, as a result of Hudson's machinations, it included a rather curious kink south of York. This was to survive for another twenty-one years.

Hudson's fate, and the associated collapse of the Railway Mania, ushered in a sober and constrained period when railway companies began to realize that more could be gained by co-operation than by uneconomic and possibly ruinous competition. One manifestation of this was the formation of the North Eastern Railway by an Act of Parliament dated 31 July 1854; Hudson's old company, the York and North Midland, was one of the three main constituents. The NER turned its mind to improving the East Coast route in the early 1860s and obtained an act for constructing a new line from Doncaster to York via Selby on 23 March 1864. Its official end points were Shaftholme Junction, north of Doncaster, and Chaloner Whin Junction, south of York, the intention being to replace the Knottingley deviation with a new and direct main line. Unfortunately, the NER soon fell upon a troubled period which delayed many of its capital projects. Disregarding an unpleasant strike in 1867, the main damage was done by one Henry J. Trotter of Bishop Auckland, a disgruntled shareholder who wrote a series of letters to newspapers and aroused widespread suspicion regarding the company's financial methods. Public confidence was restored at a public meeting in November 1867, but not before Trotter's outbursts had wiped £750,000 from the value of company stock. After his claims were refuted, the stock soon returned to its previous level, but the company was visibly shaken and deferred all new capital projects as a precaution.

One consequence of this was that the new main line via Selby was not opened for traffic until 2 January 1871. It crossed a flat, low-lying area and demanded little in the way of engineering works. From Shaftholme Junction, it ran almost due north to join the Leeds, Selby and Hull line just south of Selby station. The latter metals were then used to pass through Selby station and over the famous swing bridge, before the new line turned away to the north again at Barlby junction. Just under thirteen miles later, it reached Chaloner Whin Junction, where it ran parallel with the original Normanton line into York station. North of Selby, intermediate stations were provided at Riccall, Escrick and Naburn but the only engineering feature of note was another swing bridge at Naburn, hydraulically operated. Chaloner Whin became a 'proper' junction in 1902 or 1903, when connections between the two main lines were installed and a signal-box constructed.

Thus the missing link was at last provided. The crowning glory of the route was added in 1877, when the new station at York was opened – outside the city walls this time! It permitted through running by Anglo-Scottish trains and eliminated an irksome and time-consuming reversal in the old station, now scarcely able to cope with the volume of traffic. Given the magnificence of the new station, and the fact that it had to be extended as traffic continued to grow, it is remarkable to relate that one disgruntled NER shareholder dismissed it as a 'monument of extravagance'.

The subsequent history of the line from Selby to York is subsumed in the greater story of the East Coast main line, but space does not permit a detailed study here. The railway races of 1888 and 1895 have already been mentioned. Other significant developments include the introduction of sleeping-cars in

Ex-LNER class B1 No. 61255 passes Barlby North signal-box, north-east of Selby, with a train of mineral wagons in April 1965. At Barlby Junction the Selby-York and Selby-Hull lines divided

Frank Dean

1873, restaurant-cars in 1893 and water-troughs in 1900. The significance of the restaurant-cars may be lost on a modern reader for, until their introduction, a twenty-minute lunch-stop had to be allowed at York for passengers to 'refuel'. It might be added that they paid extortionately for their meals and had to consume them at a rate which usually wrought havoc upon their digestive systems! Corridors began to appear on trains from the 1890s onwards and, with them, it was possible to provide a primitive form of lavatory. The significance of this lies in the length of the journey times – eight and a half hours from London to Edinburgh by the contemporary 'Flying Scotsman'. It is little wonder that, after a railway accident, the most serious injury was rupture of the bladder.

After the railway races, the East and West Coast companies agreed that, in the interests of safety, they should not undercut a London to Edinburgh journey time of eight and a quarter hours. Somehow this arrangement lasted until 1932, by which time it was a complete anachronism, for development had been going on apace and Anglo-Scottish expresses were being delayed deliberately. As soon as the agreement was abolished, forty-five minutes were cut from the non-stop schedules at a stroke. This inaugurated a new period of record-breaking and improvement in which times were reduced each year until the streamlined 'Coronation' expresses began running in 1937; these reduced the journey time from King's Cross to Edinburgh to a mere six hours, a staggering achievement for a steam locomotive. Unfortunately, the Second World War brought all this to an abrupt end and the schedules suddenly stretched out to ten hours, for there were more important tasks than conveying passengers at speed. A measure of how badly the war strained the railway can be gauged from the fact that when the non-stop 'Flying Scotsman' was reinstated on 31 May 1948, it offered a timing of 7 hours 50 minutes in both directions – and that was a substantial improvement over the wartime schedules.

The line between Selby and York acquired a brief notoriety during the harsh winter of 1946/7. While some of the surrounding branch lines were closed for six weeks or more, the main line was not blocked for any significant length of time – that is, until the thaw came. When it did, the low-lying area between Selby and York soon became flooded, and main-line trains had to be diverted; by a small irony, one of the diversionary routes was the pre-1871 main line via Knottingley and Church Fenton. Fortunately, the flood waters were relatively static, so the railway authorities had to do little more than wait for them to subside and the line to dry out. Damage was very slight, and the main-line trains were soon running again.

The 1950s saw rationalization and further modernization carried out on the line. The installation of colour-light signalling at York was completed in May 1951 (a long-term project, which had been interrupted by the war) and Chaloner Whin signal-box was closed as a direct result. The small wayside stations at Escrick and Naburn succumbed on 8 June 1953, with Riccall holding out for another five years until 15 September 1958. On 15 March 1959, the prototype 'Deltic' diesel locomotive ran over the line, completing the run from London King's Cross to Newcastle in 3 hours 56 minutes – four minutes faster than the best pre-war timing. The Deltics entered regular service on 1 June 1961, and from this date onwards diesels gradually encroached on steam workings, sending many reliable locomotives to the scrapyard prematurely. In the timetable for summer 1962, the Deltics were scheduled to celebrate the centenary of the 'Flying Scotsman' by running non-stop from London to Edinburgh in six hours; presumably the publicity material failed to mention that the steam-hauled 'Coronation' expresses had done precisely this twenty-five years earlier!

1965 was officially the end of steam traction on the East Coast main line. On 31 December that year, the North Eastern Region of British Railways ran a steam-hauled relief train from Newcastle to York and back to signify this. Steam disappeared altogether from the north-east on 9 September 1967. A minor rationalization in this year was the closure of Naburn signal-box, which became redundant when the swing bridge there was fixed permanently in place. The

The Old East Coast main line at Riccall, looking south towards Selby, showing the signal-box and station. The station was closed to passengers on 15 September 1958 and to goods on 6 July 1964

Frank Dean

prototype High Speed Train ran over the East Coast route on various days in June 1973, attaining speeds of 131, 141 and 143 mph in successive trials and training runs; these finally and decisively smashed the old steam records. HSTs were introduced into regular service in 1976, but in September 1983 the Selby avoiding line was opened and the section from Selby to Chaloner Whin closed completely. The new line leaves the 1871 route at Temple Hirst, about five miles south of Selby; it then skirts round the town about three miles to the west and heads north to join Hudson's original Normanton line near the tiny village of Colton, six miles south of York. At the time of writing, the line from Temple Hirst to Selby had been reduced to single track and conveyed only the occasional local train from Selby to Doncaster; the new main line was being electrified and powerful class 91 Electra locomotives were waiting in the wings to take over electrified services to Newcastle in 1991. Meanwhile, the railway rambler can wander in safety between Riccall and Chaloner Whin and ponder all that has been; as this narrative reveals, it was no minor railway that ran there.

The Line Today

When the rails from Selby to York had been removed, the trackbed was divided at Riccall, and the two sections, to the north and south of the station respectively, were sold off separately. The section from Riccall to Selby was purchased by the Department of Transport and converted into a new, much needed bypass for the villages of Barlby and Riccall, while the section from Riccall to the outskirts of York was acquired by Sustrans Ltd and converted into a railway path and cycleway. This was the first time that the company had attempted anything quite so bold and it acquired long-term responsibility for all of the bridges together with a small number of sitting tenants – an unusual position for a path-building charity to find itself in! When the ballast had been removed (for use in the York outer ring road) and a new concrete deck laid across the swing bridge at Naburn, the cycleway conversion began in earnest in June 1985.

The main section of the path runs from Bishopthorpe (near York) to Barlby (near Selby) and was opened officially on 28 November 1987. This rather overstates the length of the railway conversion, for south of Riccall the route

When Sustrans Ltd took over this part of the East Coast main line, it assumed long-term responsibility for the maintenance of all engineering structures on it. This bridge over a minor lane at Naburn has just been repainted

switches to the old A19; the only exception is a short length between Riccall and Barlby where the Department of Transport provided enough land for a cycle track alongside the new bypass. The problem here, of course, is noise. However, with the main route established, it then remained only to construct the necessary links into York and Selby. These were completed during the course of 1988.

Like other Sustrans schemes, the list of parties involved reads like a *Who's Who* of national and local government. The main contributors on this occasion were Selby District Council, York City Council, the Yorkshire Rural Community Council Agency, the Countryside Commission, the Manpower Services Commission and the Department of Transport. The section from Bishopthorpe to Riccall is being planted with trees in the manner of a grand avenue and should present a most attractive sight in twenty to thirty years' time; anyone who travelled over this route will remember it both for its flatness and the general lack of trees.

In the long-term, Sustrans also hopes to construct a path from Selby to Doncaster, Barnsley, Manchester and Liverpool as part of a long-distance project commissioned by Barnsley Borough Council. Most of the route will use abandoned railways or canal towpaths; it was considered 'usable' in 1989, but in need of major works to bring it up to the standard of a Long Distance Footpath as accepted by the Countryside Commission or Department of Transport. Between 27 May and 3 June 1989, a large party of walkers and cyclists travelled over the route in order to publicize the scheme and exert pressure upon politicians to support it. For good measure, they included the Selby & York Railway Path and the recently converted Liverpool Loop Line. Those who lasted the entire week ended up in Southport Winter Gardens, 150 miles from their starting point at York Minster. The seven and a half mile walk described in this chapter is small beer by comparison!

The Walk (7½ miles)

As described in the history above, this line closed to all traffic in September 1983. It might be expected that so recent a closure would contain plenty of relics but unfortunately this is not the case, due to the rationalization and streamlining carried out by British Rail prior to closure. For example, while the station building at Naburn survives, its platforms were removed in order to prevent High Speed Trains dislodging pieces of masonry in their slipstream. Elsewhere, the story is much the same: the site of Escrick station is betrayed only by the former station yard, while Riccall station appears to have vanished without trace beneath the village's new bypass. Even the signals have gone: being metal, they

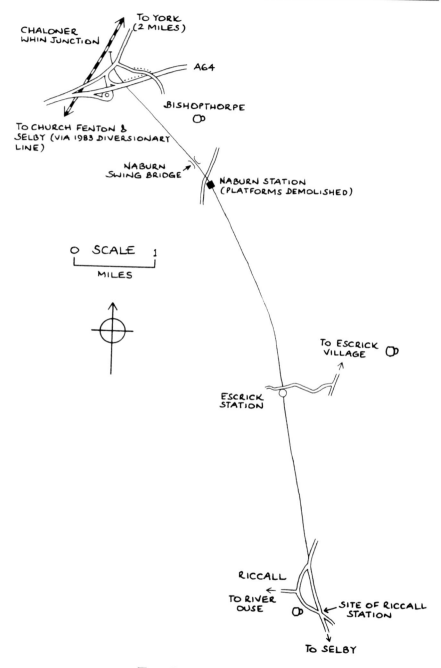

CHALONER
WHIN JUNCTION

TO YORK
(2 MILES)

A64

BISHOPTHORPE

TO CHURCH FENTON &
SELBY (VIA 1983 DIVERSIONARY
LINE)

NABURN
SWING BRIDGE

NABURN STATION
(PLATFORMS DEMOLISHED)

SCALE
MILES

TO ESCRICK
VILLAGE

ESCRICK
STATION

RICCALL

TO RIVER
OUSE

SITE OF RICCALL
STATION

TO SELBY

THE VALE OF YORK

were cut down for scrap. Their stumps remain in the ground like spent shell-cases from a long-forgotten war. At least Escrick yard had some life about it when I visited, for it was being used as a depot by the railway-path conversion team.

The description that follows traces the route of the old line from the outskirts of York to Riccall, where the trackbed now accommodates the new A19 trunk road. This arrangement has the advantage of making York the base and return point, a practical consideration as it is such a centre for bus and train services.

The path may be picked up at grid reference 587483, where there is an access point from a minor road to Bishopthorpe. It runs alongside the road for a short distance before swinging sharply to the right and passing under it. It then follows the busy A64 for about a quarter of a mile (entirely segregated) before reaching the trackbed at grid reference 583481; here an old railway bridge provides a convenient way of passing under the main road and into the relative peace and quiet of the countryside. If the walker turns north at this point, he can walk back to the site of Chaloner Whin junction, though it is a desolate spot these days. It might conceivably appeal to train-spotters, inasmuch as all southbound trains from York must pass this way: their destinations are as diverse as London and Penzance.

It is not long before new housing encroaches on the old permanent way at Bishopthorpe, but a through route has been provided even if it doesn't follow the course of the line exactly. Just south of the village, there are abundant apple trees to the east of the line and it is tempting, here as elsewhere, to think of them as being the result of some core tossed long ago from the window of a passing train. In all probability, they are simply an orchard left untended – a more prosaic explanation! A lone apple tree further south is more likely to be the fruit of some 'railway projectile'.

Most of the bridges on the line are of a stark modern style, with brick abutments and a concrete span; they undoubtedly replace earlier structures which may have looked more appealing. The major engineering work on the line is Naburn swing bridge (grid reference 598465), which crosses the navigable River Ouse but, like the others, it would win no beauty contest. It is a metal structure of two separate spans, that to the north being movable until 1967. This sits on a large turret, housing the machine room, which can be inspected from the riverside path; a few large cogs can be seen in its dark chamber, with a metal shaft disappearing upwards into the roof. The signal-box sat on top of the bridge astride the two tracks; one pair of its supports still remains in place. A few hundred yards south, the line passes Naburn Marina on the west, and then Naburn station, the marina serving the needs of pleasure cruisers on the river. Close by the station, a viewing tower has been built on the trackbed utilizing a large number of ex-BR concrete cable-ducts. This is actually the tenth mile-post from Selby and, if it sounds a little extravagant for such a purpose, it may help to explain that it was built on a large scale in order to give a distant view of York Minster to the north.

The line now curves gradually to the south before commencing a ruler-straight run of over three miles to Riccall: no wonder the trains could achieve such high speeds. The site of Escrick station intervenes at grid reference 617419, but other than the trackbed with its shallow cuttings and embankments there are few distinctive features of either railway or natural origin. Finally, the red expanse of an industrial working comes into view to the east; this turns out to be the yard of a company which makes tiles and agricultural pipes. Shortly afterwards, there is another viewing-tower and then the railway path ends, at the start of Riccall bypass (grid reference 623384); this used to be the site of a level crossing, so the road-makers could hardly have had it any easier.

Its main-line pedigree certainly makes the route extraordinarily direct, but this ruler-straightness creates an immediate problem for the path-builder: how to avoid monotony? As if the engineering characteristics of the line are not enough, the surrounding countryside is also completely flat apart from some undulations near Escrick. Not surprisingly, some have described this landscape as bleak. On a good summer's day, it certainly creates a feeling of great openness, and the views across the surrounding cornfields, with trees punctuating the distant skyline, are very pleasant; but it is a different tale on days of cloud, wind and rain. The path-builder's solution to this problem has been twofold. Firstly, features of interest have been created along the route, using redundant railway concrete; cable-ducts and drainage frames have proved the most versatile materials. These have been fashioned into viewpoints, children's play areas (complete with concrete tunnels), seats, picnic sites and, at Escrick, a large circular maze, which spreads out across the trackbed in a shallow cutting. Modern railway engineers would be somewhat surprised if they revisited the line! Secondly, extensive tree planting has taken place, with species such as horse chestnut, copper beech, rowan and elm. At present the planting is not so close as to restrict future views, and it is to be hoped that a few sections will be left unplanted for the sake of variety. The only regrettable thing is that some of the young saplings are faring rather badly, perhaps as a result of residues left behind by weed-killing trains.

There are several information boards along the route, as well as a number of interesting cast mile-posts which have been manufactured specially for the cycleway; this is very commendable as it again adds interest. Most of the original railway mile-posts have been removed, the few survivors remaining as headless concrete stumps. Their upper parts have no doubt been removed for sale at Collectors' Corner or 'appropriated' by collectors, keen to deposit part of the former East Coast main line in their living-room or back-garden. Some waymarking has already taken place, and there are plans at the York end to develop a network of cycle lanes, for which the old railway could act as a useful feeder, both for commuting and leisure journeys.

All in all, the path-builders have made a cheerful and imaginative attempt to bring interest and variety to the line but, until it settles into its new role, it is

This maze has been constructed in a shallow cutting just south of Escrick station and incorporates a large number of reused concrete cable-ducts left behind by BR

bound to wear the look of a recent industrial casualty. It will also take time for plant- and animal-life to become established, as British Rail is hardly in the business of creating wildlife colonies. Perhaps some latter-day philanthropist could scatter wild-plant seeds along the line, like the Victorian clergyman who scattered primrose seeds from the window of his carriage on Devon's lovely Lynton and Barnstaple Railway? Every year, the banks there are a glory of flowers, though few ever see them now that the line has closed. When I visited, things between York and Selby still had a long way to go, though north of Escrick a marbled-white butterfly landed on my shirt and stayed there for the next half-mile. Tame butterflies? Perhaps a portent of things to come!

Further Explorations

Passing as it does through the great and very flat Vale of York, this path presents a rather untypical view of Yorkshire. A visit to the excellent Scarborough and Whitby Railway Path will redress the balance, with over twenty miles of dales and rugged coastal scenery, while the Hudson Way, from Market Weighton to Beverley, makes an attractive walk through the Wolds. Both of these are described in detail in other chapters. Unfortunately, other railway walks in the area are still in the planning stage: the most notable possibilities include the great 'Trans-Pennine Trail', mentioned above, and a new railway path from Selby to Market Weighton, described briefly at the end of Chapter 6. In my opinion, the 'Trans-Pennine Trail' is a good bet, given the involvement of Sustrans Ltd and Barnsley Borough Council, but the Selby–Market Weighton path is rather a dark horse; we will have to wait and see how serious the proposals were.

The network of Yorkshire waterways presents an alternative source of walks, although care must be exercised in one's choice of route, particularly if heading off west towards Leeds. A walk among the skeletons and ghosts of industry is not everyone's idea of heaven! The main possibilities locally are the River Ouse, the River Derwent and the Pocklington Canal from Thorganby to Pocklington. The Ouse can be followed from Riccall to Selby (a public footpath runs along the east bank), making an attractive alternative to following the road.

On a slight tangent, the River Derwent gave its name to the Derwent Valley Light Railway, one of the lesser known anachronisms of English railway history. This line ran from York to Selby via the Derwent Valley and was constructed to serve the rich agricultural district to the south-east of York. It was promoted in 1898 by two rural district councils under the terms of the 1896 Light Railways Act. Powers were granted in 1902 but transferred to a company of local landowners in 1907, the line finally opening throughout on 21 July 1913. By some extraordinary quirk, the DVLR escaped the grouping in 1923 and nationalization in 1948, and continued to operate as an independent company until 1981, when its final section of track from York to Dunnington was closed. Between 1934 and 1969, it did not even possess a locomotive, preferring to hire motive power as required from the LNER and later the North Eastern Region of British Railways. This unusual arrangement came to an end in 1969, when the company purchased two surplus diesel shunters from its state-owned neighbour. While the trackbed of the DVLR is not open to the public, the company deserves a mention on account of its long survival as a relic from a bygone age. One or two of its village stations survive for those with the time to find them.

The last feature of interest has got to be the National Railway Museum at York, which occupies a converted locomotive round-house a few minutes walk from York station. The museum contains one of the largest and most important railway collections in the world, but two of its exhibits are particularly appropriate to readers of this series. From the furthest west of the area covered, there is a pair of antique carriages from the early Bodmin and Wadebridge

Railway; while from almost the furthest north, there is the powerful beam engine which once stood at the head of Weatherhill Incline in County Durham. As far as these walks are concerned, that offers a nice touch of symmetry.

Transport and Facilities

Map: Ordnance Survey: Landranger Series Sheet 105 (recommended)

Buses: Arriva North East
www.arrivabus.co.uk
Telephone: (Traveline) 0871 200 22 33

Trains: National Rail Enquiries
www.nationalrail.co.uk
Telephone: 08457 48 49 50

Selby and York are still connected by rail, which is very convenient for anyone who wishes to walk or cycle the entire length of this path. There is an hourly service from Monday to Saturday and a two-hourly service on Sunday.

The bus provision is also very good. One service is the no. 42 operated by Arriva which provides a regular bus from Selby Bus Station to York Piccadilly from Monday to Sunday.

As for other facilities, Selby and York are the obvious centres; the intervening villages seem microscopic by comparison. A pub at least can be found at Barlby, Riccall, Escrick and Bishopthorpe (home of the Archbishop of York's Palace), but walkers should note that Escrick was ill served by its station: the village lies over a mile to the north-east. The area is exceptionally well served by breweries, for Tadcaster, the county's brewing capital, lies but a few miles west of the cycle path. The Ordnance Survey map still shows three breweries in the town and these are owned by Bass, John Smith's and Samuel Smith's respectively. John and Samuel Smith are reputed to have been brewing brothers who fell out with each other in the eighteenth century; their breweries still have a welcome touch of interest. John's produces the potent Imperial Russian Stout, a jet-black concoction first brewed for the Court of the Empress Catherine II of Russia, while Samuel's ferments its beer on Yorkshire slate and is the only brewery which still employs a cooper – an ancient craft which has practically disappeared with the advent of modern metal casks. At the other end of the scale, there is the tiny Selby brewery, a small family concern which restarted brewing in 1972 after a gap of eighteen years.

The Alban Way looking towards Hatfield. The view is framed by the huge bridge which carries the existing main line from London St Pancras to St Albans and Bedford

The privately owned and beautifully preserved station at Felstead on the former Braintree–Bishop's Stortford line with a fine display of summer flowers

This bridge carries the Weaver's Way over a tributary of the River Bure between Felmingham and Aylsham. The concrete spans were probably produced in Mr Marriott's concrete shop at Melton Constable

Hornsea Town station viewed from the former approach road; note the grand passenger entrance. This was one of only two stations in Yorkshire which terminated in a turntable, an added attraction for visiting holiday-makers

A view of the trackbed between Kipling Cotes and Cherry Burton on the Hudson Way. The Wolds have been left behind as the path heads toward the coastal plain. This route may one day again see trains, since there is a well organised campaign locally to reinstate the direct railway between York and Beverley

Naburn swing bridge on the old main line between Selby and York. The turret on which the bridge pivoted is just visible behind the tree to the left.

Staintondale station is by general consent the most attractively preserved on the Scarborough and Whitby Railway Path, and perhaps that is not surprising when one considers that a son of the last station-master now owns it. In the best railway tradition, floral displays still figure prominently

This close-up view of the magnificent Hownes Gill Viaduct between Consett and Waskerley conveys a strong impression of its towering grandeur. It is 730 ft long, 150 ft high and was constructed between 1857 and 1858 from two and a half million white fire-bricks

8
THE SCARBOROUGH AND WHITBY RAILWAY PATH

Introduction

If the North Yorkshire Moors conjure up visions of open heathland stretching away for miles in every direction, it needs to be added that they also include villages and dales as delightful as any of those seen in television programmes such as *Last of the Summer Wine* and *All Creatures Great and Small.* In one episode of the series *Poirot,* the area even masqueraded as the Lake District, much to the chagrin of one observant correspondent who complained to the editor of the *TV Times!* However, what may not be so widely known is that the North Yorkshire Moors National Park extends right to the coast; and a splendid section of coast it is too, stretching from just east of Whitby to a few miles north of Scarborough. For just under eighty years, a single-track branch line threaded its sinuous way between these two towns, hugging to ledges cut into rocky cliffs, winding around valleys, striding over becks that tumble down to the sea and serving scattered communities to whom, in winter at least, the railway was a veritable lifeline. It was a real roller-coaster of a route too, as the gradient profile reveals, and the frequent sea-mists or 'frets' from the North Sea could make the rails so wet and slippery that trains were unable to pass its two summits.

Like many holiday lines, the Scarborough and Whitby Railway had something of a Jekyll and Hyde character, even in its best years, for it was extremely busy in the summer and distressingly quiet in the winter. Other railway writers have bemoaned the problems of maintaining a public transport system which was worked to capacity only on seven or eight weekends during high summer, so the arguments will not be repeated here: they can be imagined if not already familiar. Yet for all this, the railway authorities acknowledged the splendours of the route – and tried to cash in on them – by running scenic excursions until within two years of closure. Thanks to the good offices of Scarborough Borough Council, which purchased the line and converted it into a long-distance footpath, these scenic splendours are not lost forever. To enjoy them, however, the modern visitor must don a pair of walking-boots instead of ordering a ticket at the booking-office window.

History

The idea of building a coastal railway between Scarborough and Whitby was being circulated many years before the line finally opened in 1885. One of the first schemes was promoted in 1848 by the obscure Scarborough, Whitby, Stockton-on-Tees and Newcastle and North Junction Railway but, unfortunately for anyone who seriously wanted the line, the company was a product of the Railway Mania and soon disappeared without trace. It is notable in history for little more than the extraordinary length of its name. Another scheme appeared in 1863, when a Scarborough, Whitby and Staithes Railway was proposed. This had the backing of the then independent Cleveland Railway, which was seeking access to Scarborough, but the powerful North Eastern Railway opposed it and the public proved unwilling to subscribe the £450,000 capital required. Despite its failure, however, the idea rekindled interest in building a line from Scarborough to Whitby, and three further schemes were promoted during the course of 1864. The first envisaged a narrow-gauge tramway between Scarborough and Cloughton, worked by horses initially, but with the option to convert to steam if successful. The second scheme envisaged a contour railway running from Scarborough to Sleights on the existing Esk Valley line. The idea was to minimize engineering works and exploit the mineral resources of the area, particularly limestone and ironstone. It offered the shortest connecting route between the two towns but had a summit of 700 ft and a constant 1 in 50 rising gradient for a full six miles, which made it impractical from an operational point of view. The third proposal, for a coastal railway, was the best supported and a bill for this was duly presented before parliament; this received the Royal Assent on 5 July 1865. It authorized the raising of capital up to a limit of £275,000, allowed five years for construction, and required that work commence simultaneously from both ends of the line.

As might be expected, the North Eastern Railway opposed the new scheme, claiming that it already ran an acceptable Scarborough-Whitby service via Malton. On their line, however, passengers were required to change trains at either Malton or Rillington, and promoters of the new railway were quick to point out that the NER route was also exceedingly long; the new line would shorten the distance to a mere nineteen miles. Undeterred, the NER rapidly constructed a new curve at Rillington and, on 1 July 1865, introduced express trains from Scarborough to Whitby via Pickering; the journey time was one and a half hours. (It is interesting to note that, if the seven miles between Rillington and Pickering were relaid, this service could be reintroduced today.) Unfortunately for the NER, a severe depression hit the north-east the following year, with the result that the Rillington curve closed; it was never reopened. By then, however, the rival Scarborough and Whitby Railway had ground to a halt, and it seemed that their scheme had come to nothing. The company's engineer and contractor had surveyed the route in April 1865, hoping to start construction in August of that year, but there were difficulties in raising capital and the scheme gradually lost momentum. Little more happened between then and 1870, when the company's powers finally lapsed.

1870 might thus have been the end of any plans for a coastal line linking the two towns had it not been for an entirely different scheme which emerged in that year. This proposed an isolated Scarborough–Whitby line, unconnected at either end. It would start from Gallows Close in Scarborough and run to near the abbey at Whitby, with a 1 in 5 incline down to Gideon's Timber Pond on the River Esk. The bill for this new Scarborough and Whitby Railway was passed on 29 June 1871: it authorized capital up to £120,000 and allowed three years for the compulsory purchase of land and five years to complete the line. Construction work commenced on 3 June 1872, and by August 1873 seven miles at the Scarborough end were ready for ballast. At the same time, however, though the permanent way at Whitby was staked out, the land there had not yet been purchased.

During the course of 1872, the directors wisely came to the conclusion that junctions with the NER were required at each end if their line was to be viable, and a bill for these alterations went before Parliament in the 1873 session. It was passed on 26 May and included provisions for extra capital of £40,000 to be raised. Funds were slow coming in, however, and eventually dried up: as a result, work came to a standstill in 1877, with money owed to the engineer, contractor and others. A grim two-year period then followed, when it looked at times as if the whole scheme might have to be abandoned, but, after a number of false starts, renewed efforts were made in 1879 to complete the line. These came to their fruition on 12 August 1880, when a new Act revived the powers of the 1871 and 1873 Acts (now lapsed) and allowed for further capital of £80,000 to be raised. New engineers were appointed and tenders invited for the construction of the line; the lowest came from John Waddell and Son of Edinburgh, who were accordingly awarded the contract. Waddells started work in 1881 and completed the line within four years, including the magnificent Esk Viaduct at Whitby, which linked the east and west banks of the River Esk. This impressive structure was erected in 1883: it contains an estimated 5½ million bricks and weighs approximately 26,000 tons. We are lucky in having a good record of its construction thanks to Frank Sutcliffe, the noted Whitby photographer, who took many fine shots of this and other parts of the line as they were being built.

The official opening took place on 15 July 1885, public services commencing the following day. Local people had good cause to celebrate, for the line's completion verged on the miraculous. Five schemes had preceded the successful one, and that had cost £649,813 to complete – over five times the initial capital of £120,000. Anyone who walks the line today will readily appreciate why the cost was so hopelessly underestimated. The inaugural train made a single return trip from Scarborough, enabling the various dignitaries and promoters to enjoy a luncheon at The Crown Hotel, Whitby, followed by a sumptuous banquet at The Royal Hotel, Scarborough. The train was provided by the North Eastern Railway and the official party included its directors, for the Scarborough and Whitby company had concluded an agreement in 1884 that the NER should operate its line in return for half of the gross receipts. Its capital had been so stretched by the construction that the acquisition of locomotives and rolling stock was clearly out of the question.

Unfortunately, the working arrangements did not run smoothly, and it is fair to say that the two companies now settled down to a period of mutual antagonism. There was undoubtedly fault on the part of the NER, which was not particularly bothered either to promote the new line or to route traffic by it. On top of this, the rates it charged were considered to be unreasonably high. Such grievances induced the secretary of the Scarborough and Whitby Railway Company to bombard his counterpart at the NER with an almost ceaseless stream of complaints, while the company's promotional literature exhorted passengers 'to ask for tickets by the COAST ROUTE, and TO SEE THAT THEY GET THEM'. This slightly anarchic state of affairs continued until 1 July 1898, when the NER purchased the line for £261,333 – paid entirely with its own stock. This was substantially less than the cost of the line, but it had proved unprofitable from the start. Certainly the antagonism between the two companies involved did not help, but the population of the intervening area was extremely sparse and excursion traffic never made up for the lack of a proper local trade.

With the 1923 grouping, the line passed into the ownership of the London and North Eastern Railway, which used it for testing various types of Sentinel steam railcar. This established a tradition: in the 1930s, the first diesel-electric railcar, *Tyneside Venturer,* was employed on the route, working a circular scenic tour which originated at York – out via Malton and Pickering, back via Whitby and Scarborough. These tours became an established feature of the line and, together with the introduction of cheap fares, greatly increased its traffic. By summer 1933, this had risen to such a level that it could scarcely cope and a committee was formed to determine ways of improving the situation for 1934. The most significant result was the creation of platform 1A at Scarborough. This was constructed at the south-western extremity of the station and avoided the necessity of Whitby trains having to cross other lines, which were already heavily congested with holiday traffic. The only unfortunate aspect, from a passenger's point of view, was that the platform was nearly a quarter of a mile from the booking-office window! To compensate for this, all Whitby trains actually left Scarborough three minutes later than shown in the public timetables: this provided a little 'panic time' in which last-minute passengers could make it to the carriage door. While on the subject of odd operating features, it is also worth mentioning that through trains had to reverse at both

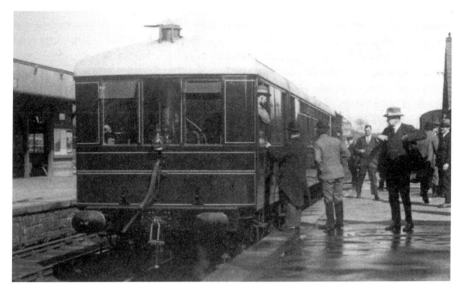

The station at Robin Hood's Bay used to be a passing place on the single-track branch from Scarborough to Whitby. The line was used frequently to test types of experimental traction, and here Sentinel-Cammell No. 22, in LNER varnished teak livery, is seen at the southbound platform after successfully towing a horse-box up the 1 in 43 gradient from Whitby on 6 April 1927

H.G.W. Household

ends of their journey, for the junctions at Scarborough and Whitby both faced away from their terminal stations!

Unfortunately, the increase in traffic was short-lived. After the Second World War, road competition increased and the line again descended into loss-making. The appalling winter of 1947 blocked the roads and stopped the buses for eight weeks; not even trains could withstand such extremities of weather for long. At Ravenscar, the snow reached the arm of the signal at the end of the platform and even the snow-plough could not get beyond Staintondale. After six weeks, an emergency train managed to reach the village, intending to take passengers to Scarborough for essential shopping, but its return journey was blocked by snowdrifts every half-mile, and the dispirited villagers had to jump off and walk back before it had reached Staintondale. The train averaged about one mile per hour. Various economy measures were introduced in the 1950s, but they were not enough to remedy the situation. Scalby station was closed on 2 March 1953, although a small number of trains continued to call there during the summer months for the benefit of holiday-makers in the camping-coaches. Hayburn Wyke, the smallest station on the line, was converted to an unstaffed halt on 23 March 1955 and Fyling Hall followed suit on 5 May 1958. Diesel railcars were introduced in that year but they proved no more immune to the notorious sea-frets than steam engines: on 19 January 1959, a three-car unit proved unable to traverse the line even when one of its coaches was detached, and its passengers were finally conveyed to Scarborough by bus.

By 1964, the financial situation was dire, even during the summer. In one especially bad week, the staff responsible for Cloughton, Hayburn Wyke and Staintondale were paid £160 in wages but collected only £6 in fares. Ominously, the only railway vehicles which recorded a profit were the stationary camping-coaches. Freight services were withdrawn first, the last goods train running on 4 August 1964. The passenger services followed seven months later on 6 March 1965. Local residents fought long and hard against the closure and even the Transport Users Consultative Committee acknowledged that they would face 'serious hardship' if the trains were withdrawn; but all to no avail. At least the line went out in style: on the last day, a double-headed steam-hauled enthusiasts' special ran, in addition to the usual service of diesel railcars. But then that was it: no more scenic excursions, no more slippery rails – on the face of it, no more anything.

Scalby station, looking north, in about 1912. The site now accommodates a small housing development called Chichester Close

J. Robin Lidster Collection

The Line Today

Following closure, the line was lifted in 1965, although the section from Hawsker to the junction at Whitby was left in place so that it could carry traffic from proposed potash workings in the area. This scheme was temporarily shelved in 1970 (although planning permission had been obtained) and it appears that the rails were never used again; nothing had happened by 1972, and in 1985 Scarborough Borough Council acquired the trackbed to extend the railway path into Whitby. A short stub remained in use at Scarborough rather longer, for the large yard at Gallows Close was retained until 1981. Even then, a few rails were left at the east side of the yard to serve a coal depot, but these too were removed in 1985. With them, the last operational section of the Scarborough and Whitby Railway was closed, exactly one hundred years after its opening.

The development of the railway path reflects the line's piecemeal closure. The initial section ran from Hawsker to the outskirts of Scarborough; Whitby to Hawsker was added in 1985, and in 1988 it was possible to walk without obstruction all the way to Gallows Close, although it was difficult to tell whether or not the final half-mile was on any sort of official basis. The site at Gallows Close is rather large and it seems improbable that it will escape redevelopment, but it would be very convenient if the path could be led through, as the former yard is only a short walk from Scarborough bus and railway stations.

The number of obstructions on the walk is extremely small, given its considerable length. The Esk Viaduct at Whitby is fenced off (hardly surprising); a short section of line at Robin Hood's Bay has been used for a car-park and residential gardens; a detour has been made around Ravenscar Tunnel, where bricks are reported to be falling out of the roof; and another detour is necessary at Scalby, where the former station has been demolished to make way for a small housing estate for the elderly. However, taken as a whole, the preservation of so much of the line, and so many of its sixty-one bridges, is a remarkable achievement. Without doubt, it now makes one of the finest railway walks in the country.

The Walk (23½ miles)

The following notes describe the walk from north to south. There is no particular advantage to this; it is simply that I happened to be staying nearer the Whitby than the Scarborough end of the line. While visiting Whitby, energetic walkers may be interested to pay a brief visit to Whitby West Cliff station (grid

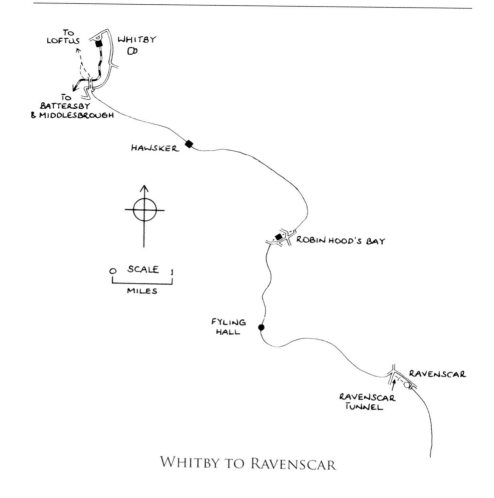

WHITBY TO RAVENSCAR

reference 890111), on the former line to Staithes and Loftus. The station, of course, is closed, but the buildings survive intact, being used by the Yorkshire Water Authority. The outside is practically unchanged since the last train departed in 1961 and could be mistaken for part of an operational railway, but closer inspection reveals that the trackbed area is now cluttered with extensions and other paraphernalia. However, it is still possible to identify the buildings on both platforms, including the signal-box at the south-west corner of the site.

The main walk begins in Larpool Lane on the outskirts of Whitby, at grid reference 896095, close by the impressive, brick-built Esk Viaduct. This is 915 ft long, 120 ft high and stands on 13 arches but, as noted above, does not form part of the walk. It is sad to relate that the structure is beginning to show signs of its age and may have to be demolished; it is arguably the most impressive industrial monument in Whitby and deserves to be preserved, perhaps using funds from the Railway Heritage Trust. For anyone who doubts the ability of those responsible to safeguard the viaduct's future, it can be viewed from the north bank of the River Esk by an interesting path which starts at Bog Hall near Whitby station. From Larpool Lane, the main path to Scarborough leads away to the south; the first section was only completed in 1985 and is not yet heavily used. To begin with, it looks more like a typical country path through woods than a former railway line, but the views open out as Hawsker station is approached (grid reference 924079), and the impressive ruins of Whitby Abbey can be seen over one's shoulder to the north. Hawsker station is now used by the local Scout group and, while a few external alterations have been made over the years, its railway origins are still very clear. Shortly after leaving Hawsker, the line begins to climb around the cliffs to Robin Hood's Bay and impressive coastal views appear to the east. The gradients on this section are as high as 1 in 39 so it is not surprising that trains had problems with adhesion in bad weather. The Bay remains the dominant visual feature for some six miles and can usually be seen, so long as there are no trees – or sea-frets – in the way.

A steep descent leads into Robin Hood's Bay but, at grid reference 953057, the line is blocked by garden extensions. The walker should turn left and then right and proceed downhill as far as the main road. Cross over this into Station Road, noting a new car-park on the right which was built on the former railway sidings. Beyond the car-park, the old station buildings remain on the right, largely unaltered. Part of the main building now accommodates the local old folks' club, while the former post office and refreshment room (a separate timber building outside the station) is now in use as a hairdresser's. This unusual addition was built on to the signal-box which can be seen behind it. The walker should now continue south-west down the old station drive to a minor road at grid reference 947053, where an underbridge has been removed; the path recommences opposite.

The walker now enters a wooded section which is well used by horseriders and has good access to local camping-sites, spiritual successors of the former camping-coaches. Along the way, a railway-installed concrete stile will be noted, made redundant and purposeless by the conversion of the railway itself into a footpath; it stands forlornly beside the trackbed like an out-of-place modern sculpture. By the time Fyling Hall station is reached (grid reference 944029), the woodland has become very dense, creating an atmosphere of enclosed seclusion. The path takes a sudden swing to the right immediately before the station platform, which is easily missed: a faint track leads straight ahead past its remains, rapidly being engulfed by bushes and sycamores. Having descended into Robin Hood's Bay, the railway must now regain height to reach the summit at Ravenscar (631 ft above sea level), so a long climb begins, along which the magnificent coastal views once more return. Walkers will enjoy the bright heather which cascades down the steep moors right to the very edge of the path, though this is a relatively modern phenomenon: steam locomotives had to work very hard on this part of the line and they usually set fire to anything that ventured to grow so close to the site of their endeavours! Shortly before Ravenscar, Brickyard's alum quarry is passed on the right and a line of wooden sleepers can be traced in the grass, the site of a former siding. This was once an area of considerable industrial activity for, apart from the alum quarry, Whitaker's brickworks stood by the line and a narrow-gauge incline brought additional traffic in the form of ganister, quarried one and a half miles away on Stony Marl Moor. The narrow-gauge railway was dismantled in the 1930s, although the quarries remained active until about 1965.

Shortly before Ravenscar Tunnel, the path swings away to the left and climbs up to meet a minor road at grid reference 980016. The tunnel is approached by a cutting and, in summer, its northern portal can only just be seen through undergrowth and overhanging foliage. At the lane, the walker should turn left and immediately right into Station Road. A glance at the map will reveal that there isn't very much to Ravenscar, but that did not stop the railway builders placing their station rather inconveniently at the southern end of the village (grid reference 985013). This is partly explained by the fact that, at the turn of the century, the Peak Estate Company Ltd offered 750 acres at Ravenscar for development into a new seaside resort. The scheme failed due to the lack of easy access to the beach, in addition, of course, to the cold winds and damp fogs from the North Sea. The demolished station and the row of shops which still stands nearby were to have been the nucleus of this new development.

The line now begins a two-mile descent to Staintondale at 1 in 41. Ravenscar station was built on a short section at 1 in 1571 but the gradients at each end were so steep that the change could be seen in the inclination of the carriage roofs as they departed. Gradually, the countryside becomes less rugged and, in summer, heather slowly gives way to golden cornfields. As the line descends into Staintondale, it plunges into woodland again and passes right between the two platforms of Staintondale station at grid reference 999978. This is the best preserved of all the stations on the line and is a most attractive sight when bedecked with flowers, echoing the days of 'Best-Kept Station' awards. Perhaps this is hardly surprising, for it is owned by one of the sons of the last station-master. The line then continues south as a wide woodland path, cool and welcoming after the heat of the sun on a hot August day. At Hayburn Wyke, the station house and platform survive, but the station buildings, which were all of timber, have been removed. Despite the air of economy, the house and platform represented an improvement on the original station of 1885, which stood on the opposite side of the line and was constructed entirely of timber – something of a hazard to passengers in winter, when it was difficult for them to keep their footing on the icy wooden platform. Its replacement is punctuated with little

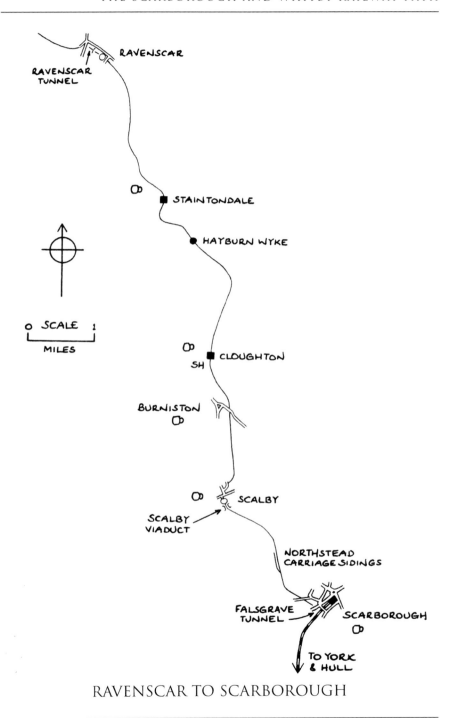

RAVENSCAR TO SCARBOROUGH

The goods shed at Cloughton survives complete with canopies and platforms. Miraculously, a porter's trolley still adorned the site in 1988, although it has probably 'gone for a walk' by now

openings which allow water from the nearby hillside to trickle down on to the trackbed; some still retain their cast iron gratings.

The views open out again as Cloughton is approached, but the gently undulating farmland makes it difficult to recall the grandeur that has gone before; passengers travelling north could have had little indication of what lay ahead. Cloughton station (grid reference 012942) is privately owned but the path passes right in front of it and through the yard, where a goods shed still stands, complete with canopy. Remarkably, in 1988 a discarded porter's barrow remained here, rusting away in the grass, but it is too much to hope that it will survive for long. The rest of the yard has been turned into a picnic area. The line may now be followed with ease to the A165 at Burniston (grid reference 016927), where the walker should cross the road diagonally to the left to pick up the continuation of the trail. By now, Scarborough can be seen in the distance – the end is in sight! On approaching Scalby, a new housing development occupies the trackbed and the walker must negotiate a number of residential roads where some waymarking would be helpful. The path leads into Field Close Road, where it is necessary to turn left; proceed to a T-junction with Lancaster Way and turn left again to reach Station Road, the main road from

A view of Scalby Viaduct, which spans the Sea Cut from the River Derwent

Scalby to Scalby Mills. Chichester Close can be seen diagonally to the right: this occupies the site of the old station and still gives access to the trackbed just north of Scalby Viaduct. However, anyone hoping for an attractive view of the River Derwent will be sorely disappointed unless they are exceptionally tall, for the viaduct's parapets are over six feet high. A profuse growth of trees in the area makes it almost impossible to photograph the structure.

Continuing south, residential housing creeps up on the line and it soon assumes the character of a parkland walk. Beyond an overbridge at grid reference 025899 it suddenly opens out into a large park, the site of Northstead carriage sidings. There were originally ten roads here for the storage of carriages during the summer, together with locomotive coaling and watering facilities. Towards the south of the site, a huge bridge (now demolished) used to carry a footpath across the railway. The sidings were dismantled in 1965 and the area remained something of an eyesore until reclaimed and grassed over in the 1980s; to the untrained eye, it now looks like a perfectly ordinary recreation ground, though the tell-tale traces of a turntable pit can be found at the north end. The official walk may very well end here, but there was nothing to say so in 1988 and I carried on regardless; it seemed a reasonable assumption as there was no accompanying change in the walking surface. Between Northstead and Gallows Close, the line appeared to be double track but was in fact two reversible lines running parallel – one to Whitby, the other to the carriage sidings. In just over a quarter of a mile, the walker will be standing in the vast empty expanse of Gallows Close goods yard, with the northern portal of Falsgrave Tunnel visible in the distance; the size of the yard is revealed by the width of the road bridge which crosses its mouth. The tunnel is only 260 yds long and Scarborough station lies at the end of it.

It will be understood that the following directions are liable to change following redevelopment of the site, but on my visit it was possible to leave Gallows Close by a large gate on the left which stood in front of a disused weighbridge; this, incidentally, appears on the 1898 plan of the yard, which also shows that the buildings opposite used to be stables. Beyond the gate, the walker should turn right, proceed as far as a T-junction and there turn left for the bus and railway stations, which are only a quarter of a mile distant. It goes without saying that, if in future the end of the path is moved further north, the walker should comply with any signs and directions which are given. However, waymarking on the route is almost non-existent and it seems hard to imagine that council workmen will suddenly appear with signposts and information boards! Perhaps they ought to.

Further Explorations

After tackling the twenty-three and a half miles of this walk, the average rambler may want to explore the local pubs, or prefer to take a bus home and have a bath. However, for those who still demand more, there are parts of the Rosedale branch of the North Eastern Railway and the Historical Railway Trail from Goathland to Grosmont – part of the original horse-drawn Whitby and Pickering Railway.

The Rosedale branch of the NER ran from Battersby (on BR's existing Esk Valley line) to Blakey Junction, where the 'main' line continued to a set of isolated calcining kilns above Rosedale Abbey, while the east branch diverged by reversal on to a long loop around Rosedale Head to Low Baring. The line was opened on 27 March 1861 and closed officially on 13 June 1929; during its life, it conveyed about ten million tons of Rosedale ironstone, the chief incentive for its construction. The trackbed can be traced from Battersby Bank Foot, at Ingleby

Greenhow (grid reference 588066), to Blakey Junction (685988); most of this eleven-mile stretch forms part of the Lyke Wake Walk and is shown as a public footpath on the relevant Ordnance Survey maps. In *Railway Rights of Way,* Rhys ab Elis states that the two branches from Blakey Junction may also be walked, but this is borne out neither by the OS maps nor the signs around the terminus at Rosedale, which make it quite clear that the route is private.

The Historical Railway Trail from Goathland to Grosmont is a far easier walk at a modest three and a half miles: it is even possible to catch a steam train back on the preserved North Yorkshire Moors Railway. As mentioned above, the trail formed part of the original Whitby and Pickering Railway, opened in 1836. This was a horse-drawn affair and included a three-quarters of a mile incline between Goathland and Beck Hole, which by July 1847 represented a serious bottleneck, for it stood in the way of steam locomotives from Whitby and Pickering which were working to and from each end. As a result, a deviation line was constructed at a cost of £50,000 and opened on 1 July 1865. It might be expected that the original line closed on the same day, but parts of it remained in use until October 1951, when the fortnightly train to the tiny hamlet of Esk Valley was withdrawn. The creation of the present footpath (presumably the work of the North Yorkshire Moors National Park) is fairly recent, for in 1972 a number of the bridges were still missing; they have since been replaced with modern steel foot-bridges, which rest on the original stone abutments. Apart from the incline, the original tunnel at Grosmont (119 yards) remains open as an integral part of the walk.

Grosmont is also the home of the North Yorkshire Moors Railway, which runs as far as Pickering over eighteen preserved miles of the former line from Whitby to Malton. It closed on the same day as the coastal route from Whitby to Scarborough – a black day indeed for rail travellers in this part of the county. Moves to reopen the line commenced in June 1967 and culminated in an official opening by the Duchess of Kent on 1 May 1973. Nowadays, the railway is flourishing and at certain times of the year offers a better service than that provided by British Railways in the early sixties. This, of course, is achieved by running no trains other than a few Santa Specials between November and March – always the dead part of the year, which dragged so many rural branch lines into loss-making and ultimate closure.

Transport and Facilities

Maps: Ordnance Survey: Tourist Map 2
Ordnance Survey: Landranger Series Sheets 94 and 101
Ordnance Survey: Outdoor Leisure Map 27 (recommended)

Buses: Arriva North East
www.arrivabus.co.uk
Telephone: (Traveline) 0871 200 22 33

East Yorkshire Motor Services
The Travel Office,
Ferensway Coach Station,
Hull, Humberside
http://www.eyms.co.uk/
Telephone: 01482 325679

Trains: National Rail Enquiries
www.nationalrail.co.uk
Telephone: 08457 48 49 50

There are still trains to Whitby (from Middlesbrough) and Scarborough (from York and Hull). The line to Whitby is particularly attractive and is highly recommended, especially as there are occasional worries about closure – hopefully unfounded. The services are of a seasonal nature and are understandably better during the summer than the winter. In particular, there are no Sunday trains between the beginning of October and the beginning of the following May. Services on the line from Hull to Scarborough also used to run from Monday to Saturday only, but British Rail introduced a Sunday service in 1989 and their local enquiry office advised that this would continue if it proved a success. However, it would be wise to enquire locally if you are thinking of using it during the winter months – it may not be there!

The situation with regard to buses is thankfully straightforward and is summarized in the table below. The services of use to railway ramblers is Arriva's route 93/X93, which runs hourly during the winter and half-hourly during the summer (June to September); and East Yorkshire's routes 15 and 115, which run half-hourly throughout the year. Most of the services run well into the evening; there is also a reduced number of Sunday journeys.

Bus Services Between Whitby and Scarborough

Place	Service	Days of Operation
Whitby	Arr 93/93X	Daily
Hawsker	Arr 93/93X	Daily
Robin Hood's Bay	Arr 93/93X	Daily
Ravenscar	Arr 93/93X	Daily
Staintondale	Arr 93/93X	Daily

Place	Service	Days of Operation
Cloughton	Arr 93/93X	Daily
Burniston	EY 15/115	Daily
Scalby	EY 15/115	Daily
Scarborough	Arr 93/X93	Daily

Arr – Arriva North East; EY – East Yorkshire Motor Services

Being a holiday area, it is easy to find refreshments in Whitby, Robin Hood's Bay and Scarborough, but facilities are rather sparse elsewhere. An ice cream is the most that can be hoped for at Ravenscar, but the Shepherd's Arms at Staintondale (grid reference 993982) is well placed. It is situated about a quarter of a mile from the line as the crow flies, but twice that distance via public footpaths and country lanes; it is also uphill all the way. However, as a reward, it sells food and has superb sea-views. Things improve at Cloughton, by which time the walker has reached the outer limit of Scarborough commuterdom; there are pubs here, at Burniston and at Scalby. Yorkshire still has a good number of breweries belonging to both national and regional companies, and this is reflected in a better-than-average choice of ales. From outside the county, Cameron's of Hartlepool are particularly well represented. It is a full twenty-three and a half miles from Whitby station to Scarborough station, so anyone who attempts the lot is entitled to a drink, if only to anaesthetize their aching feet!

9
THE WASKERLEY WAY
CONSETT TO WASKERLEY

Introduction

Any railway rambler from outside the area who stumbled upon County Durham could be forgiven for thinking that he had arrived in heaven: it is simply littered with railway paths. This generous provision originates largely from the Countryside Act of 1968 which required local authorities to provide recreational access to the countryside. Prior to this, there were very few well-defined pedestrian routes of access in the area, despite a considerable demand from out-of-county visitors and a great east-to-west flow of trippers from the large urban centres around the Tyne and Tees rivers.

From this point of view at least, it can be regarded as fortunate that the Act coincided with a great decline in the county's traditional heavy industries. This in turn led to British Rail closing many of its long-surviving freight lines, which the county council promptly acquired for conversion into green lanes. Three routes became available around Consett within six years. The Derwent Valley branch was the first to go, in November 1963, followed by the Lanchester Valley line in 1966, and the western stub of the Stanhope and Tyne Railway in 1969. The eastern section of this ancient line held out until 1985, but its fate was inextricably bound up with that of Consett steelworks. When the works closed, the line became an anachronism and suffered the same fate.

Much of Consett's history is predictably concerned with the great industry which once sustained it, but it has other, more unlikely claims to fame; for example, the world's first Salvation Army band was formed here in 1879. In the late 1980s, it became the meeting place of four separate railway paths. This chapter is concerned with one of them, originally the earliest line to pass through Consett – the Stanhope and Tyne Railway.

History

The idea for a wagonway from Stanhope to the River Tyne originated in 1831.

The main incentives were limestone from the quarries above Stanhope, lead from the smelters at Stanhope and Rookhope, and coal traffic from various collieries along the way. The terrain was extremely uneven, but inclines were an accepted part of wagonway construction and were not regarded as a problem; in fact, quite the reverse, for they avoided the need for costly engineering works. As a result, the line featured a large number of inclines, and later improvements were based around their removal, although the two most westerly, at Crawley and Weatherhill, survived until the end.

The promoters of the Stanhope and Tyne Railway deliberately decided not to seek parliamentary powers, in an attempt to conceal the magnitude of their scheme – after all, they planned some thirty-four miles of wagonway and could expect considerable opposition. They relied instead on a succession of wayleaves, rights of way rented by the railway from adjoining landowners. Way-leave negotiations began in 1831, and the sums agreed were initially very reasonable: the average on the western end of the line was about £25 per annum per mile. However, as the area under negotiation approached South Shields, the promoters' plans became obvious, and they were forced to accept rates up to and in excess of £300.

Construction work began in July 1832, and by October had progressed a full eight miles from the start at Stanhope. The most serious obstacle was Hownes Gill, a glacial gorge just outside present-day Consett, which stood directly in the path of the railway. This was 150 ft deep and 800 ft across. Recognizing that a bridge would be expensive and would delay the opening of the line, the railway constructed instead inclined planes down either side of the ravine. These were to be the cause of serious delays to traffic for many years to come. The rest of the construction proceeded rapidly throughout 1833, and the section from Stanhope to Consett opened on 15 May 1834, the rest of the line following on 10 September the same year.

The arrangements at Hownes Gill soon acquired a reputation as the bottleneck on the system. Wagons were lowered into and raised out of the ravine in cradles, but only twelve an hour could be handled in this way at best. Quite simply, the early traffic almost exceeded Hownes Gill's ability to cope with it. William Bouch recommended construction of a bridge as early as 1844, but his suggestion was not acted upon, presumably due to financial difficulties. These became acute as a result of the gigantic annual way-leaves bill, which, by 1837, was causing a hefty annual deficit. The cost of operating the railway was £5,998 per annum, but the way-leaves exceeded this, costing £6,300 per annum; the two combined did not leave much of the company's income. The directors did not reveal this dangerous state of affairs for several years, but in 1839 their hand was forced when the railway lost five thousand pounds' worth of coal traffic to a rival line. This was the last straw, and an Extraordinary General Meeting was held on 29 December 1840 to discuss the situation. The company was bankrupt: there was nothing to do but dissolve it and suspend services while a rescue package was arranged. A new company was formed to work the eastern section from Consett to South Shields, while the western section was sold to the Derwent Iron Company. This concern had recently been established at Consett and quickly intervened when it saw its supplies threatened by the railway's difficulties. The sale of the line from Consett to Stanhope was concluded in early 1841 and the iron company reopened the route in 1842. Things then continued much as usual until the entry of the Stockton and Darlington Railway on to the scene.

The S & D was seeking to extend its territory north-westwards by means of subsidiary companies, the Bishop Auckland and Weardale Railway being one example. This was incorporated in 1837 and opened a line from Bishop Auckland to Crook on 8 November 1843. The Derwent Iron Company was keen to establish a southern outlet for its products and offered to sell its line to the S & D if the company would construct a connecting line from Crook to the original Stanhope and Tyne Railway. This it did in 1844. The new line was known as the Weardale Extension Railway and ran from Crook to the top of Nanny Mayor's Incline. It opened for traffic on 14 May 1845, the junction of the two railways being named Waskerley Park. The iron company then sold its route to the S & D, which merged the two lines under the grand title 'The Wear and Derwent Junction Railway'. This was a wholly-owned subsidiary of the S & D, and had its headquarters at Waskerley. This became a well-known railway village, renowned for the toughness of its railwaymen – hardly surprising in view of the bleak moorland terrain in which they lived. A locomotive depot, large enough to accommodate four engines, was opened in 1846. This was followed by the construction of sidings, stores, railway offices and a wagon repair shop. By 1854, traffic was heavy enough to necessitate the construction of an additional engine shed.

The S & D was not wholly geared towards freight and inaugurated a passenger service between Consett, Stanhope and Crook on 1 September 1845. At the Consett end, this stopped on the west side of Hownes Gill, for there was still no bridge over the gorge, and passengers had to complete their journey on foot. Additionally, the service was rather slow due to the inclines and the fact that the lines were already busy with mineral traffic. As if these disincentives were not enough, the terrain between Stanhope and Waskerley was very thinly populated. The combined effect was to make the Stanhope to Waskerley part of the service a failure, and it disappeared in 1846; the main passenger axis then became the stretch of line from Crook to Consett.

Waskerley lost its status as a railway headquarters in 1847, when the S & D formed the Wear Valley Railway by amalgamating the Wear and Derwent Junction Railway with the Bishop Auckland and Weardale Railway. A few months later, it took over the newly formed company by means of a 999-year lease, thus becoming the third legal owner of the metals from Stanhope to Consett. During the 1850s, it made significant improvements to the route by bridging Hownes Gill and replacing Nanny Mayor's Incline. Hownes Gill had remained a bottle-neck, although an increase in capacity was achieved in 1853 when funicular railways were installed either side of the gorge and the former inclined planes taken out of use. The funicular railways could take three wagons at a time, and increased the line's capacity to about 600 wagons a day, but the S & D was still not satisfied and in 1856 took the bold decision to bridge the gorge. A design by Thomas Bouch was approved in December that year and the new viaduct opened for traffic on 1 July 1858. It remains a masterpiece of engineering elegance. The decision to bypass Nanny Mayor's Incline was also taken in 1856. A survey was made of a route from Burnhill to near Whitehall, which would enable steam locomotives to reach Waskerley from Consett via a two-mile deviation. The land was purchased early in 1857 and the contract awarded in August that year; the new line was opened on 4 July 1859, and Nanny Mayor's Incline closed on the same day. The Crook to Consett passenger service was now consolidated by the provision of an extra platform at Rowley and new stations at Burnhill and Carr House (Consett). Burnhill was constructed for the convenience of the railway families at Waskerley, just over a

Hownes Gill Viaduct stands just to the south-west of Consett on the ancient Stanhope and Tyne Railway. It was designed by Thomas Bouch, later responsible for the ill-fated first railway bridge over the River Tay. The original piers at Hownes Gill were considered inadequate and were strengthened with buttresses at an early date; the buttressing can be clearly seen in this reproduction of an old print from about 1860

H.G.W. Household

mile away, and a connecting footpath was provided for their use. Carr House station closed in 1868, when a new link was opened from Hownes Gill to connect with the Derwent Valley line from Consett to Newcastle.

With these major changes complete, the line now assumed a more settled existence. The lead traffic from Stanhope gradually declined, but limestone traffic remained heavy and reached a peak during the First World War, due to increased production at the Consett ironworks. The passenger service between Consett and Crook settled down to a basic pattern of four trains per day in each direction, an arrangement which lasted with only minor variations until after the grouping of 1923. In the 1930s, bus competition began to make serious inroads on the railway's passenger business and freight traffic between Consett and Crook gradually dried up as the main flow was in the opposite direction, from Consett to Tyneside. Only at Burnhill did the passenger figures hold up reasonably well, and that was due to the large number of railway families living at nearby Waskerley. Unfortunately, their concessionary fares meant that the station was not exactly a big revenue earner. These developments led to the passenger service between Consett and Tow Law being withdrawn on 1 May 1939, while the section from Burnhill Junction to Tow Law was closed to all traffic seventeen days later. These metals were not removed until 1952, which may show a certain reluctance on the part of the railway to embrace closure whole-heartedly.

Despite the passenger decline, freight traffic was still very good. Lime continued to travel from the kilns at Stanhope, substantial quantities of sand came from quarries at Parkhead and there was a respectable stone traffic from Rowley – nearly 20,000 tons in 1934. The Second World War delayed further contraction, but decline set in again in the 1950s. On 28 April 1951, British Railways closed the section from Weatherhill to Stanhope, including the famous inclines at Weatherhill and Crawley. The goods traffic was now confined to sand and fluorspar from Weatherhill and Parkhead, explosives from a War Department depot at Burnhill and limestone from Rowley. (The limestone was not actually quarried at Rowley, but was transferred there from lorries, on the last leg of its journey to Consett steelworks.) In 1952, the long abandoned rails from Burnhill to Tow Law were lifted, and in 1953/4 the engine shed and other buildings at Waskerley were demolished, leaving only a weighbridge and goods office. Next, the lines at Burnhill junction were simplified, the line from Burnhill to Rowley reduced from double to single track and all signalling west of Consett dispensed with. It was thus a greatly simplified railway which saw in the new decade in 1960.

A daily goods train continued to run from Consett to Parkhead and Weatherhill, the old stations at Rowley and Waskerley remaining open as public goods depots. However, Waskerley could not have generated much traffic at this time, due to its remote moorland location and subsequent depopulation. It was accordingly closed, along with Parkhead, on 2 August 1965, Rowley suffering the same fate on 2 June 1966. The branch was now hanging on by the skin of its teeth. The section from Burnhill to Weatherhill was closed on 29 April 1968, followed by the section to Consett on 1 May 1969, made inevitable by the closure of the War Department depot at Burnhill; this provided the last regular traffic over the line so that it was sustained for the last twelve months by its deadliest cargo. There was still sand traffic from Parkhead but it now had to either go out by road or be transported down into Stanhope for shipment via the Wear Valley line. These changes probably arose from price increases and changes in accounting methods brought about in the time of Dr Beeching.

Dismantling commenced at the Weatherhill end late in 1969 and was completed in the first few months of 1970. The once thriving community of Waskerley is now almost a ghost village and wears an air of bleak desolation; every part of it looks round-shouldered and weather-beaten. On a brighter note, Hownes Gill Viaduct has been designated as of 'special architectural or historical interest' and should be preserved for the foreseeable future. Today, this is the only indication of the importance of this once vital mineral line.

This striking view was taken from the top of Weatherhill Incline and portrays the bleakness of the surrounding countryside to good effect. Note the two sets of telegraph-poles to the right of the picture, one for the railway, the other for the lonely road which leads down to Crawley and Stanhope

Revd D. Littlefair Collection

The Line Today

Following the line's closure by British Rail, Durham County Council acquired most of the trackbed from Consett to Stanhope, including Hownes Gill Viaduct which is still receiving on-going maintenance – a very long-term commitment. At present, the Waskerley Way uses only the seven miles nearest to Consett, but it is intended to extend the route to just above Stanhope when a working quarry near Parkhead finally closes. There were only four bridges on the line, but three of them have been demolished and replaced with embankments in line with council policy. While enthusiasts may regret this, it does greatly reduce the maintenance costs.

At the Consett end, a grand junction of railway paths is to be made between the Waskerley Way, the Derwent Walk, the Lanchester Valley Walk and the Consett and Sunderland Railway Path. This will probably form the largest junction of railway paths in the country, and is already overlooked by an old smelt wagon rescued from the steelworks – an appropriate sentinel in such a location. At the time of writing (November 1989), this development was not complete but walkers could get from the Waskerley Way to the Derwent Walk or the Consett and Sunderland Railway Path without difficulty. Cyclists could also pick up the Lanchester Valley Walk by using minor roads between Consett and Lanchester. The main outstanding problems were the construction of the Consett bypass, which would affect the Consett and Sunderland path, and the extension of the Lancaster Valley Walk from Hurbuck to Consett. The county council actually owned the land, but needed to reach agreement with a local landowner through whose property the route would pass. John Grimshaw of Sustrans Ltd was also keen to see improvements to the surface of these tracks, and hoped that the council would place some of this work with his organization in due course.

The Walk (7 miles)

The Waskerley Way starts at grid reference 098493, a remote location just south-west of Consett. It was rather awkward to get to when I visited, but this should improve as links between the four Consett railway paths are developed. The ideal place to start will probably be, if it is not already, the site of the former Consett railway station (grid reference 112507), which is a few minutes' walk from the present day bus station. Failing this, my approach was to leave Consett by the A692 to Castleside. In 1988, this led past a new Presto supermarket on

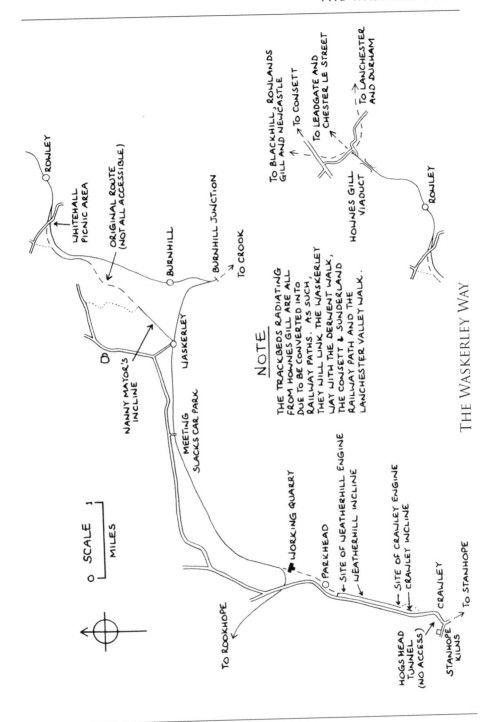

NOTE

THE TRACKBEDS RADIATING FROM HOWNES GILL ARE ALL DUE TO BE CONVERTED INTO RAILWAY PATHS. AS SUCH, THEY WILL LINK THE WASKERLEY WAY WITH THE DERWENT WALK, THE CONSETT & SUNDERLAND RAILWAY PATH AND THE LANCHESTER VALLEY WALK.

THE WASKERLEY WAY

the edge of the town: this convenient landmark may now be a Safeway supermarket, due to a recent takeover. The road then slopes downhill, surrounded by fresh bare fields where Consett steelworks used to stand. About three-quarters of a mile after passing the supermarket, a tiny lane turns off to the left at grid reference 097500. This should be followed for approximately a third of a mile until it passes under the ancient Stephenson Bridge (grid reference 098494); this once carried the line to Consett, Leadgate and Chester-le-Street, and should now be carrying pedestrians and cyclists following the same route. Immediately after the bridge, turn right and then right again to reach the trackbed. The Waskerley Way now leads off towards the south-west, but first it might be worth looking back towards Templetown, where a number of large metal gantries stood bleakly against the sky. If they have now gone, the demolition of Consett steelworks and the subsequent landscaping of the site are complete.

Immediately beyond the start of the walk, Hownes Gill Viaduct is met. This is 730 ft long, 150 ft high and by general agreement the finest viaduct in the county. The views are equally impressive, though the sight of the tree-tops below can be quite dizzying. The viaduct was constructed between 1857 and 1858, using over 2½ million fire-bricks; these alone cost £4,037. Most pocket-

The view from Hownes Gill Viaduct between Consett and Waskerley is no less impressive than the viaduct itself (see p. 129 and colour photograph). The village of Castleside is in the middle distance; the hills of Northumberland lie beyond

calculators would run out of noughts before they had computed the cost of building such a structure today. The viaduct is best viewed from the ground, and to this end there is a useful path which the council has constructed, leading from its northern corner down into the valley below.

Just before Rowley station (grid reference 088479), an overbridge has been infilled so that the walk climbs a short embankment to meet the road which used to pass over the line. The station site lies immediately beyond, now used as a car-park and picnic site. The attractive station building has been removed and is now preserved at Beamish Open Air Museum, where it stands alongside a short length of operational railway. The station remained in use as a goods depot years after closure to passengers, an important traffic being stone from local quarries.

The line continues to Whitehall picnic area (grid reference 077478), which lies the other side of a demolished underbridge. The main route is on a slight embankment here but, just before the demolished bridge, the walker should look out for a branch which diverges on the right and then runs roughly parallel to the main track at a lower level. This was probably the start of a siding which led to the quarry of the Derwent Ganister Company, installed in 1889 at a cost of some £80. Up to this point the scenery has been typical of many of the valley lines which wind their way west from Durham, but the trackbed now enters increasingly bleak and impressive moorland. A solitary overbridge still stands at grid reference 071476 and the council leaflet shows the route of Nanny Mayor's Incline starting just beyond this on the right. Unfortunately I missed this, due to the distraction of a frightful gale which was driving the rain in sideways, but there is a better opportunity to view the incline at Waskerley.

The line now enters a series of cuttings and embankments which were constructed so that the incline could be bypassed. Like Hownes Gill, this was an unwelcome barrier which denied access to steam locomotives and had to be overcome. The deviation line was dug out by pick and shovel and laid to double track, which was extended north-east as far as Rowley; this reveals both the value and volume of the mineral traffic which used it. At grid reference 067463, the cuttings finally give way to an impressive embankment, which reaches a maximum height of 60 ft above the valley floor. It is rather unusual in that it sags in the middle, giving the impression that the builders were not too worried about levelling it off; perhaps it didn't matter on a line that was so steeply graded anyway.

By now, the wind had reached such a ferocity that I found it almost impossible to walk in a straight line, so I was grateful for the next cutting, which offered some welcome protection; this led past lonely Bee Cottage with its collection of hives, although there were no bees in evidence on this occasion! The cutting finally opens out just before Burnhill Junction (grid reference 064444), where the Weatherhill freight trains were forced to reverse after closure of the Weardale Extension line to Tow Law and Crook. This route is now blocked by a fence, beyond which lies a tree plantation, so the walker, like

This cutting on the approach to Bee Cottage is part of the diversionary line which made Nanny Mayor's Incline redundant on 4 July 1859. It was dug entirely by pick and shovel

the trains before him, must now turn sharply right and continue almost due west.

After a short climb, the line levels out and follows the contours to Waskerley. This was once a busy railway centre but has now shrunk to the small and remote community which remains here today; there must be little inducement to live on these wild moors now that the railway has gone. Much of the evidence of Waskerley's past has disappeared, but the remains of a small platform can be picked out on the south side of the line, and Nanny Mayor's Incline still runs downhill to the north-east. The old formation is surprisingly wide and can be seen disappearing into the distance for nearly a mile; little vegetation gets a grip in this wild terrain. A bridleway follows the incline for two-thirds of its distance, from 052453 to 059461, but then turns sharply to the left to reach Middles Farm and Horsleyhope. It is hard to imagine that passenger carriages once travelled this way on the short-lived Stanhope to Consett service. A description of this survives from 1854 and it sounds rather like something from Will Hay's famous railway comedy *Oh, Mr. Porter!* On the downhill run, two composite carriages with outside handbrakes ran loose, behind a few loaded wagons. There was no separate accommodation for the guard and, when the trains were full at weekends, the luckless man had to ride outside on the buffers. One wonders what the NUR would have to say about that! A small church survives in the village but, like many nowadays, it is usually locked. The graves date mainly from the 1930s and 1940s; it is a mystery why there are no earlier graves, unless they were associated with the redundant Methodist church, which is now used as a barn.

The walk continues for another mile west, to Meeting Slacks car-park (grid reference 032454), where there used to be a siding. The car-park is not very large, and its boundary is marked out with old stone sleepers. Some of these bear the impression of railway chairs, while one still contains a pair of twisted railway spikes. This is the official end of the Waskerley Way, but the council has already done some work on the section to Edmundbyers Road, and the walker would have no difficulty in continuing for another two miles. Here, however, a working quarry straddles the line, and it is necessary to switch to the nearby road. When the quarry closes, the walk will be extended to Crawley, which is just above Stanhope on the northern slopes of the Wear Valley. The obstruction is preceded by the site of the junction with the privately worked Rookhope branch, which curved away to the west at grid reference 003433; the trackbed offers a convenient means of reaching the road. The Rookhope branch reaches a height of 1,670 ft above sea-level and was considered such a venturesome project that the Stanhope and Tyne Railway would have nothing to do with it. At that altitude, it was particularly prone to snow-drifts and was blocked practically every winter. In 1889, drifts of between 3 and 6 ft were recorded as late as May.

Three-quarters of a mile after the quarry, the trackbed is used as a bridleway, and follows the course of the incline between Weatherhill and Crawley engines; this can be joined at grid reference 997422. At Weatherhill, incidentally, the Stanhope and Tyne Railway reached its maximum height of 1,445 ft above sea-level. Weatherhill engine has now been removed and is preserved at the National Railway Museum in York. This was the second machine on the site and dates from 1919, the first having become 'life-expired' as a result of the vast quantity of limestone it hauled up the mile-long incline. The trackbed cannot be followed beyond the point where it joins the B6278 in Crawley (grid reference 993405), but Stanhope is only three quarters of a mile away by road, or slightly more by one of the many footpaths which lead down into the town. The line terminated at quarries and lime-kilns clustered around the south of Crawley.

The council leaflet on the Waskerley Way refers succinctly to the rugged beauty of the walk: 'The views ... of wooded valleys and wild moors speak for themselves.' They certainly do; even in wild weather, this walk makes a deep impression on the senses, perhaps especially so. On the open plain west of Waskerley, the landscape is barren and uncompromising; it conjures up Shakespearian images of a blasted heath, for this is a vibrant landscape, symbolic in its simplicity. When the wind blows, the lone walker can feel very exposed and very vulnerable.

Further Explorations

The railway rambler who wants to try some further explorations in these parts had better have plenty of time and a good pair of boots! At present the county council has reclaimed approximately forty-eight miles of old railway, and there are another forty-five miles to come. Unfortunately, the rate of development slowed down when the Department of the Environment insisted that MSC labour was used on council reclamation schemes; previously, contractors had been used. Things must be even more difficult now that the MSC Community Programme has finished. However, to set against this, Sustrans Ltd has recently entered the field and was instrumental in converting the line from Consett to Chester-le-Street and Sunderland. The company's list of collaborators includes, as well as the councils of Derwentside, Chester-le-Street, Sunderland and County Durham, the Countryside Commission, the Department of the Environment and for good measure, Northern Arts, which provided a substantial grant to create sculptures at each mile point.

The main routes are listed in Appendix B, but it is worth sketching in the overall picture. When the network is complete, there will be three walks from Durham, four from Consett, three from Bishop Auckland and two from

Sustrans Ltd are keen to add interest to their paths by creating exciting sculptures such as this exmple on their Consett to Sunderland route

Barnard Castle. This, without exception, will be the best network of railway walks in the country. As for the present, the established walks are covered by an attractive pack of route cards available from the county council; these deal with the Derwent Walk, the Waskerley Way, the Brandon-Bishop Auckland Walk, the Lanchester Valley Walk and the Deerness Valley Walk. There are over forty-five miles of old railway line in this one pack alone! Copies can be obtained from the address in Appendix A; the cost is very reasonable and can be ascertained beforehand by telephone.

A new railway path from Spennymoor to Bishop Auckland was nearing completion in August 1988, while work had started on the Tees Valley Walk from Barnard Castle to Middleton-in-Teesdale. This is a very long-term project due to the high capital cost involved (mainly arising from bridges and viaducts), but a short section is already open from Lonton to Mickleton, including a viaduct over the River Lune. The county council also owns most of the line from Bishop Auckland to Barnard Castle, but proposes a more limited reclamation on this due to the sparse population of the area through which it passes; the idea is to create a public right of way along the line and then sell the trackbed off. This type of conversion will need a good deal of forethought and care, as the Downs Link in West Sussex (see *Railway Walks: GWR & SR*) was created using a similar policy and cannot be judged a complete success. Some new owners have made parts of this route rather unattractive, creating considerable difficulties for the countryside wardens who have to put things right.

If the prospect of all this walking is a bit much, it might be an idea to visit Beamish Open Air Museum, not far from Chester-le-Street. As mentioned above, this includes a small working railway based around the re-erected Rowley station, but there is much more besides, including working trams, an old colliery and a reconstruction of an entire street from the turn of the century. When Frank Atkinson, the founder, first mooted the idea for the museum in the 1950s, he was greeted with some astonishment and incredulity, but the massive success of the project utterly vindicates his vision. The only caveat is that visitors should allow plenty of time and avoid obviously busy periods such as bank holidays; the crowds at Beamish can be unbelievable! While in the area, it is also worth visiting the Causey Arch (grid reference 201559) and the nearby Tanfield Railway, which is just off the A6076 Sunniside to Stanley road. The Causey Arch is a large and impressive structure, now in the care of Durham County Council; completed in 1727, it is the earliest railway bridge in the world, and originally conveyed a wagonway to a nearby colliery. The Tanfield Railway houses a collection of Tyneside steam locomotives (principally industrial) and is relaying track southwards from Marley Hill.

To the south of the county, the Railway Centre at Darlington deserves a special mention. This is housed in Darlington North Road station, which was built in 1842 as the terminus of the Stockton and Darlington Railway and is probably the oldest railway station in the world. Exhibits include Stephenson's

Locomotion No. 1 and a selection of locomotives in the apple-green livery of the North Eastern Railway, which amalgamated with the Stockton and Darlington in 1863, and worked the moorland line to Stanhope for many years.

There is much else to see in the county, for Durham is justly proud of its industrial heritage and has taken early steps to preserve as much of it as possible. It offers a cornucopia of interest to the modern rambler and railway historian.

Transport and Facilities

Maps: Ordnance Survey: Landranger Series Sheets 87 and 88
Ordnance Survey: One-Inch Map Sheet 84

The Waskerley Way is another route where the modern Landranger maps are not very convenient: the old railway is tucked into the bottom right- and left-hand corners of two adjoining sheets. However, the entire route is shown on the discontinued one-inch map, which can usually be obtained (along with many other Seventh Series sheets) from the address given in Appendix A.

Buses: Go North East
www.simplygo.com
Telephone: (Traveline) 0871 200 22 33

Weardale Motor Services
www.weardalemotorservices.co.uk
Telephone: 01388 528 235

Trains: National Rail Enquiries
www.nationalrail.co.uk
Telephone: 08457 48 49 50

Considering that the railway passenger service between Stanhope and Consett was withdrawn in 1846, most readers will not be surprised to discover that there are no direct buses between Stanhope and Consett via Waskerley or any other route. The ideal solution, once again, is to cajole that long-suffering friend into helping out with a second car. However, this suggests an unfairly bleak picture of public transport, for bus services in the north-east are generally good and it is possible to get reasonably close to the two ends of the line at Stanhope and Consett, although this creates a substantial walk of some fifteen miles.

Stanhope must be approached via Bishop Auckland, a town well served by buses and local trains from Darlington which ply back and forth on one of the area's few surviving passenger branch lines. At Bishop Auckland, the walker should change on to a Weardale service 101 to Stanhope. This runs every hour until 7 p.m. from Monday to Saturday, with five Sunday services in the afternoon and early evening. An exciting development in 1988 and 1989 was the re-introduction on summer Sundays of a passenger train service from Bishop Auckland to Stanhope. Two return trips were made, one in the morning and one in the late afternoon, either of which would be invaluable to anyone who wanted to walk the entire route. The initial service was experimental, so contact the station at Darlington for the current situation.

Consett, alas, lost its railway passenger service on 23 May 1955 and, since then, residents and visitors alike have had to rely on buses. However, there are good services from both Newcastle and Durham, the latter being particularly convenient due to the close proximity of its bus and train stations. The main service is the Simply Go service 15/15A, which runs from Durham to Consett until shortly after 11 p.m.; the journey time is a very reasonable forty minutes.

As for refreshments, the walker will have no difficulty in finding pubs in Stanhope and Consett but, in between, the provision is a little more sparse. The only viable stopping place is the Moorcock at Waskerley, which is located about three-quarters of a mile north of Waskerley station at grid reference 050467. The pub has an efficient and welcoming fire (very necessary in these parts) plus the county's largest beer-garden – 3,000 acres of open moorland.

Given the overall remoteness of the area, it is a good idea to take a packed lunch. For that matter, it is sensible to take some warm protective clothing in case the weather takes a turn for the worse. In places on these moors, the only thing between the walker and the heavens is the sky – there is no protection from any winds that blow. The fact that it may be summer is no guarantee of gentle, sun-kissed breezes, as I know from personal experience!

10

THE DERWENT WALK

CONSETT TO SWALWELL

Introduction

The Derwent Valley has long been a popular retreat for Tynesiders wishing to escape from the hurly-burly of Newcastle; writers talk in glowing terms of its beauty, its steep, wooded hillsides and the gurgling burns that flow down to join the River Derwent. It is little wonder that the Derwent Walk established by Durham County Council in 1971 is the most popular railway path in the area.

The railway originally formed the northern part of the so-called Consett branch; this ran from Durham to Newcastle in a large west-facing loop, which took in Lanchester, Consett and Rowlands Gill. Even allowing for the industrial and mining development which accompanied the railway, the route remained predominantly rural, with only localized pockets of industry. The Lanchester part of the route opened in 1862 and contemporary commentators wrote in bucolic terms of agricultural labourers looking up from their work in the cornfields to see the passing of the first train. Of course, the railway itself has now gone and, were it still there, the modern farmer would view it from the cab of a tractor. However, the mines and much associated industry have gone too, and with them this delightful area has lost the disfigurement of smoke and colliery pit-heads. Anyone who viewed the north-east as a waste land, full of industry and slagheaps, would find a walk along the Consett branch today something of an eye-opener.

The Derwent Valley part of the route is also a veritable feast for the railway rambler, for it features no less than four substantial viaducts. From an engineering point of view, this puts it in the same league as the Great Central Way and the Keswick Railway Footpath. Wandering along this green, woodland path with its dramatic viaducts, high embankments and deep cuttings, it is easy to forget the history of the line, yet the Derwent Valley was once the battleground where rival companies fought over competing claims to a share of the valuable traffic to and from Newcastle. For one tantalizing month in the summer of 1861, it looked as if the Derwent Valley line would be constructed as part of a major trunk route from West Auckland to Newcastle, carrying trains of the London and North Western Railway to and from Liverpool. Such a line would have required colossal engineering works, but then it was designed to link into the Stainmore route, which already had breathtaking viaducts at Deepdale and Belah. Had the route ever materialized in this form, it would have made one of the greatest railway journeys in the country.

History

The first proposals to construct a railway through the Derwent Valley arose in 1844 during the Railway Mania, when a Newcastle, Shotley and Weardale Junction Railway was suggested. The scheme came to nothing, but in 1859 a Newcastle and Derwent Valley Railway was proposed, to run from Scotswood Bridge (on the Newcastle and Carlisle Railway) to Hownes Gill. This attracted the interest of a number of companies which wanted an independent route to Newcastle, namely the London and North Western, the North British and the Stockton and Darlington Railways. The scheme therefore represented a considerable intrusion into the territory of the North Eastern Railway, which regarded Newcastle as an important hub of its network, even though it did not exercise a monopoly in the city.

November 1859 saw the first shots fired in what proved to be a lengthy and costly battle for control of the Derwent Valley. In that month the promoters of the Newcastle and Derwent Valley scheme deposited their plans with the local authorities, but the NER had rushed its own surveyors into the field and deposited plans for a rival scheme at the same time. It became obvious that the 1860 Parliamentary session would be crucial and the NER prepared its ground by courting the S & D with a view to amalgamation. As a result, it effectively detached the S & D from the enemy camp and caused the bill for the Newcastle and Derwent Valley Railway to fail. Any rejoicing by the NER was short-lived, however, for its opponents were incensed, and retaliated by opposing every NER bill currently before the House. All three, including the NER's own Derwent Valley bill, accordingly failed later in the session.

Worse was yet to come, for in 1861 the NER's opponents presented a bill for a proposed Newcastle, Derwent and Weardale Railway. The original scheme did at least have the merit of breaching NER territory with a relatively minor branch line; this proposed to invade it with a heavily-engineered main line, some thirty miles in length. The new railway would run from Newcastle to West Auckland, where trains would continue via the Stainmore route to Tebay and Liverpool; a large number of branch lines were also envisaged to tap into the lucrative mining and manufacturing traffic in the area. Against this Goliath, the NER fielded the Blaydon and Conside Bill, which was exactly the same as its previous presentation and proposed an NER branch line from Blaydon to Consett.

There was intense rivalry in the 1861 Parliamentary session. The NER and its supporters denounced the proposed Newcastle, Derwent and Weardale Railway as 'useless and unnecessary', but protagonists of the scheme were extremely well prepared and undermined most, if not all, of the substantial objections. As a result, the House of Commons approved the preamble of the ND & W Bill, but rejected the Blaydon and Conside Bill. The NER was now on the brink of defeat, so it could hardly believe its good fortune when the House of Lords overturned the Commons' decision on 27 July 1861; its opponents were equally dumbfounded. However, the NER's confidence was shaken and it decided to finish off the ND & W scheme by a method more reliable than the debating chamber – diplomacy and compromise. In 1862, it accordingly approached the LNWR and NBR with a view to reaching an agreement on the routing of trans-Pennine traffic and access to Newcastle. Concessions were made and when the Blaydon and Conside Bill was presented for the third time in 1862, nothing stood in its way. It was finally passed on 17 July that year.

Now that the threat of a rival scheme had been removed, the NER did not need to hurry itself and, as a result, there was no construction activity for the next two years. However, in April 1864 the troubled Consett ironworks were put on a sound financial footing, and this revived the railway's interest in the line; it now had a potential customer, and a big one at that. Work commenced in 1865 and was largely complete by early 1867. The Irish navvies who constructed the line certainly had their work cut out, for the list of engineering works in the Derwent Valley is impressive. Apart from the five viaducts (the one at Swalwell is not part of the walk), there were several high embankments and deep cuttings, some of which required stone retaining walls to a height of 4 ft to prevent slippage on to the line. Goods services were inaugurated on 18 June 1867, passenger services following six months later, on 2 December. Stations were provided at Shotley Bridge, Ebchester, Lintz Green, Rowlands Gill and Swalwell, although the latter was not ready for the official opening due to difficulties in obtaining the land. The line was laid to double track between Lintz Green and Rowlands Gill in order to allow plenty of room for trains to pass.

At the Consett end, the new line formed an end-on junction at Blackhill with the existing Lanchester Valley line from Durham. The whole circular route became known as the Consett branch and was regarded (if not always operated) as a single entity. The initial passenger service along the Derwent Valley was three trains in each direction daily, but this was increased to four in 1869. At the end of that year another improvement was made when third-class carriages were added to the

A westbound special headed by two ex-LNER 2-6-0 locomotives, Nos 62022 and 62023, seen crossing Rowlands Gilt Viaduct in 1953

N.E. Stead Collection

trains, following local representations. Passenger traffic expanded right up to the First World War and, as it did so, the services were correspondingly improved. By 1914 the timetable had reached its peak, with twelve trains per day from Newcastle to Blackhill and nine in the opposite direction; various extras and short journeys completed the picture. This pattern remained fairly static until 1920, when bus services in the valley began to have a serious impact on railway passenger traffic; as noted elsewhere, this was largely due to wartime improvements in the reliability and efficiency of the internal combustion engine. The impact of the buses was particularly rapid and damaging because, with the exception of Rowlands Gill, none of the stations were centrally placed. In addition to this, some of them involved steep climbs from the villages they served, which were situated on the valley floor.

The freight traffic was a lot more resilient; it had been important from the start and continued to grow. The main customers were collieries, coke-ovens, brickworks, paper-mills, dairy farms and the livestock mart at Blackhill. The dairy farms, of course, provided milk, the main centres being Ebchester and Rowlands Gill. When Michael Flanders and Donald Swann lamented the disappearance of milk churns, porters and cats on seats from country railway stations, they were describing a scene that was more or less universal, even though the obvious image today might be of some rustic Devon halt. In time the collieries began to close but, at Rowlands Gill, a substantial timber traffic developed by way of compensation; most of this was bound for Liverpool.

By the 1900s the traffic generally had expanded to the point where the long single-track sections were creating unwelcome bottle-necks and, as a result, the NER decided in September 1903 to double the section from Swalwell to Rowlands Gill. This work took just over four years to complete and involved widening the viaducts at Swalwell and Lockhaugh (north of Rowlands Gill) together with the usual selection of embankments and cuttings. As in the initial construction, some of these cuttings required substantial stone retaining walls to prevent slippage on to the line. The widening of the viaducts was also carried out in an extremely careful and sympathetic manner, so that, at Lockhaugh today, the structure does not appear to have been built in two stages.

The major decline set in after the Second World War. The first victim was High Westwood station: this opened in 1909 as the only addition to the initial provision but was closed on 4 May 1942. It is believed that the timber buildings were in a poor state of repair and that the LNER was unwilling to invest money in a lost cause, such was the station's poor revenue. The Sunday passenger trains were axed next, disappearing a few years after the end of the war. In 1951, the newly formed British Railways provided the worst ever passenger service over the line, with just three trains from Blackhill to Newcastle and only two in the opposite direction. By contrast, the competing buses were now running approximately every ten minutes. In this timetable, intermediate stations were also omitted for the first time; Shotley Bridge, Ebchester and Swalwell were the first to see these 'express' trains rush through without stopping. By 1952, the passenger situation was disastrous, with only thirty-six tickets issued at Ebchester and just two at nearby Lintz Green throughout the entire year. It therefore came as no surprise when Shotley Bridge and Ebchester were closed to all traffic on 21 September 1953. Lintz Green and Swalwell suffered the same fate on 2 November the same year, although Swalwell retained goods traffic and, surprisingly, excursion train facilities. This left Rowlands Gill as the only intermediate passenger station on the branch, and it too succumbed on 1 February 1954 when the Derwent Valley passenger service was withdrawn altogether. Passenger trains continued to run from Newcastle to Blackhill via Annfield Plain, over part of the eastern section of the old Stanhope and Tyne Railway, but this too lost its passenger service the following year (1955).

Freight traffic now began to suffer badly as well, though not through competition so much as the closure of local collieries. The biggest batch of closures occurred in 1955, when parcels facilities were also withdrawn from Swalwell – a seemingly insignificant economy in comparison with the disappearance of so much valuable coal traffic. These changes were accompanied by understandable rationalizations to the track. When Swalwell was closed

A busy scene at Shotley Bridge station in the days before the First World War. In the station forecourt horses and carts with their two uniformed drivers can be seen awaiting passengers from the incoming train

Beamish, North of England Open Air Museum

completely on 7 March 1960, only Rowlands Gill provided anything approaching a regular traffic on the line, and this travelled north to Newcastle; the section from Rowlands Gill to Blackhill was already dead on its feet. When Rowlands Gill finally closed to all traffic on 11 November 1963, the whole line was brought into disuse. It was dismantled from north to south between 1964 and 1965, although Blackhill remained open for goods and coal traffic via other routes. The Derwent Valley line thus missed its centenary by a mere four years and, for a while, was left to its fate amid the silent growth of trees and weeds.

The Line Today

After it was lifted by British Railways, the line went into suspended animation, but in 1971 Durham County Council began to convert the section from Blackhill to Swalwell into a linear country park. The work was considerable, for in places the trackbed was almost blocked by gorse, birch, willow and pine; it does not take long for nature to reclaim her own. Apart from the clearance work, many viaducts and bridges had to be repaired, although a number of underbridges were demolished because they were considered 'unnecessary and dangerous' probably a euphemism for 'costly to maintain'. Happily, however, all the bridges between Rowlands Gill and Swalwell were retained.

It was proposed to restore the remaining stations to 'some of their former glory', but this could not have included the station buildings, for none survive today, if indeed they survived closure of the line in 1963. If it is any consolation, they were very plain, single-storey buildings, their modesty reflecting the fact that the contractor's finances were extremely stretched by the time of their construction. However, several of the station houses survive, and these now overlook the car-parks and picnic areas.

The trackbed was initially seeded with grass, but this proved unequal to the task and has since been replaced with the consolidated ash surface so typical of other railway paths in the area. The only significant problem today is damage by horses which are thoughtlessly cantered or galloped; I have witnessed first-hand how this tears out lumps of surface material. The damage was so severe by the winter of 1987/8 that Durham County Council imposed a total ban on horseriding while reinstatement work took place. A permit system is now used, although it does not appear to extend to the section of the path in Tyne and Wear; it should do.

The walk is administered by County Durham from Blackhill to Rowlands Gill, and by Tyne and Wear from Rowlands Gill to Swalwell. The only break in continuity is at Rowlands Gill, where redevelopment has claimed part of the old trackbed. Apart from this, it is all intact. The route opened to walkers in July 1972 and cost something in the order of £34,000 to create – a very reasonable figure by any reckoning.

The Walk (10½ miles)

The walk may be picked up in Blackhill at grid reference 101523; this is just off the A691 Leadgate-Shotley Bridge road and conveniently close to the General Hospital. This is offered as a well-signposted landmark and is not intended to suggest that ramblers will require its services! To make doubly sure, the route is described from south-west to north-east so that walkers can enjoy an almost continuous downhill gradient. Only beyond Rowlands Gill is there a short climb and this is hardly demanding at 1 in 440.

The first mile is pleasant walking, with good views over the Derwent Valley to the north. This leads to Shotley Bridge station, where a single platform survives, along with the attractive station house. Shotley Bridge was regarded as a spa until the 1920s and many early visitors travelled here by train seeking

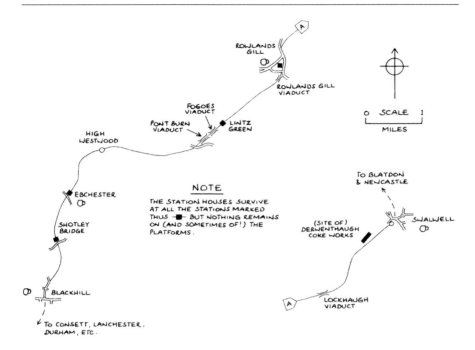

THE STATION HOUSES SURVIVE
AT ALL THE STATIONS MARKED
THUS ▬■▬ BUT NOTHING REMAINS
ON (AND SOMETIMES OF!) THE
PLATFORMS.

THE DERWENT WALK

'the cure'; as a result, it was the destination of many North Eastern Railway excursions. Nowadays, Shotley Bridge is the start and end point for two interesting and well-designed council leaflets on local farming and trees. The farming leaflet describes the route from Shotley Bridge to Rowlands Gill, while the trees leaflet describes the route in the opposite direction; a thoughtful arrangement for energetic walkers who are keen to learn! But joking apart, these leaflets add considerably to the enjoyment of the walk because they explain the views, picking out and describing individual features of interest.

Between here and Ebchester, the first of many concrete snow-posts can be found on the left-hand side of the track. The depth of snow is recorded in Roman numerals – I, II, III, IV; it is a chastening thought that the path could be buried under as much as 4 ft of snow in a bad winter. Away to the north, small commercial woodlands can be seen on the opposite side of the valley. These have been planted alongside small streams which tumble down to the River Derwent; the steepness of their valleys makes them unsuitable for other use. Ebchester station is reached at grid reference 107548 but only the station house

This stone-built bridge spans the Derwent Walk between Blackhill and Shotley Bridge. With its attractive stonework, it is typical of others on the line which have likewise been blackened by soot

now remains. In former days, this was one of the centres from which milk was dispatched; in 1934, for example, 32,640 gallons were despatched from this site. Beyond Ebchester, Broad Oak Farm dominates the views to the north. This is just inside Northumberland and occupies 500 acres of fine sandy loam; many other farmers in the valley have to contend with clay, which is tenaciously sticky when wet, and hard as rock when dry. In fact, the contractors who built the line had to remove the clay from one cutting with gunpowder! Part of the farm is used for grazing bought-in bullocks which, after twenty months of fattening up, will find their way onto Tyneside dinner tables.

The site of High Westwood station is met at grid reference 117561; a steep lane crosses the path here and there is also a small picnic area. As stations on the line go, this was reasonably sited for both the tiny community of High Westwood and the larger village of Hamsterley, but rail travellers were faced with a steep climb up the side of the valley either before or after their journey.

Small wonder that the buses found such ready acceptance. Beyond High Westwood, the line enters the area in which many of the Derwent Valley mines were situated; those at Hamsterley, Lintz Green and Victoria Garesfield brought much valuable traffic on to the branch.

This is also 'viaduct country': after descending to cross the B6310 at Hamsterley Mill, the walker suddenly finds himself on the dizzying height of Pont Burn Viaduct. This is the largest viaduct on the line and reaches a maximum height of 120 ft above the stream from which it takes its name; it has 10 arches of 60 ft each. Barely 100 yds later, the walker arrives on the slightly smaller Fogoes Viaduct. This takes its name from Fogoes Burn, and should, presumably, be called Fogoes Burn Viaduct. It reaches a maximum height of 90 ft and is built on 6 arches of 60 ft each. Unfortunately, both viaducts are surrounded by trees, which makes it difficult, if not impossible, for any photographer who wants to capture their splendour on film. They are connected by a short embankment, which, needless to say, is surrounded by open fields! The bricks from which they are constructed were made from clay deposits discovered just north of Rowlands Gill – a classic example of Victorian entrepreneurial enterprise.

Shortly after the viaducts, Lintz Green station is reached. This is a remote spot, and the station always served a very scattered community. The station house remains, together with an overbridge, from which steps, complete with kissing-gates and railings, lead down onto the two deserted platforms. These steps were erected in 1883 at a cost of £160. They led from a muddy lane which was the subject of argument and proposals for improvement; the modern walker can see that little has changed in over a hundred years! On a more sinister note, Lintz Green witnessed the murder of its station-master by an unknown gunman on 7 October 1911. Mr George Wilson was shot at about 10.45 p.m., just after seeing off the last train from Newcastle to Blackbill. He was carried into the station house, where he died shortly afterwards. Like the Polegate murder in East Sussex (recounted in *Railway Walks: GWR & SR*), no shred of evidence has ever materialized to shed light upon this senseless and inexplicable attack.

Shortly after leaving Lintz Green, the line passes into a wooded cutting where the walker should note the stone retaining-walls built to prevent earth slips; these extend for approximately a quarter of a mile. Finally, the line swings north on to the double-track Rowlands Gill Viaduct before reaching the end of the Durham section of the walk. The River Derwent is the county boundary at this point, so half of the viaduct is in County Durham and the other half in Tyne and Wear; this must make for interesting maintenance arrangements!

Rowlands Gill is now a commuter suburb, but it owes its existence to the coming of the railway and the development of local mines. The official route guide talks of bowler-hatted businessmen catching the 8.21 to town, but not all of its inhabitants were so disciplined and orderly. The local folk-song, 'Wor Nanny's a Mazer', describes a couple who decided to travel by train to the

Blaydon Races but missed the morning departure; there wasn't another one until seventeen minutes to one. They thus had plenty of time to kill, but Nanny's delight at finding a 'pubbilick hoose' near by, which served the 'best bittor beor', turned to inebriation as the long hours ticked by. Eventually, she became so drunk that the landlord had her 'hoyed ootside o' the door'. Her husband continues the lament:

> Wen aa think o' the trubble aa'd wiv hor that day
> aa'd like te borst oot and cry.

A mazer, by the way, is an historical term, meaning a 'hardwood drinking-bowl, usually silver-mounted', so a loose translation of the title might be 'Our Nanny's a Beer jug'. The strong dialect of the area is celebrated in a light-hearted local guide entitled *Larn Yersel' Geordie*.

A few instructions are necessary to get from the County Durham to the Tyne and Wear section of the walk. The Durham section ends by a minor road, where the walker should turn right. Proceed downhill to the B6314 (only a hundred yards or so) and there turn left. It is now just under a quarter of a mile to another T-junction, this time with the A694. Rowlands Gill station will be passed on the left, betrayed by yet another station house in the now familiar style; it is located at grid reference 167585. On reaching the A694, turn right, proceed past a garage and as far as the parapets of an old railway bridge. A small car-park is situated here (grid reference 167589) and the trackbed may now be regained for an unobstructed walk to Swalwell.

This section of the branch was doubled between 1903 and 1908, which necessitated widening all the embankments, cuttings and viaducts. In the first cutting north of Rowlands Gill, the railway was able to buy extra land to create better slopes, but, near Swalwell, stone retaining-walls again had to be installed to prevent land slips; once more, clay was the problem. The main feature of interest is Lockhaugh Viaduct, which is reached at grid reference 181599. Photographers will be pleased to hear that, unlike the others, this is not entirely surrounded by trees. A path leads off on the right to meadows beside the River Derwent. This is a delightful spot, much enjoyed by locals, which affords excellent views of the viaduct. Sadly, its parapets have been the victims of depredation by vandals, for several huge stones have been dislodged and plunged into the valley below.

On approaching Swalwell, the walker may be able to see traces of Derwenthaugh cokeworks on the left-hand side of the line. These were long a feature of the walk, but were in the process of being demolished in summer 1988. The works were served by their own branch line and, when I visited the area, an isolated signal-box and crossing-keeper's hut still stood forlornly amidst the ruination. Most of the works buildings had been reduced to a long heap of rubble but the land was elsewhere being restored to its original contours. In

Lockhaugh Viaduct spans the River Derwent north of Rowlands Gill and was doubled in the early years of this century – the join is just visible underneath the arches. Lockhaugh is one of four viaducts on the line

time, it may be impossible to tell that any industrial plant stood here at all.

The site of Swalwell station is met at grid reference 199619. The remains of a platform lie half-overgrown on the left-hand side, but these are easily missed. The path now enters a large open space, which accommodates a car-park, toilets, information centre and water-garden, before joining a track which runs alongside a football ground. This joins a main road at grid reference 199622. A low stone viaduct once carried the line on towards Blaydon: only a few arches of this remain today but the last of them supports an impressive railway montage which advertises the start of the Derwent Walk. Perhaps in time a similar grand entrance will be provided at Consett.

Further Explorations

Many other local walks have already been mentioned in the previous chapter, but, until recently, the list of railway paths in Tyne and Wear was rather modest. However, the Newburn to Wylam Wagonway is of interest as it passes the birthplace of George Stephenson and gives a four and a half mile walk along the north bank of the River Tyne. It starts just west of Newburn at grid reference 163655 and extends to Wylam Bridge at grid reference 110642; this is a particularly fine bowstring bridge, which can be seen from passing trains on the Newcastle-Carlisle line. Stephenson's cottage is passed at grid reference 127651. Though this is now owned by the National Trust, it is not open to the public; the exterior has probably not changed much since Stephenson's time. He moved away at the age of eight in 1789 – the year of the French Revolution. The route of the wagonway has seen many changes over the years: it was in use when Stephenson lived at Wylam and was ultimately adopted as a branch of the North Eastern Railway. It closed on 11 March 1968, having survived long enough to see service by BR diesel multiple units.

The list of railway-path proposals in Tyne and Wear is very great, although many of them are only going to be one or two miles long – a lot of the colliery branches were not much more than this anyway. Many of the proposed routes will take over old trackbeds abandoned by the National Coal Board, a fact which tells its own sad tale of industrial change in the area. However, the eastern end of the Sustrans path from Consett to Sunderland will have seven and a half miles in the county, while a footpath along the western part of the famous Bowes Railway is proposed for extension. Tyne and Wear County Council purchased a section of this line in 1976 and have restored it to working order, complete with a cable-hauled incline; the entrance is at Springwell, near Washington (grid reference 285588).

With its extensive heritage of industrial lines, many of them recently closed, Tyne and Wear is another county well worth watching for the development of its railway-path network.

Transport and Facilities

Map: Ordnance Survey: Landranger Series Sheet 88 (recommended)

Buses: Go North East
            www.simplygo.com
            Telephone: (Traveline) 0871 200 22 33

Trains: National Rail Enquiries
            www.nationalrail.co.uk
            Telephone: 08457 48 49 50

The main bus service along the Derwent Valley is Simply Go's routes 45 and 46, which follow the A694 Blaydon–Consett road. The service is extremely good, every ten minutes during the daytime and an hourly frequency in the evening and on Sundays. At the time of writing, the last return working left Consett at 10.17 p.m. and returned from Newcastle at 11.15 p.m. Monday to Friday. On Saturdays and Sundays, this service runs every half hour.

Pubs are easily found in Consett, Blackhill, Rowlands Gill and Swalwell; the most convenient intermediate establishment is the Derwent Walk Inn at Ebchester station. This stands on the site of the former Station Hotel and could conceivably be the same building, much converted. Two pictures of the old hotel hang in the bar for the benefit of customers who are any good at architectural detective work. Nearer the bottom of the valley, the attractive Chelmsford Hotel in Ebchester Village is an alternative venue for refreshments. It is blissfully easy to get to, being downhill all the way, but the steep climb back to the station gives a clear insight into why so many locals lost their enthusiasm for rail travel.

There are car-parks at Shotley Bridge station, Ebchester station, Rowlands Gill and Swalwell. At Ebchester, the car-parks for the Derwent Walk Inn and the railway path are very close together, so drivers should make sure they choose the right one! There is also no shortage of picnic areas, either at the old station sites or along the rest of the route.

APPENDIX A
Useful Addresses

DAVID ARCHER,
The Pentre
Kerry
Newtown
Montgomeryshire
SY16 4PD
Tel: (01686) 670382.
Supplier of second-hand maps.
www.david-archer-maps.co.uk

THE BRANCH LINE SOCIETY
c/o Mr. A.G. Welsh Membership
Secretary
22 Treemount Court
Grove Avenue
Epsom
Surrey
KT17 4DU
www.branchline.org.uk

CAMRA LTD
The Campaign for Real Ale
230 Hatfield Road
St Albans
Hertfordshire
AL1 4LW
Tel: (01727) 867201
Apart from the National Good Beer
Guide also publishes a useful range
of local pub guides.
www.camra.org.uk

DURHAM COUNTY COUNCIL
Sites Rangers and Ecology
Environment Department
Durham County Council
County Hall
Durham
DH1 5UQ
Tel: (0191) 383 3594
At time of going to press Durham
County was in the middle of a Local
Government Reorganisation and was
due to become a Unitary Authority
from April 2009. The new authority
will take on some of the railway paths
that are currently managed by district
councils in the area. As a result of
these changes the county's website
was being re-designed and no longer
had links to the individual railway
paths.
www.durham.gov.uk

ORDNANCE SURVEY
Customer Service Centre
Romsey Road
Southampton
Hampshire
SO16 4GU
Tele: 08456 050505 (calls charged at
local rate)
www.ordnancesurvey.co.uk

NORTHUMBERLAND RAILWAY
WALKS SOCIETY
c/o Mr. Bill Halliday Membership
Secretary
40 Shearwater Way
Blyth
Northumberland
NE24 3PU
www.northrailwalks.org.uk

RAILWAY RAMBLERS
Membership Secretary
27 Sevenoaks Road
Brockley
London
SE4 1RA.
The specialist club for exploring
abandoned railways on foot.
www.railwayramblers.org.uk

RAMBLERS' ASSOCIATION
Head Office
2nd Floor
Camelford House
87-90 Albert Embankment
London
SE1 7TW
Tel: (0207) 339 8500
www.ramblers.org.uk

SUSTRANS LTD
Head Office
2 Cathedral Square
College Green
Bristol
BS1 5DD
Tel: (0117) 926 8893
A charitable company which
constructs safe off-road routes for
cyclists and pedestrians – the main
builder of railway paths in the UK
and the driving force behind the
National Cycle Network.
www.sustrans.org.uk

TRANSPORT DIRECT
Department for Transport
55 Victoria Street
London
SW1H 0EU
Tel: 0207 944 2522
If you want to plan a journey from
anywhere to anywhere then look no
further than this DfT website.
www.transportdirect.info

Note: The third entry may seem a little out of place in a book about disused
railways, but Camra's local pub guides contain a wealth of information
besides the beers a pub happens to sell. Most of them also give opening
times, whether a pub has a garden and/or public bar (very useful if you
are not attired for the lounge), and whether they do food, and, if so, when.
Pubs are not included if they do not sell at least one beer which conforms
with the Camra definition of 'real ale', so the guides are not comprehensive.
However, they do contain a large enough selection of pubs to take some of the
guesswork out of planning a walk, and I recommend them highly.

APPENDIX B
OFFICIAL RAILWAY WALKS

Very few railway paths are dedicated public rights of way. The majority are 'permissive routes'; that is, the landowner – usually a local authority or other public body – permits their use by pedestrians (always), cyclists (often) and horseriders (sometimes). As such, they may very occasionally be closed, e.g. to permit repairs to the surface.

This list identifies all routes of two miles or more in each county, although I have taken the liberty of including a few shorter favourites, especially where they include a significant engineering structure such as the viaduct at Stamford Bridge. Some of the start points are not easily found, which is why six figure grid references are provided, although most local authorities have made great strides during the last decade in terms of improving signing and trying to make the routes start and end somewhere sensible and obvious.

If you are planning to take a wheelchair out on these routes, it is a good idea to contact the relevant authority beforehand (i.e. county council, district council, unitary authority, Sustrans, etc.) since there are a few practical difficulties. Even a walk which can accommodate a wheelchair throughout may have access controlled by locked gates. Such devices are intended to keep out motorcycles but, unfortunately, they also restrict legitimate and deserving users; your assistant may therefore need to obtain a key, although a 'radar' key already unlocks many Sustrans access controls. Please ensure that all gates are locked securely behind you.

Since work on this list was started in 1988, it reflects the county names and boundaries established by the Heath government in 1974 rather than those introduced (or, in some cases, re-introduced) by John Major's government in 1996. While it might be helpful to re-draft the appendix to reflect current local authority boundaries, they might all be changed again, and it was felt that this was unimportant compared with the need to make the locations of the walks available.

Key to abbreviations
Users
C   Cyclists
CIP   Cyclists (in places)
H   Horse riders
HIP   Horse riders (in places)
W   Walkers

Suitability for Prams, Pushchairs and Wheelchairs
NI   Route not inspected
NO   Route not yet open
UT   Usable throughout
UP   Usable in places
UX   Mostly unusable

Type of Path
DR   Disused railway
DT   Disused tramway

Distances
All distances are in miles

Railway Companies
This appendix does not identify which railway company built or operated which route, but occasionally abbreviations of company names appear in the text for an entry. Most of these abbreviations are well known, e.g.

BR   British Railways, latterly British Rail
DLR   Docklands Light Railway
GCR   Great Central Railway
GER   Great Eastern Railway
GNR   Great Northern Railway
LNER   London & North Eastern Railway
M&GN   Midland & Great Northern Joint Railway
NER   North Eastern Railway

General
NCN   National Cycle Network, usually followed by route number, e.g. NCN24
OS   Ordnance Survey
RUPP   Road Used as a Public Path

Cambridgeshire
Currently, Cambridgeshire has only one railway path of any length, although that will be joined in 2009 by Chesterton to St. Ives (see below). Other sections of publicly accessible trackbed in the county are mere fragments, since the flat fenland landscape makes it very easy to absorb old railways back into surrounding fields.

   Chesterton (Cambridge)–St. Ives: C, H, W, NO, DR, 14m. This old GER line is due to become a guided busway, so its listing here may seem surprising; but read on. Cambridgeshire County Council's promotional leaflet states: 'Pedestrians, cyclists and horse riders will also benefit from a brand new bridleway running all the way from Cambridge Science Park to St. Ives along the route of the Guided Busway.' The conversion of the old railway took place during 2007 and 2008, with final opening due in 2009. The cost is quoted as £116.2 million, with central government contributing £92.5 million. The real progenitor of the project is local traffic congestion, which is expected to worsen significantly by the time 47,500 new homes have been built in the area, as is planned by 2016; the guided busway is an attempt to provide new residents with an alternative to the car. Currently, no grid references can be supplied for this route since it is not yet open.

   Chatteris–Somersham: C, H, W, NI, DR, 6m, TL 386856–TL 371801. A public bridleway dedicated over part of the former GNR and GER joint line between March and St. Ives. The bridleway dedication stops at Somersham Fore Fen, about a mile north of Somersham, so it would be best to follow the route from Chatteris southwards in case public access stops at this point. However, the OS map shows a path continuing on to the edge of Somersham, and it is believed that this is a permissive route to the B1050 at TL 367777. In Chatteris, the bridleway starts at the south western edge of the town, where the A141 (which occupies the trackbed from Wimblington to Chatteris) turns south west.

Cleveland
Guisborough–Morton Carr: C, H, W, NI, DR, 4½m, NZ 622154–NZ 58147. The Guisborough Branch Walkway Nature Reserve, which re-uses most of the former NER branch line from Nunthorpe to Guisborough. The main access is at Pinchinthorpe (NZ 585152). The western end of the trail is about 1½ miles from Nunthorpe via public footpaths.

   Redmarshall Junction (nr. Thorpe Thewles)–Oxbridge (Stockton on Tees): W, NI, DR, 2½m, NZ 406225–NZ 425187. Part of NCN1, and once part of the NER link line from Thorpe Thewles to Thornaby. This route and the next entry are actually parts of the same line; they are separated because a one mile section of trackbed in Thorpe

Thewles is privately owned and no longer possesses the means whereby the railway crossed it. To be specific, this section used to include the twenty arch Thorpe Thewles Viaduct. Cleveland County Council had intended to retain the viaduct as part of the Castle Eden Walkway, but concerns arose about maintenance costs and public safety. Accordingly, the decision was taken to demolish the structure and, in 1979, eleven year old Helen Wilson and twenty year old Laura Grainger blasted it oblivion, having won a competition in the local newspaper to press the plunger that ignited 1,000 lbs. of gelignite packed into 2,800 holes drilled into the brickwork. A few seconds later – no viaduct.

Thorpe Thewles–Station Town (nr. Wingate): W, NI, DR, 9½m, NZ 403238–NZ 409360. The Castle Eden Walkway, part of NCN1; ends in County Durham.

Durham

For many years, Durham County Council routinely demolished rail-over-road bridges on the disused railways it purchased in order to reduce the long term maintenance costs of its railway paths. However, it retained (and continues to maintain) a considerable number of viaducts on these routes. Apart from the major trails listed below, the eastern part of the county contains many shorter railway paths, most of which are fragments of the county's once extensive colliery network. Overall, Durham runs Devon a close second in terms of all that it has achieved with its abandoned railways; for further details, see *Railway Walks: GWR & SR*. The hubs of Durham's railway path network are Broompark (near Durham City), Consett and South Hetton.

Belmont (nr. Durham)–Pittington–Hetton-le-Hole: C, W, NI, DR, 3½m, NZ 314432–NZ 323448–NZ 353471. Part of the former Murton-Sherburn line; ends in Tyne & Wear.

Bishop Auckland–Spennymoor: W, NI, DR, 4½m, NZ 222291–NZ 245337. The Auckland Walk, part of the former line from West Cornforth (Auckland Line Junction) to Bishop Auckland.

Blackhill (Consett)–Swalwell: W, UP, DR, 10½m, NZ 099514–NZ 200621. Once the direct line from Consett to Newcastle; includes four major viaducts. Now part of NCN14, but known as the Derwent Walk after the nearby River Derwent. There is a one mile link path from NZ 099514 southwards to NZ 099493, where a connection is made with The Lanchester Valley Railway Path, The Waskerley Way and The Consett & Sunderland Railway Path. This is a notable location amongst railway paths, for no less than four separate railway-based routes meet here.

Broompark (nr. Durham)–Consett: W, UP, DR, 9m, NZ 254417–NZ 099493. The Lanchester Valley Railway Path, a further part of NCN14. West of Hurbuck, there is a diversion off the trackbed where just over a mile of the old line is now privately owned. East of Hurbuck, there is a very steep-sided embankment which crosses the valley of the Smallhope Burn; the timber-built Hurbuck Viaduct lies buried beneath this structure.

Broompark (nr. Durham)–Crook: W, UP, DR, 11m, NZ 254417–NZ 163361. The Deerness Valley Railway Path, a former colliery line – although modern landscaping has left little sign of its industrial past.

Broompark (nr. Durham)–Bishop Auckland: W, UP, DR, 9½m, NZ 254417–NZ 205306. The Brandon-Bishop Auckland Walk is a long-established railway path which used to continue over Newton Cap Viaduct to the edge of Bishop Auckland. Unfortunately, in 1995, this viaduct was adapted to carry a new alignment of the A689, which makes the end of the walk at NZ 205306 (where the trail joins the road) a completely unsuitable location to park a car prior to a day's walking or cycling. However, with the aid of an OS map, one can follow the Wearside Way into Bishop Auckland; this diversion has the advantages of passing underneath the viaduct – it's an impressive sight – and keeping one away from the traffic noise.

Consett–Weatherhill–Crawleyside (nr. Stanhope): W, UP, DR, 13m, NZ 099493–NY 999424–NY 993405. The Waskerley Way, now part of NCN7, is an old railway with a lot of history. The trail takes its name from the village of Waskerley, which is just over half way along, an old railway community which now has a hint of the deserted village about it. The highlights of the walk are near the two end points – Howns Gill Viaduct just west of Consett, and Weatherhill Incline, just after the junction with the Rookhope branch (see below). Although the official trail ends just above Weatherhill Incline (at NY 999424), walkers will have no difficulty in continuing on to Crawleyside, since a public footpath runs alongside the trackbed for the drop down into the Wear Valley. Crawleyside is less than a mile north of Stanhope.

Consett–Chester-le-Street–Washington: C, W, UT, DR, 18m, NZ 099493–NZ 273535–NZ 313550. The Consett & Sunderland Railway Path, a high quality cycle trail built by Sustrans and featuring some unusual sculptures along the way, including the Beamish Shorthorns by Sally Matthews, a collection of cattle figures made from old JCB parts. The trail ends in Tyne & Wear. This route is so long because it survived as an operational railway serving the steelworks in Consett; when these closed and the line was abandoned, it was converted into a railway path almost immediately. At Washington, the trail continues to Roker (in Sunderland), but this section is not railway-based. (Note that there is a railway path from Washington to Sunderland, but it is on the other, i.e. south, side of the River Wear.)

Darlington (A66)–Dinsdale: C, W, NI, DR, 2m, NZ 327153–NZ 352137. This trail used to start at Darlington (New Road) but in c. 2007 the 2½ mile section from central Darlington to the A66 was converted into a new link road, the B6279. The trail now starts on the east side of the roundabout at NZ 327153.

Haswell–Hart: See entry for South Hetton.

Middleton-in-Teesdale–Barnard Castle: W, NI, DR, 8m, NY 952246–NZ 047175. This is virtually the whole of the Middleton-in-Teesdale branch and is walkable from the B6277 (east of Middleton-in-Teesdale station, now part of a holiday park) to the site of the Tees Viaduct outside Barnard Castle. Includes Mickleton Viaduct. There is a short diversion around the privately restored Romaldkirk station.

Seaham–South Hetton: C,W, UT, DR, 4m, NZ 429488–NZ 384453. The former South Hetton Colliery branch, now converted into a cycle trail (part of NCN1).

Shildon–West Auckland: W, NI, DR, 3½m, NZ 258233–NZ 183266. Starts near the Timothy Hackworth Museum (Soho, Shildon) and follows the trackbed of the Stockton & Darlington Railway. Includes Brusselton Incline.

South Hetton–Haswell–Hart: W, UP, DR, 10m, NZ 384453–NZ 484363. The Haswell to Hart Countryside Walk. The trail is part of NCN1 as far as NZ 408380, which is the site of Wellfield Junction. At this point, walkers and cyclists bound for Hart should bear left (east) and follow NCN14.

Station Town (nr. Wingate)–Thorpe Thewles: W, NI, DR, 9½m, NZ 409360–NZ 403238. The Castle Eden Walkway, part of NCN1; ends in Cleveland. By continuing south on NCN1, this line can be re-joined at Redmarshall Junction and then followed as far as Oxbridge in Stockton-on-Tees; see entry under Cleveland.

Weatherhill–Rookhope: W, NI, DR, 6m, NZ 003432–NY 939429. The start of this branch line is a very remote spot, about three-quarters of a mile north of the old Weatherhill Engine House. The trail, part of NCN7, is the trackbed of the former Weatherhill & Rookhope Railway, which reaches a height of 1,670 ft above sea level, thus making it the highest railway (or rather ex-railway) in the British Isles. Connects at Weatherhill with the Waskerley Way (see entry above for Consett-Weatherhill-Crawleyside).

Wellfield Junction (nr. Wingate)–Trimdon Colliery: C, W, NI, DR, 2m, NZ 408380–NZ 389362. Starts at Wellfield Junction from the South Hetton-Haswell-Hart trail, and connects at Station Town (via a short walk across the village) with the Castle Eden Walkway to Thorpe Thewles.

West Auckland–Ramshaw: W, NI, DR, 2m, precise grid references not known but the trail can be picked up in West Auckland at NZ 170267. Part of the former Stainmore route from Darlington to Tebay, converted into a public footpath in late 2005. Another section of this line has been re-used in Cumbria between Stenkrith and Hartley.

Essex

Braintree–Start Hill (nr. Bishops Stortford): CIP, HIP, W, UP, DR, 15m, TL 760227–TL 519213. Essex County Council's popular Flitch Way, which includes restored stations at Rayne and Takeley. Currently, cyclists and horse riders have been granted local access only and may not use the whole length of the trail, although parts of it are now incorporated into NCN16.

Witham–Maldon East & Heybridge: C, W, NI, DR, 5m, TL 826150–TL TL 847080. Most of this branch has been converted into a cyclepath called the Blackwater Rail Trail. The most convenient place to join the path at Heybridge is the access point near the entrance to Elms Farm Park, off Heybridge Approach (the B1018). Note that the section between Olivers Farm and Wickham Bishops is still privately owned: this part of the route includes two two timber viaducts (designated ancient monuments) which were restored by Essex County Council in 1995. The official route between Olivers Farm and Wickham Bishops follows the B1018 and public footpaths. The station building at Maldon East & Heybridge survives, with its impressive listed Jacobean style nine-arch arcaded frontage; in August 2004, it was in use as offices.

Wivenhoe–Brightlingsea: W, NI, DR, 5m, TM 053208–TM 083166. This route starts about 1½ miles south east of Wivenhoe station. The old trackbed can be reached near Alresford Grange by following a convenient footpath along the edge of the River Colne. The line is bisected by Alresford Creek thanks to a missing bridge, but there is a ford just under half a mile upstream accessible by footpaths on both sides.

Hertfordshire

Harpenden–Hemel Hempstead: C, W, NI, DR, 6m, TL 134152–TL 059074. The so-called Nicky Line, part of NCN57. The railway was renowned for its steep gradients, but is still easy going for walkers and cyclists.

St. Albans–Hatfield: C, W, UP, DR, 6½m, TL 149061–TL 232092. The popular Alban Way, now part of NCN61. Some good artefacts survive in St. Albans, including a viaduct over the River Ver, an impressive tunnel beneath the Midland main line, and London Road station which is now used as offices.

Welwyn Garden City–Hertford: W, NI, DR, 6½m, TL 255125–TL 317119. The Cole Greenway, named after the intermediate station at Cole Green. On-road links at Welwyn provide a signed connection to the Ayot Greenway (see next entry). At the Hertford end, the trackbed can be reached via the RUPP which starts at TL 321121.

Welwyn Garden City–Wheathampstead: W, NI, DR, 2½m, TL 238134–TL 186144. The Ayot Greenway, named after the intermediate station at Ayot, which is just over a mile from George Bernard Shaw's former home at Ayot St. Lawrence. The trail was upgraded in early 2007 to cope with the high level of use it now receives, which is not entirely surprising since it now forms part of NCN57.

Humberside

Beverley–Market Weighton: W, UX, DR, 11m, SE 877420–TA 037409. The Hudson Way, named after the nineteenth century 'railway king' George Hudson, who kept 'everything but his accounts' and ended his life in public disgrace and humiliation; proof, were it needed, that huge financial scandals are not a modern phenomenon.

Bubwith–nr. Shiptonthorpe (A164): W, UX, DR, 9½m, SE 708355–SE 840405. Part of the old NER line from Selby to Market Weighton, now known as The Bubwith Rail Trail; a real rural backwater, and quite delightful. At Bubwith, the best access is from SE 714357. The end of the trail near Shiptonthorpe is very remote, although Market Weighton is only about two miles east as the crow flies.

Hull–Hornsea: C, W, UP, DR, 15m, TA 106297–TA 208477. The Hornsea Rail Trail, which is also the easternmost section of the Trans Pennine Trail (NCN65). When leaving Hull, take care at Wilmington (TA 107305) to follow NCN65 to the north east, and not NCN1 to the north. Once beyond Sutton on the Hill, this is another extremely rural route. Hornsea is delightful, with its sea front recalling the genteel days of Victorian and Edwardian seaside holidays. The LNER poster which declared that 'Skegness is so bracing' might have said the same of the whole east coast!

Hull (Marfleet)–Keyingham–nr. Patrington: W, NI, DR, 11m, TA 123297–TA 300234. This is most of the former branch line from Hull to Withernsea, although it should be noted that the last four miles between Patrington and Withernsea are privately owned and therefore not part of the trail.

Stamford Bridge–Gate Hemsley: C, W, UT, DR, ½m, SE 712552–SE 705556. The shortness of this route, part of NCN66, should preclude it from this gazetteer. However, it is notable since it includes Stamford Bridge Viaduct, which was restored in 2005, having narrowly escaped demolition in 1991. The structure comprises fifteen brick built arches and a central cast iron span. The eastern part of this line, between Market Weighton and Beverley, has been in use as the Hudson Way for many years. The Gate Hemsley end of the route is in North Yorkshire; the village is reached via a trail alongside the A166.

Lincolnshire
Anton's Gowt–Boston: C, W, DR, NI, 2m, TF 300475–TF 324445. Part of the former GNR line from Lincoln to Boston, now incorporated into NCN1. For further details, see entry for Lincoln–Bardney.

Horncastle–Woodhall Spa: W, UP, mainly DR, 6½m, TF 256680–TF 217647. The Spa Trail, now part of the Viking Way. The start points are TF 258694 in Horncastle and TF 194631 in Woodhall Spa, with a canal towpath and public rights of way being used to bypass the privately owned sections of the line.

Lincoln–Bardney: C, W, UT, DR, 9m, SK 983708–TF 112691. This trail forms part of NCN1 between Hull and Harwich and is known as the 'Water Rail Way' due to the proximity of the River Witham, local canals and drainage channels. The restored Bardney Lock Viaduct is a notable feature near the southern end of the trail. In 2006, Sustrans secured funding for the rest of NCN1 into Boston, but it is not known if more of the route will be moved on to the old Lincoln-Boston railway.

London
The demand for land in London is insatiable, so it is perhaps surprising that any old railways there have become rail trails at all. The route from Custom House to Beckton is continuous, but the route from Finsbury Park to Alexandra Palace requires the use of an A to Z atlas; fortunately, the detours are easy since there are plenty of roads and paths locally.

Custom House–Beckton: C, W, UT, DR, 1m, TQ 410809–TQ 431815. Part of the former GER branch from Custom House to Beckton which was not re-used as part of the Docklands Light Railway. Starts just east of Custom House station and then follows a ruler straight course to the A117 opposite the DLR station at Beckton.

Finsbury Park–Highgate–Alexandra Palace: CIP, W, UP, mainly DR, 4m, TQ 313873–TQ 287880 and TQ 284891–TQ 292899. This trail starts near Finsbury Park station and can be followed with ease to Highgate Tunnels, where it links into a backstreet near Highgate underground station. North west of Highgate, London Underground has reclaimed part of the trackbed for a new depot for rolling stock on the Northern Line. (It is surprising to see rows of electric trains parked in a cutting where railway ramblers used to walk freely in the early days of the club.) However, the path around the western edge of Highgate Park offers a convenient detour which remains close to the old line until it can be rejoined at Cranley Gardens. From Cranley Gardens, the trackbed is a cycle trail which passes over St. James's Viaduct before reaching Muswell Hill Primary School, formerly the site of Muswell Hill station. The path then reaches the grounds of Alexandra Palace, where the trackbed is privately owned and inaccessible. However, footpaths allow the line to be traced from nearby, while a detour via adjacent Dukes Avenue leads to Alexandra Palace station, which has now been fully restored as a community centre.

Norfolk

Aylsham–North Walsham: W, NI, DR, 5m, TG 207281–TG 279302. Part of The Weavers Way, a long distance footpath of 56 miles linking Cromer with Great Yarmouth. Was formerly a section of the M&GNR branch line from Melton Constable to Great Yarmouth. See also entry for Bengate–Stalham (another section of the same line).

Aylsham–Reepham–Hellesdon–Norwich: C, H, W, UP, DR, 21m, TG 195264–TG 225093 (Hellesdon). Marriott's Way, now extended into central Norwich as the Wensum Valley Walk and forming part of NCN1 between Reepham and Norwich. The route utilises part of the former GER line from Wroxham to County School, which passed under the M&GNR's line from Melton Constable to Norwich at Themelthorpe. British Rail linked these two lines together in 1960 via the new 'Themelthorpe Curve', which was constructed for the use of freight trains from Anglian Cement and Concrete Works at Lenwade. The closure of this line (i.e. Lenwade to Wroxham via Themelthorpe) in 1983 paved the way for the creation of this rail trail. The surface has been improved in recent years, but there are still a few trouble spots in wet weather, e.g. at Themelthorpe.

Aylsham–Wroxham: C, W, NI, DR, 9m, TG 195265–TG 303187. The Bure Valley Footpath and Cycle Way, which runs alongside the narrow gauge Bure Valley Railway throughout its length. The BVR finishes at Hoveton, which is just north of Wroxham station on the still open line from Norwich to Cromer. The route started life as part of the the GER line from Wroxham to County School.

Bengate (North Walsham)–Stalham: W, NI, DR, 4½m, TG 207281–TG 279302. A further section of The Weavers Way; see entry for Aylsham–North Walsham.

Norwich, Old Lakenham–nr. Chapelfield Grove: C, W, DR, ¾m, TG 230060–TG 229077. Part of the old GER line from Victoria Junction to Norwich Victoria, now known as the Lakenham Way following a £429,000 improvement scheme.

Stow Bedon–Hockham Heath: W, NI, DR, 3m, TL 940966–TL 927925. Part of the former GER line from Thetford to Swaffham, now known as the Great Eastern Pingo Trail – an 8 mile circular route on the eastern edge of the Breckland area. Access is off the A1075 near Stow Bedon, with car parking in the old railway station yard (TL 940966). Three-quarters of a mile before the site of Wretham & Hockham station, the trail merges with the Peddars Way as it heads north-west along the course of an old Roman road.

Swalfield–Old Hall Street: W, NI, DR, 1½m, TG285316–TG298329. Part of the 20 mile long Paston Way, which links North Walsham with Cromer. Originally part of the Norfolk & Suffolk Joint Railway, a combined GER and M&GNR company which once connected the same two towns.

Northumberland

Greenshaw Plain (nr. Hexham)–Langley: W, NI, DR, 7m, NY 893661–NY 828613. Part of the former NER branch from Hexham to Allendale. The western end of Hexham northern bypass (A69T) has taken over the first three quarters of a mile of the trackbed out of Hexham, but the seven miles from Glendue Sidings (NY 893661) to Langley are now a footpath. Glendue Sidings were situated at the point where the trackbed diverges from the A69T.

Haltwhistle–Alston: CIP, W, UP, DR, 12m, NY 710632–NY 717467. The South Tyne Trail (part of NCN68), a scenic rural branch line which continues into Cumbria, q.v. Connects with Lord Carlisle's Railway (see entry above) at Lambley. Between Alston and Kirkhaugh, the trail runs alongside the narrow gauge South Tynedale Railway. The principal engineering feature en route is the towering Lambley Viaduct. In 2005, Railway Ramblers made a substantial contribution towards the restoration of Alston Arches Viaduct, just south of Haltwhistle station on the Newcastle-Carlisle line. It is believed that the trail now starts from the Alston bay platform at Haltwhistle station.

Deadwater–Kielder: W, NI, DR, 1½m, NY 603969–NY 623941. This route is labelled on the OS Explorer map as 'Bundle and go to Kielder Stane Walk', which is possibly the worst name ever devised for a trackbed walk; presumably, it has some other significance which is lost on railway ramblers. It is part of the former Border Counties

Railway between Riccarton Junction (in Scotland) and Reedsmouth. This route has not been checked personally, but the information was supplied in 1988 by the Forestry Commission and should be reliable. (Source: Rhys ab Elis, *Railway Rights of Way*, Second Supplement, 1988, Branch Line Society.) Only short and isolated sections of the BCR are accessible to the public: there is another one at Falstone village, where a mile of the old trackbed has been dedicated as a public bridleway: it runs west from NY 725875 to Kielder Dam, beyond which the line is now submerged.

Lambley–Tindale: W, NI, DR, 3½m, NY 662586 NY–621591. Part of Lord Carlisle's Railway – a scenic former colliery line from Lambley to Brampton Junction, which straddles the border with Cumbria. The link to Brampton Junction is not yet open, so walkers are advised to start from Lambley and divert on to local footpaths, bridleways and lanes until such time as access is negotiated all the way through. In February 2007, Sustrans reported that the extension from Tindale to Brampton was in the planning stages, and expressed the hope that the route would be open throughout 'within the next couple of years'. Unconfirmed reports have been received that the route is now open as far west as Hallbankgate, but please do not trespass beyond Tindale if this is not the case.

Newburn (Newcastle)–Wylam Bridge: W, NI, DR, 4½m, NZ 163655–NZ 110642. This route should be a 'must' for all railway ramblers, since it passes the cottage where George Stephenson was born (NZ 127651). Unfortunately, although owned by the National Trust, the cottage is not open to the public. The eastern part of the route is in Tyne & Wear.

Wannie Circular Walk: W, NI, partly DR, 6½m, NZ 037865–NZ 034886 towards Morpeth and NZ 037865–NZ 011870 towards Reedsmouth. Named after the Wansbeck Valley Railway, this walk is based in the grounds of Wallington Hall (NZ 029842), a large National Trust estate near Scot's Gap, and covers sections of the branch lines to Rothbury and Reedsmouth Junction. Access is at Scot's Gap (NZ 038864). When initially established, the walk was open only from June to October due to lambing and other farming activities. This may have changed, but please enquire locally before arranging a visit outside the months listed. (Contact Wallington Hall, Cambo, Morpeth, Northumberland, NE61 4AR; tel. 01670 773600.) If you are in this area, the 390 ft long Twizell Viaduct (which crosses the River Twill north east of Coldstream) has been renovated and made part of a public path. Perhaps one day this will form part of a longer railway.

Suffolk

Hadleigh–Raydon: C, H, W, UX, DR, 2½m, TM 030422–TM 060404. The western end of the GER's rural branch line from Bentleigh to Hadleigh, now known as The Hadleigh Railway Walk.

Haughley Junction–Brockford & Wetheringsett: W, NI, partly DR, 6m, TM 042627–TM 129659. This trail, the Middy Railway Footpath, was opened by Mid Suffolk District Council in 1995, but uses local rights of way to join together short sections of trackbed and is not a railway path in the usual sense of the term. The Mid Suffolk Light Railway Society has established a railway centre at Brockford & Wetheringsett station, where an admission ticket entitles visitors to walk a further section of trackbed in its ownership.

Southwold–Blythburgh: W, UX, DR, 3½m, TM 505766–TM 481748. The eastern end of the narrow gauge Southwold Railway, which closed in 1929. A modern footbridge carries walkers over the River Blyth on the plinths of the railway's original swing bridge.

Sudbury–Lavenham: This is actually three separate routes (The Valley Walk, The Melford Walk and part of St. Edmund Way) which are close enough to form a longer walk of about 9m, with nearly 7m on the southern section of the old railway from Sudbury to Bury St. Edmunds.

Sudbury–Long Melford: C, W, UT, DR, 2½m, TL 861447–TL 874458. A popular walking and cycling trail known as The Valley Walk. Arriving in Long Melford from the

Sudbury direction, head north along the B1064 to pick up the The Melford Walk, which is signed off this road at the site of a demolished rail-over-road bridge.

Long Melford: W, UX, DR, 1¼m, TL 861447–TL 874458. The Melford Walk, a linear route along the trackbed to the east of the village, which includes a number of intact railway bridges. At the north end (which comes out in Bull Lane), turn right to reach the A134; St. Edmund Way lies about a mile north along this road on the east side. However, rather than walking along this busy main road, I recommend this route: (1) Follow the minor road to Acton Place as far as TL 882460; (2) Turn left here on to a bridleway (Roydon Drift) and follow this to TL 876468 just north of Lodge Farm on the A134; (3) At TL 876468, turn right on to a footpath which meets St. Edmund Way just before it joins the old railway for the final 3 miles into Lavenham.

North of Acton Place–Lavenham: W, UX, DR, 3m, TL 884475–TL 910495. Part of St. Edmund Way incorporating The Lavenham Walk at its eastern end.

Tyne and Wear

At the time that Tyne & Wear was abolished, its county council had plans to create many cycle trails on former colliery lines. Fortunately, this project went ahead under Gateshead Council, which now maintains most (if not all) of the routes listed below. This council has also set up a helpful website which can be viewed at www.cycle-routes.org/cycle-gateshead/general/leisure.html. It really is worth exploring this site, since it provides detailed schematic maps of each route, and even gradient profiles.

Allerdene (Team Valley)–Wrekenton–Pelaw: C, W, NI, DT, 4m, NZ 255586–NZ 272595–NZ 295623. This trail follows most of the trackbed of the Teams Colliery Waggonway, which connected coal mines at Ravensworth Park (in the Team Valley) with coal staithes at Pelaw Main on the River Tyne. It is a rather hilly route, thanks to the waggonway's inclines, and includes two fairly short on-road sections.

Blackhill (Consett)–Swalwell: W, UP, DR, 10½m, NZ 099514–NZ 200621. The Derwent Walk, which starts in Durham, q.v. Most of the minor rail-over-road bridges on this trail have been demolished, but by way of compensation it includes four substantial viaducts.

Consett–Chester-le-Street–Washington: C, W, UT, DR, 18m, NZ 099493–NZ 273535–NZ 313550. The Consett & Sunderland Railway Path, the westernmost 14½ miles of which are in Durham, q.v.

Hebburn Colliery–Wardley–Springwell Bankfoot: C, W, NI, DR, 4½m, NZ 321652–NZ 306617–NZ 285590. Part of the Bowes Railway Path, which connects at Springwell with the historic Bowes Railway. See also the entry for Springwell Top-Marley Hill (below).

Marley Hill (Andrews House Station)–Dunston: C, W, NI, DT, 3m, NZ 209573–NZ 232614. The Tanfield Railpath, which follows the trackbed and inclines of the Tanfield Railway. There are three inclines altogether: Lobley Hill at 1 in 18, Fulgar Bar (Baker's Bank) at 1 in 20, and Sunniside at 1 in 50. Published sources give various figures for the gradients, these being those published on the Gateshead Council website listed above.

Newburn (Newcastle)–Wylam Bridge: W, NI, DR, 4½m, NZ 163655–NZ 110642. See entry under Northumberland, where this path finishes.

Springwell Top–Marley Hill (Andrews House Station): C, W, NI, DR, 4½m, NZ 278575–NZ 210572. A further section of the Bowes Railway Path. Starts at the western end of the current Bowes Railway operation and provides a trackbed-based link to Andrews House station on the Tanfield Railway. Forms part of the Great North Forest Trail. Cyclists should note that this is a hilly route and not suitable for racing or road tyres.

Sunderland (High Newport)–South Hetton: C, W, UT, DR, 8m, NZ 381541–NZ 378452. Part of NCN1. Connects at South Hetton with the Haswell to Hart Countryside Walk (see entry under Durham).

Washington–Sunderland: C, W, NI, DR, 5½m, NZ 322542–NZ 395565. This trail follows part of the old Penshaw-Sunderland line. On reaching South Hylton, it runs alongside the Tyne and Wear metro, which was extended to this point (via Sunderland) in 2002. The trail ends by Park Lane station in Sunderland city centre.

Yorkshire, North

Grosmont–Goathland: W, NI, DR, 3½m, NZ 827050–NZ 833014. Known locally as the 'Rail Trail', this public footpath follows the course of the old Whitby & Pickering Railway and includes the Beck Hole Incline. Stations on the North Yorkshire Moors Railway serve the villages at either end of the route. The public bridleway from NZ 835013 to SE 845994 (Goathland to Moorgates, 1½ miles) looks suspiciously like a continuation of this trackbed and would repay investigation.

Ingleby Greenhow (nr. Battersby)–Blakey Junction: C, W, UX, DR, 11m, NZ 592061–SE 683990. Part of the former Rosedale Railway and now, for part of its length, incorporated into the Lyke Wake Walk. The section of trackbed listed here has been dedicated as a public bridleway which is popular with mountain bikers, but note that a few very short sections have been washed out. At Blakey Junction, the line divided, with separate branches going to Low Baring (3½m) and Bank Top, above Rosedale Abbey (3½m). While no public right of way is shown on the OS map above Blakey Junction, it is believed that there is no practical impediment to walking these trackbeds, and local ramblers' websites include reports of doing so. The website of 'Subterranea Britannica' states that the whole branch is now a 'recognised footpath'; see www.subrit.org.uk/sb-sites/sites/r/rosefale/index1.shtml. The views from the trackbed around Rosedale are spectacular, as are some of the railway's cuttings and embankments.

Slapewath–Boosbeck: C, H, W, NI, DR, 1½m, NZ 641158(?)–NZ 659171. Part of the former NER line from Nunthorpe to Saltburn, which in May 2008 had its status as a bridleway confirmed by Hilary Benn, Minister of State for the Environment. However, there may be an inquiry into the case (the second), so the situation could change.

Stamford Bridge–Gate Hemsley: C, W, UT, DR, ½m, SE 712552–SE 705556. This section of trackbed includes the notable Stamford Bridge Viaduct, which accounts for so short a path appearing in this list. For further details, see entry under Humberside.

Wetherby–Spofforth: C, W, UT, DR, 2½m, SE 405487–SE 365507. The Harland Way, part of NCN67 and formerly part of the NER Church Fenton–Harrogate line. The route starts in West Yorkshire and includes the whole of Wetherby railway triangle, which is bounded by SE 405487, SE 396483 and SE 398492.

Whitby–Scarborough: W, UP, DR, 23½m, NZ 893107–TA 030887. The scenic Scarborough and Whitby Railway Path, now part of NCN1, which includes the massive Larpool Viaduct just west of Whitby. If you can sample only part of the route, the section from Whitby to Robin Hood's Bay is hard to beat. This is one of the greatest railway walks in the UK with only two short diversions, at Ravenscar (around the closed tunnel) and Scalby (around re-development) respectively.

York–Osbaldwick: C, W, UT, DR, 2m, SE 603534–SE 632521. Part of the former Derwent Valley Light Railway, now incorporated into NCN66.

York (Woodthrope)–Barlby: C, W, UT, mainly DR, 9½m, SE 581484–SE 631359. This route comprises most of the York and Selby Path. Formerly part of the East Coast Main Line, it became a railway path when the Selby coalfield was extended beneath the trackbed in the 1980s, necessitating the construction of a high speed rail diversion – the first section of new main line to be built in the UK for decades. Between Riccall and Barlby, the trackbed accommodates a new road, with cyclists and walkers catered for by an adjoining cycle track. The cycle track leaves the old railway formation at Barlby and continues to Selby via minor roads.

Yorkshire, South

The area once covered by South Yorkshire has become a very good place to go exploring old railways, thanks to the walker- and cyclist-friendly policies of the local authorities. It is possible that more routes are now available than those listed below. Perusal of these entries reveals that the construction of the Trans Pennine Trail has been a great stimulus in this area to the reclamation of abandoned railways as walking and cycling trails.

Ardsley–Cudworth (West Green): C, W, NI, DR, 2½m, SE 373056–SE 375085. A branch off the Wombwell-Barnsley trail (see below).

Beighton–Killamarsh–Staveley (Inkersall Green): C, W, NI, DR, 8½m, SK 446836–SK 449824–SK 425723. Part of the Trans Pennine Trail which re-uses a section of the late lamented Great Central Railway. Only the first two miles of this route are in South Yorkshire, the rest lying in Derbyshire.

Bentley (Doncaster)–Warmsworth: C, W, UT, DR, 3½m, SE 559061–SE 549013. This route was opened at a cost of £180,000 in 2003 and now forms part of NCN62. It uses the former Brodsworth mineral line, and links with the Trans Pennine Trail at Scawthorpe.

Laughton Common–Thurcroft Colliery: C, W, UT, DR, 2m, SK 507864–SK 502889. The Thurcroft Colliery Branch, opened on 22 September 2006 as part of the National Cycle Network. At the moment, this route is of purely local significance, i.e. it connects only with minor roads and footpaths rather than other cycle trails.

Meadowhall Station (Sheffield)–nr. Ecclesfield: C, W, NI, DR, 2m, SK 391913–SK 370939. This is the start of the Chapeltown Greenway, which is intended eventually to reach Chapeltown (according to plans published in 2003). The route is based on part of the old GCR Tinsley to Barnsley line, but – although a section of the line in Chapeltown has been converted (access is at SK 357969) – there remains a gap of 1½ miles between the section listed here and that in Chapeltown.

Wombwell (Broomhill)–Barnsley: C, W, NI, DR, 5½m, SE 421021–SE 352060. Part of the Trans Pennine Trail, NCN62 and NCN67. Connects at SE 391043 with the Wombwell-Silkstone Common trail (see below), and at SE 373056 with the Ardsley-Cudworth trail (see above).

Wombwell–Silkstone Common: C, H, W, NI, DR, 7½m, SE 394040–SE 282036. The Dove Valley Trail – an early (if not the first) railway path in South Yorkshire, now forming part of the Trans Pennine Trail.

Bibliography

General

Allen, Cecil J., *The North Eastern Railway*. Ian Allan, 1974 (2nd edn).

Appleton, Dr J.H., *Disused Railways in the Countryside of England and Wales*. HMSO, 1970.

Daniels, Gerald and Dench, Les, *Passengers No More*. Ian Allan, 1980.

Elis, Rhys ab, *Railway Rights of Way*. Branch Line Society, 1985.

Forgotten Railways. (Series by David and Charles.)

John Grimshaw and Associates, *Study of Disused Railways in England and Wales*. HMSO, 1982.

A Regional History of the Railways of Great Britain. (Series by David and Charles.)

Tomlinson, W.W., *The North Eastern Railway: Its Rise and Development*. David and Charles, 1967 (2nd edn).

Atlases

Conolly, W. Philip, *British Railways Pre-Grouping Atlas and Gazetteer*. Ian Allan, 1972.

Jowett, Alan, *Railway Atlas of Great Britain and Ireland*. Patrick Stephens, 1989.

Wignall, C.J., *Complete British Railways Maps and Gazetteer*. Oxford Publishing Co., 1983.

Chapter 1

Taylor, Roger and Anderson, Brian, *The Hatfield and St. Albans Branch of the GNR*. Oakwood Press, 1988.

Chapter 2

Lombardelli, C.P., *Branch Lines to Braintree*. Stour Valley R.P.S., 1979.

Chapter 3

Clark, Ronald H., *A Short History of the Midland & Great Northern Joint Railway*. Goose & Son, 1967.

Wrottesley, A.J., *The Midland & Great Northern Joint Railway*. David and Charles, 1981 (2nd edn).

Chapter 4

Ludlam, A.J., *The Horncastle and Woodhall Junction Railway*. Oakwood Press, 1986.

Chapter 5

Goode, C. T., *The Railways of East Yorkshire*. Oakwood Press, 1981.

MacMahon, K.A., *The Beginnings of the East Yorkshire Railways*. East Yorkshire Local History Society, 1974 (2nd edn; revised by Baron F. Duckham).

Price, Peter, *The Lost Railways of Holderness*. Hutton Press, 1989.

Chapter 6

Chapman, Stephen, *Hudson's Way: The Story of the York-Beverley Railway*. York Railpress, 1986.

Chapter 7

Given that the present-day cycleway from York to Selby originally formed part of the East Coast main line, it is hardly surprising that there is an abundance of material. In addition to the general histories, the following local study is also useful:

Hoole, K., *The Railways of York*. Dalesman Books, 1976.

Chapter 8

Hayes, Raymond H., A *History of Rosedale*. North Yorkshire Moors National Park, 1987 (3rd edn).

Lidster, J. Robin, *The Scarborough and Whitby Railway*. Hendon Publishing, 1977.

Lidster, J. Robin, *The Scarborough and Whitby Railway: A Centenary Volume*. Hendon Publishing, 1985.

Chapters 9 and 10

I cannot speak too highly of the following authoritative and highly readable study, which is the best railway history I have yet encountered:

Whittle, G., *The Railways of Consett and North-West Durham*. David and Charles, 1971.

INDEX

Architecture, notable, xvi, 65, 68, 76, 83, 85, 96, 115-16
Askern, 95
Attlebridge, 39-40
Aylsham, 31, 37, 39
Ayot Greenway, 11

Bannister Green, 17, 22
Bannister, Anthony, 62, 63
Bardney, 47, 51
Barnard Castle, 139
Beamish Open Air Museum, 135, 139
Beeching Report, xx, 84
Beeching, Dr R., xx-xxi, 84, 131
Betjeman, Sir John, xii
Beverley, 66, 79-92 *passim*
Bishop Auckland, 138, 139
Bishop's Stortford, 14-27 *passim*
Blackhill, *see* Consett
Braintree, 14-27 *passim*
Burnhill, 129, 130, 131, 135
Burton Constable (*see* also Ellerby), 65, 72
Burton Salmon, 95

Castle Hedingham, 26
Causey Arch, 139
Chaloner Whin Junction, 96, 98, 99, 103
Chappel and Wakes Colne, 26
Cherry Burton, xviii, 82, 83, 85, 88, 89
Cloughton, 110, 114, 120
Cole Greenway, 11
Colne Valley Railway, 25-6
Consett, 126-41 *passim*, 142-55 *passim*
Crawley, 127, 130, 137
Darlington North Road, 139-40
Derwent Valley, 142-55 *passim*
Derwent Valley Light Railway, 106
Drayton, 41, 42
Dunmow, 15, 16, 18, 19, 23
Durham, xvi, 138, 142

East Coast main line, 93-108 *passim*
Easton Lodge, 16-17, 18, 19, 23
Ebchester, 144, 145, 146, 149-50
Ellerby, 65, 67, 68, 72
Escrick, 96, 98, 101, 103, 104, 105

Esk Viaduct, 111, 115, 116-17

Felmingham, 38
Felsted, 16, 17, 18, 19, 22
'Flying Scotsman', 97-8
Fogoes Viaduct, 151
Foredyke Stream, 70
Fyling Hall, 114, 117

Gedney, 30
Goodmanham, 79, 82, 88, 92
Goxhill (*see also* Wassand), 65, 66, 75
Grand Union Canal, 12
Great Eastern Railway, 14, 28
Great Northern Railway, 46
Grimshaw, John, xiii, xiv, xv, 132
Grimshaw Report, xiii
Grosmont, xviii, 122, 123

Hamsterley, 150-1
Harpenden, 11
Hatfield, 1-13 *passim*
Hawsker, 115, 117
Hayburn Wyke, 113, 114, 118-20
Hellesdon, 41
Hemel Hempstead, 11
High Westwood, 146, 150
Hill End, 5, 9
Hitchin, 2
Hockerill, 17, 18
Holderness, 61-78 *passim*
Holt, 36, 43
Horncastle, 45-60 *passim*
Horncastle Canal, 46, 48, 52-3, 54, 58
Hornsea, xvi, 61-78 *passim*
Hornsea Mere, 75
Hornsea Pottery, 75
Hotham, Lord, 79, 80, 82, 88
Hownes Gill, 127, 143
Hownes Gill Viaduct, 129, 131, 134-5
Hudson, George, 62, 79, 80, 86, 94-5
Hull, 61-78 *passim*, 82
Hurbuck, xix, 132

Kipling Cotes, 82, 85, 86, 87, 92
Kirkstead (*see also* Woodhall Junction), 46, 49
Knitsley Viaduct, xix
Knottingley, 95, 98

Lanchester Valley, 126, 132, 142, 144

Langleys Viaduct (Dunmow), 19, 22-3
Larpool Viaduct, see Esk Viaduct
Leconfield Aerodrome, 89-90
Lemsford Road, 5, 10
Lenwade, 33-5, 37, 39
Lintz Green, 144, 146, 151
Lockhaugh Viaduct, 146, 152, 153 London
    and North Eastern Railway, xi
Louth, 56-7

Maldon-Witham branch, 25
Manchester Central, xvii
Market Weighton, 79-92 passim
Market Weighton Canal, 91
Marriott, William, 31-2
Martin, 54, 55
Meeting Slacks, 137
Melton Constable, 32, 37
Midland and Great Northern Joint Railway,
    28-44 passim
Modernisation Plan, xx, 83
Mundesley, 33

Naburn, 96, 98, 100, 103
Nanny Mayor's Incline, 128, 129, 135, 136-7
Nast Hyde, 5, 10
National Railway Museum, 106, 137
Newburn, 154
North Eastern Railway, 62-3, 65, 81, 96,
    110-12, 143-4
North Norfolk Railway, 42-3
North Walsham, 32, 37-8, 42
North Yorkshire Moors, 109-25 passim
North Yorkshire Moors Railway, 123
Norwich, 29, 32
Nottingham London Road, xvi, xvii

Parkhead, 130, 132
Pickering, 110, 112
Pocklington, 82, 83, 84
Pocklington Canal, 91, 106
Pont Burn Viaduct, 151

Railway Path Project (see also
    Sustrans Ltd), xiii
Ravenscar, 115, 117-18
Rayne, 16, 21
Riccall, 96, 98, 99, 100, 101
Robin Hood's Bay, 115, 117
Rookhope, 127, 137
Rosedale branch, 122-3
Rowlands Gill, 142, 144, 145, 146, 147,
    151-2
Rowlands Gill Viaduct, 151

Rowley, 129, 130, 135
Scalby, 113, 115, 120-1
Scalby Viaduct, 121
Scarborough, 109-25 passim
Selby, 90, 93-108 passim
Shaftholme Junction, 96
Sheringham, 33, 36, 42
Shotley Bridge, 144, 146, 148-9
Sigglesthorne, 65, 68, 75
Skirlaugh, 65, 67, 68, 71-2
Smallford, 4, 10
Smallford Trail, 6
Southend-on-Sea, 14
Springfield (see also Smallford), 3, 4
St Albans, 1-19 passim
St Albans London Road, 8
Staintondale, 113, 114, 118
Stalham, 37
Stane Street, 17
Stanhope, 126-41 passim
Stansted Airport, 19
Stockton and Darlington Railway, 128-9, 139,
    143
Sustrans Ltd, xiii, xiv, 100-1, 106, 132, 138
Sutton-on-Hull, 65, 68, 70
Swalwell, 144, 146, 152-3
Swine, 64, 65, 68, 71

Tadcaster, 107
Takeley, 16, 19, 24-5
Themelthorpe, 33, 37
Thorpe Thewles, xvi
Trans-Pennine Trail, xiv, 101, 106

Upper Lea Valley Through Walk, 11

Wade, Joseph Armytage, 62, 63, 64
Wainfleet, 46, 59-60
Waskerley, 128, 129, 130, 131, 136
Wassand, 66, 67, 75
Watford, 2
Weatherhill, 107, 127, 130, 131, 137
Weybourne, 36
Wheathampstead, 11
Whitby, xvi, 109-25 passim
Whitedale, 65, 74
Wilmington, 62, 64, 65, 70
Withernsea, 61, 62, 66, 77
Woodhall Junction, 49, 51-2, 56
Woodhall Spa, 45-60
Wylam, 154

York, 80, 82, 88, 93-108 passim
York, Vale of, 93-108 passim